While for more than twenty years an armed
confrontation between East and West ͪ
Europe, there is today a widesprea
tensions—*détente*—on the Contin
prospects for reducing armaments
economic and political relations ac
Curtain exist. *Security in Europe* s
background to these developments
century since World War II. It dea.. ...ჟ with the
onset of the Cold War—why Russia and America
were unable to compose their differences in Europe—
and analyzes the growth of formal security institutions,
first NATO and later the Warsaw Pact. It also
shows how the onset of the Cold War set the
requirements for its own ends, and how these
requirements were met.

The emphasis in the book is on politics, from the
nature of various threats to security as they were
seen by different governments to the steps that must
now be taken if the present *détente* is to succeed.
The author delves into the political roles that the
formal security institutions came to play in each
alliance ; how the evolution of strategic doctrine in the
West built up tensions within the NATO Alliance
and made it more difficult to end confrontation ; and
how both alliances have fulfilled important
non-military needs of all the countries involved.

Apart from a supportive political-historical
background, Mr. Hunter offers his skill as a stylist
who has mastered the art of combining historical
perspective with a thorough knowledge of current
developments. Furthermore, he is neither interested
in assessing blame for the Cold War, nor in
suggesting ways to tilt the balance of power one way
or another ; but, rather, in showing how European
countries have viewed their security problem and
how institutions and military doctrines have influenced
politics. The book is thus a practical guide in that it
provides an understanding of what forthcoming
changes will mean and where they are likely to lead.
Finally, it shows what lessons can be drawn for the
future from an understanding of the past.

ROBERT E. HUNTER, a Fellow of the Overseas
Development Council in Washington, D.C., was
formerly a lecturer in International Relations at the
London School of Economics and a Research Associate
at the Institute for Strategic Studies. He is author
of *The Soviet Dilemma in the Middle East* and
co-author of *Israel and the Arab World: The Crisis
of 1967.*

SECURITY IN EUROPE

SECURITY IN EUROPE

Robert Hunter

INDIANA UNIVERSITY PRESS
BLOOMINGTON & LONDON

To
J. C. R.

Published in the U.S.A. by Indiana University Press,
Bloomington, Indiana
Published in England by Elek Books, Ltd., London

Library of Congress catalog card number: 73–186000

ISBN: 253–17865–7

Manufactured in Great Britain

Contents

Preface to the First Edition

This book on European security is intended first of all for students who began life in a world that already spelt Cold War with capital letters, and who, like me, will only know of its beginnings from their elders. If they accept what I say here as uncritically as we who grew up in the Cold War accepted what we were taught about it, then I shall be disappointed. But if it advances, even by a single step, the understanding of what is at worst called international relations and at best history, then I shall be pleased.

The ideas in this book have taken shape over many years. As a result, it would be impossible for me to thank adequately everyone who has helped me in preparing it. But in general I want to thank the Department of International Relations at the London School of Economics for seven years' careful nurturing, as well as my students, both at the LSE and in the far corners of Britain, who have borne heresy with good grace. Most of all I want to thank Philip Windsor for inspiration, guidance, and for being as good an editor as one could wish for without his actually writing the whole book himself. And my thanks to Miss Angela Hallett for typing the manuscript.

Any errors of fact are entirely my own responsibility; so is my irreverence.

> Leucis, who intended a Grand Passion,
> Ends with a willingness-to-oblige.
> (*Epitaph*, Ezra Pound)

Preface to the Second Edition

Since this book first appeared, the political climate in Europe has largely recovered from the shock of the Soviet Union's repression of Czechoslovakia in August 1968. Partly as a result, the spirit of *détente*, so often frustrated in the past, has gained a new momentum. Chancellor Brandt has given added vigour and direction to *Ostpolitik*; the NATO Allies have finally begun the slow walk towards diplomatic change; and the Warsaw Pact states have responded with hopeful initiatives of their own. A European Security Conference is no longer merely an abstraction, and preparations are actually under way, at least in the West, for some form of negotiations designed to reduce forces in both East and West Europe.

In this second edition of *Security in Europe*, I have tried to give an account of the changes that have taken place in Europe during the past three years, and to speculate on their possible course. Any account will, of course, be rapidly overtaken by events. But I believe that the basic patterns of the future are still linked firmly to the past; and that an awareness of what has gone before will be helpful to anyone who must either meet or interpret what is now to happen.

Perhaps today's promise of real change in Europe will again prove disappointing; it is, after all, far easier to see the way ahead than to travel there. Alexander Pope wrote that 'Hope springs eternal . . .'; but he completed his couplet with a chastening thought:

'Man never is, but always to be blest.'

In preparing this second edition, I have benefited from the

Security in Europe

views of many people on the first edition. My thanks especially
to Robin Alison Remington and—once again—Philip Windsor.
And my thanks to Mrs. Marilyn Weinstein for typing the new
manuscript.

Introduction

What is security? This is one of the central questions posed for the student and the practitioner of international relations alike, whether they are looking at a nation, an alliance, or international society as a whole. Indeed, many observers argue that the gaining and preserving of security—either against political, economic, or military threats—is the *only* important problem of international relations, dwarfing all the many other aspects of this vast area of activity and enquiry.

This is a bold view. But there is little dispute that problems of security must be taken seriously, regardless of the philosophical perspective from which one chooses to view international society and its many difficulties. In recent years, this has been particularly true of Europe—both East and West. In no other area of the world have these matters of security seemed to more people to be so immediately and crucially important—save perhaps the larger and encompassing issue of the Soviet-American nuclear balance. And in no other area of the world have the complexities of security been more carefully analysed and organized. Within the narrow confines of the Continent, these complexities have been challenging enough. But in addition, Europe has provided the central focus for Soviet-American rivalry, concern, and confrontation of one form or another; it is the arena in which both super-powers have, over the years, maintained the largest permanent commitment of forces outside their borders; and its respective halves continue to be seen by each as vital interests. Many of these issues may now seem boring. If so, this is a sign that security has been safely won, and all the more reason to discover how it was done.

This book, then, undertakes to explore some of the major questions raised by the development of security for the European Continent in the years following the Second World War. The approach used here may strike some as unconventional. It could be simply a description of NATO, the Warsaw Pact or both of them together; but, if so, it would miss much that is essential to understanding what has been happening in Europe. Instead, there must be an attempt to see Europe and its security problems as part of the same political whole, necessarily embracing the East European members of the Soviet *bloc*, the Allies of the United States in NATO, and the two superpowers themselves. Indeed, no one can hope to make sense of European history since the War without looking at the Continent as a single context of politics, whatever its formal divisions.

Furthermore, this book includes an attempt to look beyond the narrow requirements of European security and to take a wider perspective, drawing more general conclusions about the nature of security as it applies elsewhere in the world. This must be a tentative effort. But as new patterns of politics begin to emerge elsewhere in the world—and especially in Asia—the reader may find lessons in the European experience that, with sensitivity and caution, he can make use of elsewhere.

Where do we begin? First, there is the matter of the Cold War and its origins—a subject now widely written about, even though its lessons are still largely obscured by the continuing nature of the problems that it begat. Here, it will be necessary to discuss several important factors that have defined the nature of the Cold War in Europe, shaped its course, and prescribed the requirements for its end.

Why, indeed, did this novel form of political relations emerge from the chaos of post-War struggles to rebuild and recover? Perhaps most important, we must realize that nothing existed in the early days following the end of the Second World War that made a Cold War in Europe inevitable. A cursory look at the pattern of earlier European experience might seem to belie this observation. After all, Europe had for centuries posed serious security problems of one sort or another, and had evoked formal responses, whether a loosely-structured balance of power system, a network of alliances, or the highly-structured League of Nations. But did these patterns have to repeat themselves in Europe after the War? For that to be true—indeed, for it to be true for any part of the world—certain assumptions had to be fulfilled. Statesmen had first to believe that there was some *absence* of security—a matter that always depends as much on a state of mind as on physical evidence in any situation where there is no actual aggression.

In post-war Europe, the sense that somehow security was absent derived to a great extent from the lack of any clearly-defined rules by which states could conduct their relations with one another, secure in the knowledge that everyone knew what he could and could not safely do. At the same time, two new European powers had suddenly emerged from the flux of war: the United States and the Soviet Union. These two great powers, the major victors in the War, suddenly found themselves dominating the Continent, but without the experience and understanding of European politics they needed in order to cope with each other or with the many states that fell within the compass of their actions. For them, there was not even a legacy of political rules that they might, by force of habit, try to apply in the changed circumstances of 1945.

There began, therefore, a search for ways to provide the necessary rules, or at least to reduce the uncertainty that the absence of rules presented. Today, it is widely believed that this process was conducted largely in the realm of *military* policy and organization, because of the need to put defence against aggression ahead of any other concern. But this was not really so. Indeed, as the following discussion will stress, the problems of European security, whether viewed from the East or from the West, were not related at first to military matters. Instead, security in Europe meant political organization, political stability, and the task of achieving economic recovery and strength. This was security in its broadest sense—and was an approach of more sophistication than has often been evident in later deliberations about European problems.

It was only after the early post-War years that the military dimension of security was added to the political and economic; and this addition represented a significant step in transforming what was essentially a political conflict into something far more complex and demanding. And this, it will be emphasized here, was a costly way of providing some order for political relations on the Continent—and of meeting the need to introduce elements of certainty and confidence into those relations.

The development of a system of security in Europe, therefore, began with a widespread awareness that the absence of such a system would be undesirable. Of course, it would be foolish to argue that there were no fundamental conflicts of interest on the Continent, particularly those between the United States and the Soviet Union. They were both real and considerable. But it is important to distinguish between the existence of those conflicts and the forms that they took, including the methods chosen to resolve them. The discussion that follows in this book will indicate that these methods did not necessarily require the forming of two opposing military *blocs*.

The choice of forms and methods depended primarily on the ways that statesmen and publics came to view the potential threats posed to different European countries and to the political interests of the Soviet Union and the United States in Europe. It was these perceptions, or rather misperceptions, that shaped the structure of the Western Alliance system—NATO—and the interlocking web of treaties that were concluded by the Soviet Union with its satellite nations, later supplemented by the Warsaw Pact. This process was not automatic or instantaneous; instead it was made up of a long series of discrete steps that, taken together, led political conflict from the realm of politics and economics to one whose principal dimension was military. Unfortunately, once that military dimension was firmly established, it largely eclipsed political and economic developments across the lines of what had emerged as two halves of Europe. Regardless of what the prospects for such developments had been beforehand, they died with the onset of the military phase of confrontation.

Indeed, from the time of NATO's foundation in 1949 until at least the early 1960s, the entire fabric of European security was dominated by a central paradox: that in the very act of providing some fixed and certain ideas about the nature of security on the Continent—ideas symbolized by the creation of two opposing and clearly-defined *blocs*—the architects of confrontation had both given an added impetus to the Cold War and taken the first step towards signalling the Cold War's end. This point cannot be overstated. It is now apparent that the creation of something that could be called a *status quo*, set in a formal structure of East-West confrontation that was clear to everyone, provided the basis for ending those mutual hostilities that were founded on a lack of certainty about the manner in which political relations on the Continent were to be ordered. The rules were now set; and one could reasonably expect that they would provide the basis for a relaxation of tensions and for slow and painful negotiations to alter the nature of confrontation and conflict to the mutual benefit of the two separate and opposing sides.

But there was a complicating factor, that was again more a matter of the conflict's form than its nature. By achieving a *status quo* through the building of alliances whose purposes and methods were specifically military in nature, the nations concerned with Europe's security imposed on it a logic of confrontation that had to be followed through, step by step, until there was a strategic stability in Europe to match the political stability conferred for no other reason than that two *blocs* had been born.

April 4, 1949—the day the North Atlantic Treaty was signed in Washington—was therefore both the final moment in the creation of a Cold War that the West, at least, would conduct largely in military terms, and the first moment in the process needed to bring that Cold War to a close. Yet despite this fact, it took the nations involved, along with their institutional offspring, more than a decade to work through the appropriate military logic and gain a sense of strategic stability that could be equal to their views of the various threats they faced. Only then could they use the political stability of 1949 as the basis for a political *détente* between East and West in Europe.

This process was further complicated by yet another factor: the role played by institutions in shaping and defining both the nature of conflict in Europe and the manner in which the logic of confrontation would be carried through to its end. This is a much neglected subject for study. Yet it may be argued that all security problems in Europe since the Second World War— if not most security problems in the world generally—were a compound of genuine conflicts of interest, the view that men took of these conflicts, and the institutions that were built to embody them. For example, within the Western Alliance, a sense of threat did less to shape the internal politics of the North Atlantic Treaty Organization than the other way around. Throughout the years, these internal politics—especially the role played by the United States within the Alliance and the collateral uses for which it was designed—largely determined the way in which NATO countries both interpreted the Soviet threat and chose means for reacting to it. In this way, the logic of confrontation gained a political complexity that today seems astonishing.

In the East, on the other hand, the web of bilateral treaties and the Warsaw Pact have never become as important in the Soviet scheme of things as NATO has been throughout for the United States. The Russians' use of their Alliance has had no consistent pattern over the years; and even when the Warsaw Pact was most significant—as during the 1968 invasion of Czechoslovakia—it has never rivalled NATO as a means for channelling super-power influence to dependent states. Yet institutions are still important in the eastern half of European confrontation; and the picture that emerges is even more complex than that in the West.

The foregoing analysis, which will be amplified in the following chapters, has led me to approach the problem of European security in the following manner. First, I have presented a sketch history of the way confrontation began in Europe after the Second World War; and I have tried to explain why it led both to the essential paradox of the Cold War—that its end was implicit in its beginning—and to the military logic that dominated most of the past twenty-two years.

The second chapter discusses the concept of threat. But this is not the simple concept that it usually appears to be; it is far more subtle and complex; and we must try to understand it in order to see why confrontation in Europe took the peculiar forms that it did, and how we have to approach the problem of bringing about change. The nature of the threat has been, above all, a matter of perception, along with the complex psychology that leads men to transform political ideas into mandates for action.

Third, I have introduced the mundane but important subject of formal institutions, beginning with the creation and development of NATO. How, indeed, did the institutional character of NATO affect the way confrontation progressed? How did it shape Western responses within the logic that confrontation imposed? Similar questions could be asked about the Warsaw Pact; but I have said less about the Pact here because of the smaller role it played, as an institution, in shaping the more general context of security that has embraced the entire Continent.

Fourth, I have thought it necessary to discuss the basic strategic factors relating to twenty-two years' worth of European security problems. The whole question of strategy is one of the most revealing and least understood aspects of European

B

politics during this period. Strategic factors have not only changed in response to demands imposed by confrontation; but they have also proved to be important as a way of helping the NATO Allies, in particular, to work out their far more important political relations with one another through debates on what were ostensibly strategic issues. Strategy has appeared to be both immediate and concrete; politics has always appeared to be less so. As a result, the Allies have often had to approach political problems in the guise of strategy. Here, too, NATO has played a more important political role as a diplomatic instrument of the United States than the Warsaw Pact has done for the Soviet Union. This has again led me to pay greater attention to NATO than to the Pact, despite the gradual increase in the latter's importance since the mid-1960s.

The same reasoning also applies to a section, contained in the middle of the fifth Chapter: a comparison of the diplomatic uses to which Alliance systems are put, not only in Europe, but generally. This discussion will help to highlight some of the factors common to security in Europe and elsewhere; and it will help to highlight those differences that show Europe's problems to be unique. For this purpose, I have referred here to the Central Treaty Organization, another Alliance system sponsored by the United States. CENTO lends itself to comparison with NATO as an Alliance used by a super-power for diplomatic purposes; and it, too, has its own internal political 'dynamic'.

Sixth, there is also in the fifth chapter a further discussion of the diplomatic uses of alliances: in this instance, the specific, non-military aspects of NATO, in both theory and practice. This is a topic rarely treated in detail; but it is of central importance in understanding the political context within which we must view what is happening in Europe, today—whether political, strategic, or economic. In particular, a number of political problems relating to European organization and development were more or less submerged by the overriding demands of military confrontation. Indeed, the creation of the

European Economic Community stemmed to a considerable extent from NATO's failure to meet some of its original purposes. How this came about can be seen clearly in the various efforts that various Allies have made over the years to use NATO for non-military purposes.

This leads naturally to the final section: a discussion of the process of *détente* in Europe, including the resurrection of underlying political problems once the logic of military confrontation had been worked through to its conclusion and the Cold War had come to an end. *Détente* as we know it today is the culmination of two decades of developing patterns of European security. It is an amalgam of political, economic, and strategic factors that will all have an impact on the way changes will, if ever, take place on the Continent. 'The past is prologue'; and although it would be impossible to predict with accuracy what will happen next, it is valuable to try outlining the conditions that must be met for changes to take place, and to suggest at least some tentative courses of action.

This method of dealing with the history of European security, topic by topic instead of chronologically, has required some repetition of fact and argument. I have done this, however, in order to strengthen the presentation of each subject, and hope that the reader will bear with me.

ROBERT HUNTER

February 1972

Chapter 1

Beginning of the Cold War

Twenty-three years after the North Atlantic Treaty was signed, it has become popular to look back on one of the great marvels of diplomacy—the structure called NATO, which has survived a period more than equal to that between the first and second world wars; it has given Europe a period of relative peace and security that would have seemed unreal in the context of the pre-war world; and it has continued, 27 years after the end of World War II, to keep the United States bound to the defence of a collection of European nations.

This has certainly been a success for Western diplomacy. But behind the self-congratulation also lies a large measure of misunderstanding—not least on the part of people in the fifteen countries that make up the North Atlantic Alliance. For in twenty-three years, the estrangements and cultural divisions that have set country apart from country, and continent apart from continent, are still apparent. This is now true in less measure perhaps, as we have seen a slow resurgence of spirit in the Common Market; America and France, which seemed farther apart in 1968 than in 1948, have regained at least the appearances of cordiality; and Britain is about to join the European Community on January 1, 1973.

There are many reasons for this development, not least of which is the perception by various allies of 'closeness' or 'change' in their relations. After all, the euphoria of early co-operative ventures within NATO has given way to the familiarity that breeds contempt. There is no longer anything left of the sense of urgency which the Americans were able to convey to their potential allies in 1949. But of all the pressures that led observers in the late 1960s to concentrate on the divisions within NATO one of the most important was the conventional wisdom that there should have been *unity*.

This is not an uncommon problem with any institution. But with NATO, the problem has been particularly acute, since there has always been a need—at least in times of threat—to give an *appearance* of unity that would help deter attack, or at least Russian political adventures. But the sophistication of this idea has often been lost, both because the outward facade of NATO as an institution has been accepted as real, and because the high expectations held for NATO, by many well-intentioned and perhaps far-sighted people, has tended to reinforce this idea of NATO as something very special in international relations.

The NATO facade of unity and integrity has proved a particularly dangerous illusion. This illusion was built up as the Alliance acquired buildings, a flag, uniformed military officers of thirteen nations (Iceland has no armed forces and France has now dropped out), elaborate communications, and its own glossy magazines. Indeed, over the years, a code of NATO behaviour grew up, against which the performance of individual member states has been measured. Never mind that few countries—did any?—have ever managed to live up to major elements of the code (most important, the number of troops maintained in readiness has almost always fallen short of goals). The Allies still fostered a public appearance of solidarity and normal functioning in the institutions of their Alliance, as though NATO were practically another government with a constitution, instead of a collection of more or less sovereign states that had subscribed to a treaty; and a treaty, after all, is a good deal less demanding than a domestic constitution.

But through laziness, perhaps, the NATO code of desirable behaviour came to stand for reality. Indeed, when the French Government revalued the worth of NATO against its costs—a computation central to the continuation of any treaty arrangement—this act was greeted by some other Allied governments almost as though it were treason. Nor was this just a tactic designed to swing the Government of President de Gaulle back into line through an appeal to the sainted traditions of the Alliance. There was actually a belief that the French were rupturing a code of behaviour that had value for its own sake, regardless of the purposes—military and political—that it was actually designed to serve. The French were drawing graffiti on the facade of NATO: and this was effrontery—*lèse-majesté*—quite beside any real damage that might have been done to the structure beneath.

This response was perhaps inevitable in a structure about which so much had been written and spoken in so many countries, and in whose name so much had been done, not least by heads of government who needed to appeal to some outside, almost mystical, authority to get needed appropriations out of niggardly parliaments. But there were other reasons, as well. One of these could be called a sense of tidy-mindedness, most noticeable in the Americans, that reflected again the problems of a coalition among nations basically foreign to one another. This problem recurred throughout the period of this study, and was particularly important in the Allies' discussions during the early 1960s of the questions of the so-called Multilateral Force and the sharing of nuclear weapons.

The other major factor in making apostasy a crime—namely, the high expectations held for NATO—was even more important. But this subject is so intricate, and so full of implications for the overall development and character of NATO and other forms of Western co-operation, that it must be reserved for a longer discussion on its own. The significant point to make at this stage is that the conventional wisdoms about NATO were themselves of considerable importance in directing its course, and, in particular, in leading to the appearance of uniformity and broad common purpose that its facade and bland communiqués seemed to indicate.

But in understanding NATO, we must go behind this facade, to probe the subtle political currents that have formed and shaped it, to examine the compromises and the ambiguities that are both the source of its unprecedented success, and the most tangible source of its later division and discord. We must begin with the nature of European security problems in the period following the Second World War, when there was no recognizable balance of power or other mechanism to give an air of certainty to political and security relationships among European states.

It has become natural for a generation growing up in the post-war world to accept the division of Europe into two *blocs* as the established order of things; to see the Iron Curtain as stretching limitlessly backwards in time (as it can be directly apprehended in one's own life); and even to accept a view that countries beyond the frontiers of the NATO countries are in permanent darkness. The division of Europe may seem the only real and hard fact in the context of European politics as conducted by the super-powers: it has been ordained that Europe should be divided—it was a natural occurrence—and all the rest can be seen in terms of preserving this division, without dangerous alterations on either side.

This is a compelling view, reinforced by the formal nature of the opposing *blocs*, and by the tangible character of the two institutions, NATO and the Warsaw Pact. But it is a view that has rarely had validity, and has always been accepted more firmly in some countries—in particular the United States— than in others. This view also belies the substance of European security, and the means by which it was achieved.

The immediate post-war period began on a note of naïve hope in the West, particularly in the United States. Perhaps with even more widespread conviction than in 1918, Americans saw the conflict just ended as the war to end wars. The principal victors, the United States and the Soviet Union, seemed to many to share a common commitment to prevent a recurrence of divisions in Europe on questions of peace and security. The United Nations was seen as the embodiment of a new and enduring system of collective security, the forum within which the major powers would be able to make decisions necessary to preserve world peace.

Within two years of the end of World War II, however, there was the most profound disillusionment in the West. The Soviet Union quite obviously had different views concerning the interests that were to be confirmed by collective security arrangements. Nowhere were these differing views more apparent than in Europe, where the Western powers found what they regarded as Soviet obstruction at almost every step as they tried to liquidate the legacy of confusion and political uncertainty left by the war.

The basic facts of this period are well known. But the difficulty in turning these facts into history has always lain in assigning 'blame' for the breakdown of co-operation that had been built up—and exaggerated—during the war. Until recently, Western accounts, written mainly by Americans, have tended to speak in terms of Soviet villainy, and assigned to the Russians the motives essential to the gradual establishment of a Cold War and, with it, the necessary development of a North Atlantic Alliance. But in recent years, the pendulum of analysis has swung the other way, and has led to a spate of criticisms directed at the United States—criticisms that assign to a form of American imperialism the prime motive force in breaking down Soviet-American friendship. This kind of analysis is primarily American too, and has led to a vigorous debate among historians of this period. Unfortunately, this is a debate without common ground, as two sets of American moralists attempt to ascribe villainy, where it would be more appropriate to see mistake, misapprehension, or misperception in both Moscow and Washington.

The truth of the matter is probably of less importance than the attitudes these two styles of criticism represent. In the former case—an idea of Soviet imperialism—there was both a Western ideological purity and American naïvety about both the limits of trust and the nature of political interests. In the latter case—an idea of American imperialism—there has developed a sense of Western guilt in face of new evidence that detracts from earlier, uncritical rationalizations of Western action.

But aside from today's problems of changing perceptions about the late 1940s, at that time conflicts of interest between the Soviet Union and the United States were widely seen, at least in the West, in terms of their detraction from an acknowledged ideal of unity. This way of looking at problems not only made the individual issues less amenable to bargaining and resolution, but it also contributed greatly to the climate in which a venture like NATO would gain support.

Soon after the end of the war, there developed disagreements over the meaning of the Yalta decisions of 1945—disagreements caused by mutual misunderstanding, distrust, Soviet expansionism, or perhaps a combination of all three. Here lay cause for concern in the West, but this did not yet mean that there should be new security arrangements, as such, for the Continent. There were widespread fears in the western part of Europe, but these were fears of communism, spurred on by economic devastation, not fears of Soviet aggression. Throughout the period in which communism was a major threat, particularly in France and Italy, little thought was given to problems of a military nature. Among other things, it still seemed possible in Western Europe to regard Russian (or Communist) activities as ambiguous, and there was still some willingness in the West to take account of the incredible devastation visited upon the Soviet Union during the war—despite the millions of Russian troops still mobilized. Indeed, one of the most significant facts about the formation of NATO is that the process began after the major internal threats to Western European countries were beginning to subside. The French Communists began to lose strength in December 1947; and the Italian Communists lost heavily in the general elections of April 1948—a year before the North Atlantic Treaty was signed.

The political structure of the Continent, however, was

missing something very real that could have prevented the onset of a Cold War and the development of opposing security organizations dividing East from West. There was, quite simply, no common understanding about the nature of security, and no certainty about the source of security in the future. We must remember, after all, that in the interwar period there had been the most elaborate arrangements designed to preserve security—arrangements noted for their intricacy and allowing for shifts in loyalties among nations in order to preserve something of a balance of power system. And these shifts in loyalties (as with the Nazi-Soviet Pact) took place despite the developing ideological politics of the twentieth century.

In view of the history of European Alliance systems, therefore, how could one conceive, in the late 1940s, of arrangements for security in the broadest sense—some sort of certainty against the emergence of new Hitlers or the vicissitudes of power politics—that did not include firm understandings among the various European powers? In the circumstances, it is surprising that European nations continued as long as they did after the war without any such arrangements, although from the first there were formal agreements among the major powers. An Anglo-Russian treaty had been signed in 1942 and a Franco-Russian treaty in 1944. But it was not until 1947 that there was a major treaty in the West, linking France and Britain, and even here—in all three treaties—the putative aggressor was envisaged, not as the Soviet Union or any Western power, but quite specifically as a resurgent Germany.

Germany was, indeed, the key to all the security problems in Europe after the war and, in many ways, it remains the key to those problems today. Much has been written about the failure of the Western Allies to secure access rights to Berlin as part of the agreements reached at the Yalta Conference. But these discussions merely tend to obscure the very real conflicts of interest that developed over Germany among the occupying powers.

To begin with, there was the question of the psychological attitudes towards the former German aggressors held by each of the Allies. Here, American readiness to forgive actually created a source of tension. Whereas the Americans wished to avoid the problems that followed the First World War—including German revanchism that was bred by Allied insistence on reparations—the Russians retained a great reservoir of understandable bitterness. They were not alone. The French continued to regard the Germans with great suspicion, and were certainly much closer to the Russians than to the Americans in their attitudes on the administration of the four zones of Germany. This is a fact that has often been ignored in face of the wealth of Cold War oratory, and it still motivates some French European policy, including the vaunted Franco-German treaty of rapprochement that was concluded in 1963.

American officials in the late 1940s took little account of these Russian and French sensibilities, ignoring the latter and putting the former down instead to Russian expansionist aims. This is not to say that such aims were not there, but rather that the necessary dialogue—a process of bargaining over the future of Germany—was made more difficult by a philosophical difference over the treatment of the defeated enemy.

A similar problem obtained with regard to the nature of governments in European nations, and Germany in particular. Differences of attitude became apparent first with the constitution of a Government for Poland, when the Anglo-American desire for a democratic government encountered the Russian desire for regimes in eastern Europe which would be subservient to Soviet interests. Here were potent causes of mistrust. Even worse, they indicated that there was no common understanding between Russians and Americans about the nature of the security problems in Europe. For the Americans, there was only the question of trying to prevent another European war, presumably begun by Germany, that would again drag in the Americans to decide the outcome and, with it, the balance of power in the world. But for the Russians the nature of the regimes in eastern Europe—and in Germany—was of crucial importance in providing the Soviet Union with defence against attacks from the West, a much more compelling motive for security than a generalized opposition to war. It was clearly in the Russian interest to be able to create a *cordon sanitaire* in reverse, giving the Soviet Union a sure defence that the diplomacy of the 1920s and 1930s had not provided. And it is quite understandable that the Russians would see the American penchant for democracy and representative government—particularly in highly nationalistic countries like Poland that had little reason to love the Russians in 1945—as posing a threat to Russian security. Unfortunately, in the controversy, what may have been misunderstandings came to be seen by each side as deliberate attempts by the other to deny something of importance: for the Russians, their security; for the Americans, the promises, made during the period of the 'Grand Alliance', to make arrangements for a firm post-war peace benefiting all the nations that had been victimized by Germany.

This problem was repeated within Germany itself. What was to become of this defeated country? In a very real sense the origins of NATO owe more to the demand for Germany's unconditional surrender—i.e. in its elimination as an 'actor' in the European arena—than to anything else. Just as the defeat of Japan led to the search in Asia for a replacement for Japanese power, so the end of German power left the entire centre of Europe in grave uncertainty about its future. Would there be another German threat? How was it to be prevented? How was this divided country to be administered? And could the German nation be administered in a way that would benefit the interests of all the major powers?

This last question was the most fateful. For as long as there was common agreement about the demands of European security—i.e. the defeat of Germany—then the actual disposition of the defeated territories was of secondary importance. But when there appeared to be no common understanding on the future of all of Europe—as the disagreement on Poland seemed to promise—then the strategic potential of Germany began almost immediately to take on importance, and has retained that importance to this day. In short, could anything be done with Germany, either as one nation, two, or four?

Still, this question might not have taken on such importance if there had not been the problem of uncertainty about future European political and economic arrangements, felt particularly acutely by the officials administering the American zone of Germany, but by no means limited to them. They exhibited a great deal of impatience to resolve the dilemmas of Germany, impatience stemming largely from very practical, humanitarian grounds. After all, formalizing an administration, particularly a common administration, would greatly aid the problem of economic recovery. It was a worthy aim, but it conflicted directly with the Russian insistence—and to an extent that of the French—on putting security considerations first as far as Germany was concerned. Therefore, each American attempt to institute a 'rational' process of administering the defeated enemy was greeted by the Russians with hostility and resistance, and that response in turn led the Americans to suspect Russian motives still further.

The result for Europe—and for Germany—was a gradual crystallizing of opinion in East and West of particular views about the future of the Continent, and in particular, about the future of the four (later two) zones of Germany. It may be argued that the Americans were unwilling or unable to take sufficient account of the hard strategic realities that were seen by the Russians. It may be argued, in turn, that the Russians were overly suspicious of American idealism (which would seem, to the Russians, to work in the political favour of America, as well—a view with considerable merit). But in any event the upshot was a greater desire in the West to create a degree of certainty about the future—the establishment of some framework for treating with the future of Germany and Europe. In Russia, there was a greater desire to do likewise, except within Germany itself. Here, the Russians were content to have the future of Germany remain uncertain, just so long as it was not unified and powerful and they retained control of at least their portion of it. And this view came into conflict directly with the American view of the efficient administration and recovery of Germany, a view held almost without regard to the problems that this could pose in the future for all those European countries (Russia included) which had been invaded by a powerful German state.

As this discussion indicates, the background to the formation of NATO can be seen as a process of misunderstanding and genuine differences of view about the manner in which the economic and political life of various European countries should be organized. But these differences of view were not so much in conflict that there need have been a division of the Continent into two hostile and armed *blocs* in order to resolve the matter. The difficulty lay, rather, in the failure of either side to clarify the terms in which they could talk about both European recovery and the future of Germany. There were, in effect, no guidelines, except those rather haphazardly drawn up as the frontiers of military occupation during the wartime conferences. There was no firm understanding between the United States and Soviet Union about what had to be done to avoid a conflict of interest—and this was a philosophical as much as a political problem; nor were there any firm agreements on a division of political and strategic interests in Europe around which real bargaining could take place.

Therefore, this discussion so far has illustrated what is perhaps one of the most important points to be made about the whole post-war history of European security: namely, that the onset of the Cold War really reflected the inability of both Russia and America to find ways either of overcoming their misunderstandings, or of deciding where there was scope for bargaining. Having never struck a balance of advantage, they were unable to come to terms with the demands of avoiding conflict, or with the demands of feeling secure in a continent that had no military divisions but whose peoples still felt considerable uncertainty about their political future. For

the Russians and Americans—or the Europeans in between—
to do otherwise was probably too much to ask of diplomats,
particularly since those in Moscow and Washington were
unused to the complexities of great power responsibility.
In the end, there was one way out of uncertainty—that is,
the gaining of a form of psychological security. This entailed
bringing into being institutions of a military and political
security and forming opposing military alliances that would
freeze the only basis for an agreed *status quo* that seemed to
exist.

Such is the stuff of Cold War—when hostility and mistrust
act upon uncertainty about the balance of power. A 'context of
conflict' is produced—perhaps without anyone's willing it—in
which the political possessions of each side are carefully
husbanded, and every move of the new 'enemy' is invested,
rightly or wrongly, with hostile intent. A Cold War can be
avoided where the real areas of contention are clear, and the
consequences of change predictable—that is, where it is clear
what can be the subject of bargaining, and what cannot. But
in the hostile atmosphere of a Cold War, there is no such
separation of vital from negotiable interests, as the implacable
nature of conflict supersedes reason in the ordering of security
affairs for mutual benefit. So it was with the Americans and the
Chinese, at least until a new climate of diplomacy began in
1971; so it was with the Americans and the Russians in the late
1940s.

But if a Cold War begins at least in part because of uncertainty in ordering political and security affairs, the end of a
Cold War requires at least the removal of that uncertainty.
And this, indeed, is just what both NATO and the Soviet
Alliances in Eastern Europe (later the Warsaw Pact) managed
to achieve. The *end* of Cold War, therefore, actually *began* with
the establishment of NATO and the Soviet alliances. These
were acts which gave the first concrete form to post-war
security in Europe, and provided a context for approaching
these problems. But, unfortunately, it took many years for

this to become apparent. In particular, the anomalous status of Germany had yet to be settled. Even more important, the very establishment of a military means of reducing uncertainty in Europe (NATO and the Soviet Alliances) helped to increase the tensions that made any appreciations of the new 'certainty' difficult if not impossible to define.

Since that time, we have witnessed at least two phases of relaxed tensions: the 'spirit of Geneva' in 1955, and the generalized *détente* following the Cuban Missile Crisis in 1962. Neither period really saw a change in strategic factors; both, instead, were concerned with the way in which what were really established patterns of European division would be viewed, and the extent to which other factors—tension and threat—would impinge upon the basic elements of the strategic equation.

So next, we must consider the problem of threats, and the implications of various threats for the formation and history of NATO and European security, in general.

Chapter 2

The Threat

It is now the conventional wisdom that NATO was formed in response to a real and immediate Soviet military threat to Western Europe, and that this threat has only begun to fall off in recent years in response to the success of NATO. It would be difficult to analyse the second half of this appreciation—there is certainly some truth in it, even though perhaps not the whole truth. But the first part—the initial Soviet military threat—bears closer examination. As already suggested in Chapter 1, there was scope for misunderstanding between East and West from the end of the Second World War, and a desire for certainty in dealing with the amorphous and unstructured politics of a ravaged Continent.

But the North Atlantic Treaty was not signed until April 1949. Before that, there had only been a rudimentary Brussels Treaty signed by Britain, France, Belgium, the Netherlands and Luxembourg in March 1948—a treaty of solely diplomatic importance. And even after the North Atlantic Treaty was signed, it remained little more than a diplomatic guarantee until Allied Command Europe was formed under General Eisenhower in April 1951. How, then, did the process of the emerging Cold War take on its military character? Why did the reduction of political and strategic uncertainty in a period of misunderstanding and conflicts of interest have to be done in this way?

This development was the result of a process of action and response. Many factors worked in one direction—that is, towards the onset of a militarized confrontation; and many of them had to do with the way different countries viewed threats to their security, in its broadest sense. Indeed, many West

Europeans did believe that there was a form of threat from the Soviet Union during the late 1940s, just as the Russians chose to see hostile intentions in American policy. Europeans did not see the Russian threat as being of a military nature, however, but rather one concerning the role played by internal Communist parties that were helped—as in the case of Greece, at the far edge of Europe—by outside aid and political support. And the rather belated response to these threats was contained in the Truman Doctrine and the Marshall Plan, the former largely a non-military enterprise, and the latter entirely so. Even in the United States, the Marshall Plan was seen as an alternative to a military response, and the Truman Doctrine, despite the role military aid played in it, was seen as an alternative to an active US role on the Continent. But almost nowhere was there a sense that the Russians would use their military superiority to attack westward. Indeed, Mr Churchill's 'Iron Curtain' speech at Fulton, Missouri, in March 1946 was greeted with cries of outrage at home. There is also reason to believe that this address was more of a self-fulfilling prophecy than a warning of potential disaster. And even then, as his phrase about the Iron Curtain indicated, Churchill was prophesying, not a Soviet advance westwards, but the division of Europe, indeed, a division running *east* of Germany.

Despite these views, as they were actually recorded at the time, it may still seem natural to suppose that the creation of NATO presupposed a threat to the vital interests of Western European countries. But this assumption hides the real subtleties of European politics, both in the post-war period and later. Indeed, isolated comments like the one that 'all the Russians need to get to the English Channel are shoes' only masked the ambiguities of the situation, and only seemed prescient after the fact, and in part because of it.

To begin with, there was always the problem of perspective. Since many countries were interested in European security, and since each was evaluating the behaviour of the Soviet Union, there would almost certainly be a divergence of opinion about what this behaviour meant, unless it turned into the most flagrant aggression. There were, indeed, such divisions of opinion, and in themselves they accounted for much of the impetus for the formation of a rigorous military alliance of twelve sovereign nations.

Throughout the history of NATO, and even before, the United States has held a more suspicious view of Soviet behaviour than has any European nation, with the exception of West Germany, which itself did not enter the Alliance until 1955. In many ways the American attitude is not the paradox it seems. For example, the Americans very early took primary responsibility among Western nations for dealing with the Russians on such sensitive and difficult matters as the occupation regime for Germany and the status of Berlin, about which disagreements began even before the Potsdam conference was held in the summer of 1945. Soviet intransigence—as the Americans saw it—therefore had a more profound impact in the United States than it would in European countries whose statesmen were more sceptical anyway about the possibilities of co-operation among essentially foreign nations. In that vein, the Americans held a more idealistic view of the possibilities of co-operation, and were therefore more likely to suffer profound disillusionment on this score. For this purpose of analysing Russian intentions, we may even consider Winston Churchill to be an honorary American—the self-fulfilling prophet un-honoured in his own country—and he was to be officially accorded this honorary citizenship many years later.

During the first three years after the Second World War, the period of disillusionment, there was gradually built up a case for believing in Russian aggressive and expansionist aims. Again, however, this case appealed most in the United States, the Western country most removed from the actual scene of action, and least tutored in lessons of diplomacy. To be fair to Churchill, one must note that he did see the difficulties of dealing directly with the Soviet Union (on any basis that played down relations of power). Indeed, it was in an effort to urge a particular *method* of diplomacy on the Americans (i.e. accepting a divided Europe as the basis for further diplomacy with the Russians) that he made his single contribution to post-war thinking in his Iron Curtain speech.

At the same time, most Western European states had a much more complex—not to say sophisticated—view of their relations with the Soviet Union. They were far more willing to appreciate that Soviet ambitions, whatever they might be, were more likely to be prosecuted by means that did not actually involve the use of Red Army forces. But there was a fundamental problem inherent in this difference in perspective on the two sides of the Atlantic: how could the West Europeans involve the United States in the destiny of the Continent, and particularly in its economic recovery, without also embracing the American view of the emerging Soviet 'threat'? It proved impossible to resolve this dilemma. Indeed, events made the dilemma worse. At every critical juncture, the American view of Soviet intentions seemed to be confirmed—first with the Prague *coup* of February 1948, then with the Berlin blockade, and finally with the Korean War in June 1950.

In the first instance, the Prague *coup* came at the end of a long chain of events. The Americans had proposed the Marshall Plan in June of 1947, a proposal for economic recovery in Europe that at first had even interested the Russians (Molotov came to the Paris Conference with a team of 70 aides). But then Moscow's interpretation of the American proposal shifted abruptly, and the Russians apparently came to view it as an imperialist venture—a comprehensible if unfortunate view at a time of tension and misunderstanding. The Russians also required Poland and Czechoslovakia to withdraw from the Paris Conference, and the Marshall Plan became a purely Western venture, as the Americans preferred, anyway.

As a counter, later in 1947 Moscow instituted the Cominform, a restructuring of the old Comintern that had been disbanded as a mark of Allied solidarity during the war. From then on, a confrontation was approaching in economic and political terms.

27

But it still did not include a military element, since strong evidence was yet to come of a military threat posed by either the Russians or any western power in Europe. Unfortunately, there had already developed a habit of thought in the United States that was to persist formally in the NATO Alliance for nearly 20 years, and persists yet in American views of Russian activity elsewhere. This view is that Russian military *capabilities* (troops in East Europe) implied political *intentions* of using them.

It was not until after the failure of the London Foreign Ministers' Conference in December 1947 that the question of military force in the growing conflict came to the fore. But even then it was not inevitable that the Cold War should be seen in military terms, although the American view of Soviet intentions was swinging more and more behind this interpretation.

The turning point came with the proposal for a Western Union, made by the British Foreign Secretary, Ernest Bevin, in January 1948. This was an ambiguous proposal, that was designed at first to embrace five Western European nations—Britain, France, Belgium, the Netherlands and Luxembourg. Bevin was very unclear about the scope of his proposal, beyond its being a 'spiritual union'. He did not present it as a means of opposing the Soviet Union—except, in his words, 'to organize the kindred souls of the West'—nor did he single out one or another form of threat to Western European nations as being of central importance. As a result, the proposal was seen as all things to all men. In Britain and on the Continent, governments placed emphasis upon the political and economic aspects of the Western Union, in line with the prevailing interpretations of threat to Western European countries, which, as already noted, was seen in terms of subversion and economic weakness. In addition the continental nations saw the Western Union as the starting point for a process of encompassing political integration which, in so far as it would respond to any threat at all, looked towards Germany instead of towards the Soviet Union.

It was only in the United States that the Western Union

proposal was welcomed for its military possibilities, as well. And here was the dilemma. Should the Europeans accept the American view of the purposes of this new venture—which included defence—or should they organize themselves solely according to their own lights and perhaps risk a new period of American isolationism towards Europe? This was not an idle question, since at stake was the whole structure—meaning the money—of the Marshall Plan, then stalled in Congress. It can be argued that the major reason for the timing of Bevin's Western Union proposal centred around the need to meet demands of the American Congress and the Administration. These were demands that Europeans show some incentive for self-help and self-organization. Those demands the Western Union seemed to meet, and the proposal was received as such in Washington.

But there were two difficulties with this development if the Western nations were to prevent the Cold War from being set in concrete. In the first place, the formation of an actual *bloc* in Western Europe, especially one that so clearly pleased the Americans, could only reduce the ambiguities that then existed in European politics about the division of Russian and American interests. As argued earlier, many countries would be aided by this reduction of ambiguity, as a way of countering uncertainty about their future and about the terms of any debate or bargaining with the Soviet Union on vital questions such as the future of Germany and Austria.

But for other countries, there was less advantage to be found in this process. In particular, these included the countries where domination by Russia or America had not yet been confirmed: namely Finland, Austria, Poland and Czechoslovakia. In each of these countries, there was grave foreboding that the proposal for a Western Union would lead the Soviet Union to infer a greater threat to its security, as its propaganda certainly indicated. And there was a fear that Moscow would do more than extend its fledgling network of alliances with East European states. To that point in time, the Russians' alliances seemed to

pose no direct threat to West Europe; although it is understandable that for the United States they seemed to imply
that Moscow wished to organize its 'kindred souls', and they
did, indeed, represent a parallel process in the East of structuring Cold War divisions.

This unease in the border states may help to explain what
happened next. Only a month after the promulgation of the
Western Union, the regime in Prague was overturned by a *coup*
—a *coup* that was widely taken in the West as the signal of a new
phase in Soviet behaviour. But the flurry of anxiety that followed
this event is hard to comprehend outside of the context of the
times. After all, the *coup* had been widely predicted, as a result
of the Western move towards crystallizing the division of
Europe, and it actually moved no territory across the implicit
strategic 'line' which was established at the end of the Second
World War, but which had been little more than a psychological
barrier until 1948. It may be argued that the Russians were
over-reacting (just as they over-reacted in August 1968) and
that, in turn, the Western nations over-reacted as well.

In any event, the Czech *coup* seemed to prove the Americans
right: that there was, indeed, a military threat to Western
Europe and that military preparations had to be taken to
counter it, even though the *coup* was demonstrably a political
act, despite the implicit role of the Red Army. As a result,
the treaty signed among the five Western Union powers a few
weeks later took on a predominantly military character,
although it still retained important elements of political and
economic co-operation (see Appendix I). These latter elements
are usually neglected in histories of this period. The reasons
for that—as well as the significance of these developments—are
discussed in Chapter 5.

The Prague *coup* gave the emerging Cold War a major push
towards its military phase. But even then the Europeans were
not as convinced as were the Americans of the military nature
of the Soviet threat, for they did very little to prepare themselves against it in the year that led up to the signature of the

North Atlantic Treaty. For them, the military threat was still seen to be of secondary importance, if it existed at all.

Indeed, the next major Soviet move was also sufficiently ambiguous to permit differences of interpretation in the West. The Berlin blockade seemed to prove the Americans right by showing, in a way the Prague *coup* had not, that the Russians were prepared to use military force to gain some advantage in the uncertain areas of central Europe. It is still not clear that this was so, or that a show of military force by the West—however small—would not have broken the blockade there and then.

But whatever the Russians' intentions at this point, the fact that the blockade of 1948–49 was broken without the use of military force raises the question whether this event should be interpreted as a military (as well as political) manoeuvre. Whether this argument is valid or not, the Americans were given the 'evidence' they needed to convince reluctant European statesmen. Indeed, the negotiations to create a North Atlantic Alliance were conducted under the shadow of the blockade, and culminated in a treaty whose non-military aspects were of minor importance from the point of view of the United States, although this opinion was not shared by all West Europeans (see Appendix II).

Even then, there continued to be a divergence of opinion about the actual nature of the Soviet threat. In France, for example, there has never been more than a bare majority of public opinion willing to believe in a Soviet military threat to Western Europe. Furthermore, in virtually every European member country of NATO at the time it was created, this new treaty was seen more as a diplomatic venture—an American guarantee with little that was tangible to back it up—than as the formation of a full-scale and viable military alliance. Indeed, the first years of NATO followed the pattern of development of the Brussels Treaty Organization (Western Union Defence Organization): there was a striking lack of any real acceptance of a military threat to Western Europe. The signing of the North Atlantic Treaty was followed by, even if it did not cause, the ending of the Berlin blockade. Surely, it was argued in Europe, this proved that a diplomatic show of strength was sufficient to give the Western Europeans enough psychological confidence to allow them to put into effect the far more important Marshall Plan for economic recovery? So, too, even the Americans did not contemplate backing up the treaty with military forces of their own, although they did see it as an institution within which US military aid could help Europeans to protect themselves, despite the overwhelming (potential) superiority of Red Army forces.

But once again, it was an external event—and one that did not necessarily imply an impending Soviet attack on Western Europe—that turned the tables. In June 1950, North Korea attacked her southern neighbour, in what appeared to be a war of aggression sponsored by the Soviet Union. In Western Europe, the Americans presented their view that this was part of a general Soviet expansionist effort—only a feint perhaps—and the whole idea of a military threat to Western Europe gained more currency than before. In fact, this act finally established in US minds the idea that Russian aims were global and interrelated. This idea is still evident to some extent in the lingering view of a 'seamless web' of Russian-American relations, in which a change in any aspect of their relations, anywhere in the world, is seen to have some implicit impact on all the rest.

Be that as it may, the onset of the Korean War was enough to lead to the formation of an actual organization for NATO— the Allied Command Europe—within which the Americans agreed to supplement their meagre garrison forces with four divisions plus General Eisenhower, in exchange for real efforts by the Europeans to build up forces on their own. Thus there came into being within NATO a real military presence on the ground; and this was the final act of militarizing the Cold War, almost exactly two years after the North Atlantic Treaty was signed.

Of course, it may be asked whether the presence of Red Army forces in eastern Europe, and many more in the western parts of the Soviet Union, had not already 'militarized' the Cold War. Yet evidence is ambiguous on this question. On the one hand, the Soviet Union had not used its overwhelming superiority to do more than take political advantage of opportunities in Prague and Berlin—opportunities that helped to harden divisions on the Continent but that did nothing to extend the Russian presence westward. Nor did West Europeans see Russian forces as a direct threat to them. Was Moscow merely using its forces to guarantee the nature of régimes in states it occupied—an essentially defensive posture?

On the other hand, local Communist parties in the West (and especially in Italy and Greece) had been receiving at least psychological support from the presence of Russian forces nearby, even though the Russians did seal the fate of the Greek insurgents as early as 1948 by acquiescing in the closure of the Greek-Yugoslav border and the cutting off of arms supplies.

It can be argued, however, that the militarizing of the Cold War could only take place when there were two sides deploying forces in at least implicit confrontation with one another. This view may seem to beg the question whether the Soviet Union would at some later time have attacked one or more West European countries. But this was certainly a period of Russian consolidation in Eastern Europe in which there was not yet a sense that competition with the Americans in Europe generally or Germany in particular had to be conducted in military terms. Rather, this element of competition, in so far as it has ever been more than a way of symbolizing more fundamental political conflicts of interest, could not begin until there were actually two military structures, fully manned, and military doctrines and rhetoric to go with them. This is a classical problem of confrontation: when does a political conflict take on a military dimension? Is the presence of forces enough? Or does it require firm evidence that one side or the other does indeed intend to use its forces to secure political ends?

At the same time, the creation of an actual Allied Command Europe posed this same dilemma for Russian observers. With its creation, as with the stationing of American B-29 bombers in England during 1948, the Russians had to weigh the possibility that the Americans were beginning to pose a military threat to them. Their posture in East Europe then, to the extent that it was defensive, had to take into account new western capabilities in addition to the possible internal threats to Russian hegemony in satellite states, which Red Army forces were designed to counter. Whether anyone wished it or not, therefore, there was now a military dimension to the Cold War.

Even then, the panic caused in the West by the Korean War did not last very long. Within months, the Europeans sank back into indifference concerning the possibility of a Russian military threat. It was only in the autumn of 1951 that the first great NATO exercise began in which the Americans tried to get their European allies to take seriously the demands of defence— one of a series of such exercises that will be described in more detail in later chapters.

It can be seen, therefore, that three events—the Prague *coup*, the Berlin blockade, and the Korean War—hastened the development of military Cold War in Europe. But even then, the European appreciation of the Soviet 'threat' to Western Europe was never as high as that held by the Americans, except in one country—West Germany. Indeed, it was only on the question of admitting it to NATO and beginning its rearmament that there developed significant European pressure towards emphasizing the importance of NATO's defences, and sufficient motivation by any of these countries to begin the repeated crises of confidence that surrounded the 'nuclear sharing' issues of the 1960s—to be described in Chapter 4. But these were issues that were more important in terms of possible West German diplomatic power and the relative importance within the Alliance of the United States and its European Allies, than in terms of countering an actual military threat.

As we shall see later, American support for the rearmament of West Germany led the other members of NATO to take problems of defence more seriously than they might otherwise have been disposed to do, if only as a way of retaining some influence on such a politically explosive process. Indeed, this rearmament of West Germany gave NATO a dual quality of protecting against both Russian and German potential threats. As a result, the whole armaments question within NATO had henceforth to be seen in the light of Germany's role as well as of Russia's intentions. This lent a peculiar ambiguity to the next 20 years of NATO's development.

At the same time, the introduction of West Germany into the Western system raised anxieties in the Soviet Union. Here was a more palpable form of threat—or at least the Russians were able to represent it as such to their East European satellites. This point was long inadequately appreciated in the West, and not given as much weight as it deserves in assessments of later Russian acts that related to the role of West Germany in the Western Alliance.

In Western Europe, perceptions of an actual military threat from the Soviet Union did rise somewhat in the late 1950s, during the period, 1958–61, of the so-called 'Berlin crises'. But even now it is unclear what the Russians were trying to achieve by exerting pressures on West Berlin: whether they actually harboured a motive for expansion, or were merely trying to take one political issue of the Cold War—the status of Berlin— from the realm of uncertainty into that of certainty. Whatever the Russian motivation, after the last crisis ended in 1961 with the building of the Berlin Wall, there ceased for all practical purposes to be any real strategic uncertainty anywhere in Europe and, partially as a result, there was a serious downgrading of appreciations of military threat to Western Europe, even as viewed from the United States. This was largely a psychological reaction: as long as there was some part of Europe whose status was not confirmed, it was possible to see a certain Soviet pressure to revise frontiers. But once that problem was finally settled—in particular, to prevent the further draining away of East German workers and to end the Soviet threats of a unilateral peace treaty with East Germany—there was no longer an issue that could be used as the focus for anxieties about European security itself, as opposed to unresolved political questions or, for example, Russian behaviour in the East European states themselves.

Largely as a result of this development, from then onwards there was a further intensification of what has been known as the problem of 'cohesion' within the Alliance. This problem had first arisen for almost the opposite reasons when the Russians acquired, some time between 1956 and 1958, an ability to attack the United States directly with nuclear weapons. In theory, this meant that the West Europeans could no longer be sure that they could allow their security to depend on promises made by the United States to use nuclear weapons in Europe's defence. In effect, this new vulnerability of the United States could be seen as an implicit increase in the Soviet military threat, since the counter (deterrent) to it was theoretically no longer as certain as before. Even so, this was as much a problem deriving from the practice within the Alliance of letting the US commitment to Europe's future rest in such large measure on questions in the realm of strategy, whether or not there were a real Russian military threat. As will be seen in Chapter 4, the Allies' acceptance of the US military role as a symbol for other attachments had its liabilities: this role then had to be played out in its own terms, however unimportant it might actually have been at times in its own right.

Nevertheless, after 1961 and the building of the Berlin Wall, appreciations of the Russian threat declined throughout NATO, and the willingness to take defence problems seriously decreased as well. But this process was not uniform: the Germans were the last to concede that the military threat was, indeed, going down, since they were on the 'front line' and were most

concerned with political change in Europe rather than acceptance of the *status quo*.

Of course, this reduction in appreciations made of the
Russian military threat begged an important question:
objectively viewed, had there ever really been such a threat?
But regardless of the answer to this historically unanswerable
question, the new appreciation helped to lay the ground-work
for *détente*, along with three other factors of importance: first,
the recognition of the strategic certainty of European division,
a certainty that had really been present—except possibly in the
case of Berlin—ever since West Germany entered NATO in
1955; second, the beginnings of American-Soviet strategic
stability that became apparent after the Cuban missile crisis
of October 1962; and third, the growth of East-West intercourse
in a large number of areas, particularly that of economics.

The French, of course, were the first to exploit the general
appreciation of a reduction in the Soviet military threat. But
they were not alone in having the potential to do so: other
European nations could also have exploited the emerging
détente, but apparently did not do so because they lacked the
French inclination to place higher value on gaining increased
diplomatic flexibility than on retaining the marginal advantages
that would be provided by ensuring a continued American
military presence on the Continent and preserving the psychological worth—for security—of the NATO organization.

The most important thing to note about this French attitude
was its sincerity, at least in its appreciation of the Soviet
military threat. After all, by the mid-1960s, there was very
little remaining evidence to support a thesis that the Russians
would undertake a serious military venture against NATO.
The Allies themselves concentrated almost exclusively on
possible limited aggression against flank areas in northern
Norway or the Turkish border areas; and even in these areas
the concern expressed by the North Atlantic Council was
probably intended more to give the outlying Allies a feeling
of participation in the Alliance, than to provide an objective

view of threat. Even after the Russian invasion of Czecho-slovakia in the summer of 1968, there was surprisingly little willingness by any NATO nation to believe that there had been an increase in the Soviet military threat to Western Europe. The Soviet invasion could be seen as consistent with the strategic understandings, if not the political ones, that formed at least part of the basis of *détente*. The concern about possible Russian aggression against Western Europe, as expressed by the Supreme Allied Commander, Europe (General Lemnitzer), went almost unheeded throughout the rest of the Alliance.

Yet the North Atlantic Council did take some remedial action, as though the tangible military threat had increased, and the French Government even modified its independent stand somewhat to join with the other fourteen nations in a collective warning against further Soviet military action in other areas, implicitly including Yugoslavia. These were areas where actions similar to the invasion of Czechoslovakia would change the strategic *status quo* or, as in the case of Roumania, could imply Russian preparations to do so (this was one reason for President Nixon's visit to Bucharest in early 1969).

But this NATO reaction was less a renewed appreciation of a real threat to Western Europe—there were few open avowals of this—than an appreciation that the Soviet action undercut another basis of *détente*. This was the increasing intercourse between East and West Europe, coupled with greater Russian tolerance of independent East European political and economic development. Greater efforts by NATO in the military field, which proved to be of marginal significance, would therefore be signals that *détente* in Europe could not proceed unless Soviet rule in Eastern Europe were modified. It may be argued that this was the same sort of use made of military responses to counter a non-military 'threat' that helped to change the Cold War confrontation in Europe from the political and economic realm to the military realm in the first place. Unlike 1948–49, however, there was little danger in 1968 of actually changing the terms of the confrontation.

Thus, it can be seen that over a period of nearly 20 years the establishment of a military *bloc* in Western Europe—in confrontation with a Soviet military *bloc* that was first a series of bilateral treaties and was later enshrined in the Warsaw Pact—created a logic of its own, a military logic, that then had to be followed through to its own conclusion. If East-West relations were to be conducted largely in the framework of military preparations, doctrine, and rhetoric, then this military framework had to be dealt with in its own terms before more basic political issues could be dealt with on their own.

Perhaps the most striking feature of this logic was the long-standing debate within NATO about the difference between the Russians' military capabilities and their political intentions. As alluded to earlier it is interesting to note that the Soviet Union maintained an overwhelming conventional military capability in Europe for several years before this was interpreted in the West to mean that Soviet leaders were necessarily prepared to attack westwards. It was only after the context of military confrontation was established—beginning with the Prague *coup* and the Brussels Treaty—that Russian forces-in-being came to be seen as a positive threat, whether or not the Russians intended to use them for purposes of aggression. It seems to be a general principle, therefore, that as long as there is no context of conflict, then forces in being can be explained in many ways. But as soon as that context develops, in this case almost by accident or at least in part by a process of mutual misperception, then the internal logic of conflict requires that the numbers of forces should be seen to represent the nature of the threat. At least this was the way in which the Americans always saw the problem of Soviet forces in Eastern Europe, since, of course, it was they who were directly locked into the context of conflict by being in direct confrontation with the Russians.

Beginning with the point at which the conflict was accepted in the West as one of a military nature (again, here is the process of 'selling' the American concept), then there was no

D

alternative but to accept the logic of numbers, and prepare to counter the apparent threat of capabilities-equals-intentions. Only when something like a balance had been achieved in numbers of forces on each side of the division could there again be any rational thought upon the problem. Such a balance was achieved very early on in NATO's history when one added nuclear weapons—the panoply of deterrence—to the equation. But subsequently something like an actual parity of conventional forces was achieved in the late 1960s, as well, although this development has been hotly debated in the NATO Alliance, and depends in part on definitions of the time a war would remain 'conventional'. It is interesting to note that it was the Americans, trying to stimulate a slightly greater European military effort, who first saw parity as between NATO and Warsaw Pact forces, and the Europeans, led by the British Defence Secretary in 1969, who disputed the American case and emphasized NATO's continuing reliance on American nuclear arms. This seeming paradox largely reflects the symbolic role that a US military presence on the Continent plays in demonstrating overall US concern for Europe's political and economic future. As will be discussed later, however, the American view of the balance of forces has shifted yet again, for other reasons.

It is no coincidence that, as perceived tensions decreased, NATO intelligence experts (led by the United States, which was by then most anxious for a relaxation of tensions and a bilateral *détente* with the Soviet Union) saw that earlier estimates of Russian troop strengths (the famous 175 divisions) had been exaggerated. They had been exaggerated, so the argument ran, not just immediately before the new appreciation, but from the start. Therefore, by the early 1960s, it was possible for some NATO countries to begin to see a decreasing disparity in conventional weapon and force levels between the two Alliances. This decreasing disparity then allowed the Western Allies to make some distinction between Russian intentions and capabilities. The actual process of dissociating the two factors took some time longer; it was not until December 1967 that, after further intelligence down-grading of Soviet forces, the North Atlantic Council accepted formally the distinction between the Russians' military force levels and their political intentions. This change was, of course, facilitated by other moves towards *détente*. But it does illustrate the internal demands of a logic of military confrontation, and is a commentary on the high price paid for security by all countries in Europe, East and West, for their failure to find a basis for bargaining without engaging in a costly and dangerous military confrontation. Interestingly enough, the Soviet invasion of Czechoslovakia did not mean more than a partial reversion to the old identification of capabilities and intentions in NATO's view of Soviet behaviour— although the Supreme Allied Commander, Europe, pressed for such a reversion to it, as he always had done. And this testifies to the way in which the subleties of politics can survive, once the original internal logic of military confrontation has been worked out. It is then possible to set in train a process of relaxed and rational thought about all the outstanding issues of diplomatic, economic, political and military conflict. Most important, at the time it became possible to work towards changes in European politics that could one day permit the established structures of confrontation to be replaced by less costly and risky alternatives.

Of course, Western perceptions that a military threat from the Soviet Union was no longer worth taking seriously did not mean that there was no political threat to Western interests. Indeed, the Russians have continued to pose the most serious threats to West European interests in Eastern Europe. These are interests not in subverting Russian dominance or altering strategic stability, but rather in securing more benign treatment of East European peoples. This kind of threat, however, is far less menacing to the West, even though—as discussed in Chapter 6—it does pose political problems for the cohesion of the Western Alliance.

A similar process was, of course, taking place on the Russian side—or so at least one can presume. Apparent perceptions by the Russians that tensions were becoming more relaxed also came at a time when the Western military preponderance was disappearing—in this case, preponderance denominated in relative nuclear strength and the end of America's near-invulnerability to Russian nuclear attack. These were the weapons and conditions that could most directly affect Russian security as opposed to that of the East European states. Here, however, the Russians seem to have been less impressed by their new ability to deter the United States directly with nuclear weapons, and more by the decrease in the anxieties felt by the Western nations. This led to a decrease in the latter's emphasis upon the conflict aspects of East-West relations. Numbers of forces and weapons had always mattered less for the Russians than had their appreciation of Western intentions as viewed from outside the context of the arms balance; they have always tended to view conflict as a matter to be resolved in political terms—even if this might at times require military means—rather than a matter of arms balances. Now the West seemed to be sharing that essentially political view, while the Russians in turn began to see that, up to a point, numbers and types of weapons are important in providing both strategic stability and a climate in which political problems can be approached directly. Indeed, this growing mutual appreciation by each super-power of the other's style of looking at the world has been one of the most salutary developments in their relations during the last few years, and one that underpins much of their efforts to limit the arms race and reach broad political understandings.

For years, the Russians had been concerned about Western intentions towards them—a 'threat'—but this had been less the fear of specific levels of weapons and forces, including nuclear weapons, than the observation that a context of conflict did exist. The Russians could see that there were outstanding political issues in contention—beginning with the political organization of Eastern Europe in 1944 and dominated throughout by the twin problems of Germany and Berlin. But for the Russians it was these issues, and not the mere existence of weapons, that mattered. In a way, the Western view of Soviet force levels in Eastern Europe, before a political context of conflict was created in 1947–48, characterized the Soviet view of Western armaments throughout the Cold War period. These Western armaments were seen by the Russians primarily as adjuncts to the underlying political conflict. Unlike in the West from at least 1955 to 1962, the Russians rarely saw these Western armaments as creating an environment of their own that had first to be stabilized, without reference to East-West political relations, before the logic of Cold War could come to an end.

This may seem to be almost a chicken-and-egg problem, but it is not quite that. To set in motion the process of transition from a time of threat to one of *détente*, the Western nations had first to feel the security of *numbers* that would start the process of relaxation—the change in context—to which the Russians could then respond. This is not to say that the Russians were never wary of the numbers game. They were surely sufficiently influenced by American atomic bombs in the late 1940s to be even more mistrustful of American actions; and they had always paid close attention to the role of West German forces in NATO, either because of genuine fears, or in order to impose greater discipline on the East Europeans. In this regard, the progress of West German *Ostpolitik* during 1970–71, and especially the Treaty of Moscow and the *de facto* acceptance of the Oder-Neisse Line as Poland's Western frontier, have done much to end East European perceptions of a West German threat.

Finally, Russian tendencies to be distrustful of American actions were reinforced, of course, by Marxist ideology, just as American anti-communism reinforced American mistrust of the Russians.

All in all, the philosophical differences between America and Russia about the pre-eminence of weapons in a context of confrontation, as opposed to the nature of the interests involved in the confrontation itself, made it natural that the Americans should be first to define that the Cold War had entered a necessarily military phase (at about the time of the Prague *coup*). And it made it natural that they should be first to define that it had come out of that phase (after the Cuban missile crisis).

Such was the nature of the 'threat' as it was perceived on either side during the years of NATO's formation and development. But perception of threat did more than just bring into being two military *blocs* in confrontation with one another; it also led to the creation of an elaborate diplomatic network in East and West that radically transformed the nature of relations among many states. Some of these problems—particularly those arising out of the internal organization of NATO—will be the subject of the next chapter.

Chapter 3

The Role of Institutions

When the North Atlantic Treaty was signed and ratified by the twelve governments in 1949, it was still necessary to transform a diplomatic instrument into a firm set of institutions that would be capable of expressing a collective will and, hopefully, of taking some common action to implement mutual guarantees.[1] This was so even if the Treaty were not to become an instrument for changing a political confrontation in Europe into a militarized Cold War. As suggested in the last chapter, this process of institution-building did not go very far at first nor was it concluded on a straightforward and ordered basis. Instead, the institutions of the Alliance—the 'O' in NATO— grew up piecemeal as more and more statesmen came to see the diplomatic guarantees as inadequate. But a context of conflict was coming clearly into focus. In order to make that context concrete—that is, in order to follow through with the logic of an emerging military confrontation—it was necessary to create institutional structures that would represent firm evidence of Western intentions, and particularly those of the United States. At least so it seemed, even though this view helped hasten the establishment of military modes of thought in East-West relations. And, of course, evidence of intentions had to be made clear both to the potential enemy and to all the Allies. Once undertaken, the common venture could not be seen to fail, or the resulting demonstration of disarray could be worse than having done nothing at all.

For the first year, little was done by the new Allies to create an actual organization. The twelve member states managed to constitute themselves into a Council, composed of their

[1] Greece and Turkey joined in 1952; West Germany joined in 1955.

foreign ministers, and to provide also for councils including their defence and finance ministers. Beyond that, they did little of value except to begin half-hearted attempts to co-ordinate their meagre defence efforts. Five Regional Planning Groups were set up—one, significantly, embracing intact the entire Western Union Defence Organization of Britain, France and the Benelux states. But there was no prospect that this collection of planning groups could ever prosecute a war, or even respond with any measure of success to an attack. There was, in short, no practical means of implementing the guarantees spelt out in the North Atlantic Treaty to the effect that each nation would regard an attack on any other as an attack on itself.

The only real guarantee was one given by the Americans to their new allies. And, for the time being, that was enough: the American assurances had some psychological value, and there was the vague spectre of an American atomic arsenal, although of precious small dimensions, that gave some significance to the military aspects of the newly structured East-West confrontation in Europe, for good or ill. And this implied US involvement helped to offset, at least in American minds, some of the threat that seemed to be present in mobilized and deployed Red Army forces.

But with the beginning of the Korean War the contradictions posed by an emerging military confrontation that in the West had no effective military potential became more apparent. At least the Americans found that they could present this case with more assurance of finding a sympathetic audience in Western Europe.

In this way the first real elements of military power actually to be concentrated and directed within the NATO organization were brought into being. In late 1950, the United States agreed to place four divisions in a supranational command that would be headed by General Dwight D. Eisenhower, a folk-hero in Europe and the first of a succession of Supreme Allied Commanders, Europe, all of whom have been American generals. This Allied Command Europe was charged with implementing what has become famous as the 'forward strategy'. This was the intention of defending Western Europe, should there ever be an attack from the East, as far 'forward' as possible. Such a strategy was no more than sound military thinking. But for those states lying just to the west of Germany, this forward strategy had a particular meaning: if it was to be at all effective, it had to prevent the fighting from taking place on their own soil. And this meant, quite simply, that there would have to be some form of defence of West Germany itself.

Therefore, the very act of formulating a strategy for NATO compromised the already complex quality of the West German government which had been formed in 1949. In its attempt to make its strategic doctrines as rational and sensible as possible —however implausible it might have been to try mounting an actual defence—the Alliance had arranged to include West Germany within its ambit. In other words, any further value that might be derived from continued ambiguity about the status of Germany in the context of East-West relations—in order to facilitate, for example, a resolution of conflicts over Germany at some future date—was virtually lost. But it was not entirely lost even then: after all, the Russians did not settle down to take a consistent line on West Germany until 1955 after the conclusion of the Western European Union agreements and Germany's entry into NATO. In the intervening years the Russians demonstrated their flexibility on German questions in acts such as their flamboyant gesture in March 1954 of actually suggesting that they might join NATO! But when West Germany became a formal part of the Western Alliance, the Russians then sought to formalize the permanent division of Germany in the process of organizing the Warsaw Pact. Yet even then, East German forces did not become part of the Warsaw Pact until 1956, and the declared policy of the *bloc* continued at least until then to provide for the possible withdrawal of the German Democratic Republic (GDR) from the Warsaw Pact in the event of Germany's reunification.

In any event, the logic of the forward strategy quickly made itself felt: if West Germany were to be included in the West's defence, then there would surely have to be a great quantity of soldiers and equipment available, and what better place to find them than in Germany itself? This was anyway the logic pursued by the Americans. Therefore, as early as the autumn of 1950, the North Atlantic Council took a decision in principle to permit the rearming of West Germany, a scant five years after the end of World War Two. This was an important event, for it not only signalled an effort by the Americans to allay fears about German revanchism on the part of the European Allies—at least sufficiently to get troops provided for the forward strategy. It also began four years of bitter wrangling about the most appropriate means for bringing West Germany back into the comity of nations—that is, to secure the use of German troops. And, of course, once the Germans started actually to provide troops, the United States, as well as the Soviet Union, would have to think clearly about giving all sorts of tacit or explicit guarantees to those countries in both Eastern and Western Europe that saw in the Federal Republic of Germany a greater threat to their security than they saw in either of the two super-powers. More than that, once these German troops were involved, the Russians could no longer give anybody the benefit of the doubt about the status of West Germany—though, of course, the Russians had started the process off by equipping the East Germans with a small force of *Kasinierte Volkspolizei*, by any other name an army. NATO's decision to rearm West Germany was, therefore, a signal act, not only in the context of relations inside NATO (it was the genesis of more than two decades of 'German problem' within the Alliance), but also in the context of finding ground for accommodation with the Soviet Union. It was just one more difficulty, and a central one. Of course, one might argue that clarifying the position of the two Germanies would help to bring on a period of strategic stability on the Continent that was one requirement of *détente*, but this is an historical point that is impossible to judge adequately.

In order to meet American arguments, the NATO Allies in the autumn of 1950 agreed to the raising of German forces, and at the end of 1954 the Allies finally found a method to accomplish it. In the process, there developed an ambitious venture in European integration, the European Defence Community; then the EDC was defeated in the French Chamber of Deputies; and finally the British Government brought into effect a splendid diplomatic *coup de main* in proposing a Western European Union that would include Germany and Italy in the original Western Union. Through this plan, which the British had been waiting three years to unveil, London thereby found a way of bringing German forces into being, while at the same time remaining aloof from direct political involvement in Continental affairs. In this way the British were able to appear as good and loyal NATO allies, yet at the same time preserved their chances of maintaining a 'special relationship' with the United States (see Chapter 5).

With the prospect that NATO forces actually would be raised, Allied Command Europe sprang into being on April 1st, 1951. NATO had finally become an organization (see Appendix VI). Its Supreme Headquarters, Allied Powers Europe (SHAPE) were established in temporary buildings in a suburb of Paris, where they remained for exactly 16 years, until asked to retire by General de Gaulle. This proved the adage that flourishing institutions can make do with just about any kind of real property: it is only those institutions that are dying that have the time to build palaces.

The problems facing the new Supreme Allied Commander, Europe (known universally by the acronym SACEUR), were formidable, as were the problems facing the civilian side of the Alliance. No one had ever done anything like this before—at least not in peace time. This was a grand coalition of twelve sovereign nations, each pledged to the defence of all. And the coalition included the unprecedented 'integrated' military command—although no one has ever quite understood the meaning of the word 'integrated'.

In these early days of NATO there were trials and errors, on both the civilian and military sides of the Alliance. But for every problem a committee was created, so that by late 1951, it was hard to see the institution for the committees of which it was composed. This was a not unnatural development, and reflected, if anything, the massive problems of operating such an enormous enterprise with nations which had only two basic interests in common: first, to maintain whatever defence or deterrence should from time to time be thought necessary—particularly when the Americans were successful in presenting their view of the threat—and second, to keep the United States firmly committed to the Continent, both stragetically and for the purposes of economic and military aid. And with only slight modification, primarily in the financial arrangements, these are still the only real objectives binding the nations of the Alliance together, although, as discussed in Chapter 5, there have been many attempts to broaden the mandate of the organization.

But gradually some sense began to be made of the problems of NATO'S organization. On the civilian side, three separate councils of ministers—foreign affairs, defence, finance—were consolidated into a single council, where the appropriate ministers could meet from time to time. Then the whole civilian side of the Alliance was moved from London to Paris, and a permanent staff was slowly evolved, first through a body called the Council Deputies, and then through the creation of a permanent Staff/Secretariat. This latter body was headed from 1952–57 by the able Scot, Lord Ismay, and thereafter by a succession of lesser lights.

The problems of running the civilian side of the Alliance have never been rationalized to anyone's real satisfaction. But there were some terrible handicaps. First, to preserve the appearance of unity within the Alliance, the North Atlantic Council has always effectively taken decisions by unanimous vote—that is, by not voting at all, but rather relying on the emergence of what passed for consensus. The appearance of unity was often considered more important than the reconciliation of competing interests. This method of reaching agreement is a clue to the relatively ineffectiveness of this body, as an actual deliberative and decision-taking organ, and to the limited aims of the Alliance generally. As experience with the League of Nations showed, there had to be some disproportionate weight in voting for more important powers if anything were to be accomplished through this mechanism. Hence the voting procedures in the UN Security Council—a good idea, even if they assumed too much common interest among the five permanent members. So too, the European Economic Community adopted a system of weighted voting within its Council of Ministers that extended progressively to cover more important business, although it has rarely been used; in practice, unanimity is still the rule where any matter of real importance is at issue.

But this approach did not apply to the North Atlantic Council. This was perhaps unfortunate, since this procedure of effective unanimity helped to maintain a fiction concerning the equality amongst the member states; and this fiction later helped to reinforce resentment of American domination of the Alliance. At the same time, it also meant that there was a greater need to arrive at decisions around a lowest common denominator, a point that, as often as not, involved some concept of the indivisibility of the Cold War. The Secretaries General have usually been accorded the onerous task of expressing that lowest common denominator, yet some have taken to the task with more alacrity with others. Sr Brosio, NATO'S Secretary General until 1971, was also faced with the problem of trying to reconcile an evaluation of threat, made in the simplest terms possible, with the subtle demands of a policy concerned with *détente* and the differing interests of various Allied governments in it. This has not been a particularly happy mixture. His successor Mr Luns must carry on the effort.

This reliance on a lowest common denominator of official

attitude within NATO has, in turn, meant that it has been difficult to consider accommodation with the Soviet Union at any one particular point. Thus the context of conflict in Europe was reinforced by the manner in which the North Atlantic Council was organized—though perhaps this was not too high a price to pay in exchange for having a viable Alliance at all. This dilemma is common to Alliances, and reflects another aspect of the logic of military confrontation: namely, that only by working out this logic can the Allies then give serious thought to the institutional and political problems posed by attempts to recast confrontation in any way other than the terms in which it first began.

In this way, the pattern of taking decisions within NATO may have actually delayed the end of the Cold War by inhibiting individual nations from exploiting potential understandings with the Soviet Union about the political and strategic *status quo*. Nor could the North Atlantic Council itself do much about this problem: its decisions were often no more than a process of ratifying other decisions already concluded through informal caucus or bilateral bargaining between the United States and other countries. As the pre-eminent nation in the Alliance and as the one chiefly responsible for the Western half of European security, the United States thereby almost by default helped to impose an institutional rigidity on the Alliance as a whole—a rigidity that may have been unavoidable.

Partly as a result of these institutional forms, the disparities in power within the Alliance, and its limited mandate, the civilian side of NATO largely served the following purposes during the early years: it was a means for the United States to exert its influence on its various Allies in ways that could build most consensus amongst them all; it helped to formulate ways of allocating the costs of the Alliance amongst the member states; it permitted the creation of a collective pressure on nations to meet their economic and military commitments; and it did give a sense of unity and solidarity to the Alliance that produced a certain élan within NATO. Each of these purposes was approached in different ways. Yet none was more difficult than accommodating to the disproportionate power of the United States, reflected in part by the dominance during those early years of American personnel in the day-to-day workings of the Alliance. This is a topic of such importance that it will be discussed in detail in succeeding chapters. Yet here it is worth noting that, as time went on, the pattern of American domination became less acceptable to some of the European members of the Alliance. They then tried to redress the balance—and, indeed, this effort has been going on ever since, lately with explicit, if not altogether heart-felt, American participation. Unfortunately, the format of unity in the North Atlantic Council, among other factors, inhibited the making of changes—as when the French, in 1958, proposed that responsibility for general Western interests, not just those within the NATO area, be divided among America, Britain and France. The proposal was received with coolness in Washington, and demonstrated that NATO institutions, and NATO ties, were considered in Washington, as elsewhere, to be of limited scope and effectiveness. In fact, the apparent solidarity of the NATO façade may even have prevented the Americans from comprehending the import of the French suggestion—an import that was to emerge during the French crisis within NATO during 1966–67.

Besides this cosmic question of US influence within the Alliance, however there were still the other, more mundane, purposes of NATO's civilian side, even though they too reflected the predominance of the US role within the Alliance. To begin with, among the first tasks to be faced by the North Atlantic Council—one which it has had to face ever since— was the matter of raising funds with which to operate and, of course, of raising troops to implement the forward strategy. How was the burden to be shared? Or, at the very worst, how was American aid to be apportioned among the various Allies who were to receive help under the Mutual Defense Assistance Program? After a few false starts, the Council in the autumn of 1951 appointed a Temporary Council Committee to look into the matter, and decide upon a doctrine of 'fair shares' for each of the member countries. What this committee bargained out was later adopted as the famous Lisbon force goals of February 1952—so named because of the location of the relevant Council meeting. These goals were indeed ambitious—some 96 divisions to be raised by 1954, including 25 to 30 divisions in battle readiness that would be stationed on the Central Front in Central Europe.

Immediately, a 'numbers game' began, with the 96 divisions serving as a shibboleth of loyalty to the Alliance and to the NATO 'concept'. For years, various NATO Allies were berated for not keeping up their quotas, and the whole Alliance was often said to be militarily vulnerable for not having met the force goals. In fact, of course, there was no Soviet attack throughout that time, so the missing divisions could not have been all that important, except psychologically. In addition, as long as these divisions were missing, it was hard to think of the NATO Alliance as being the military equal to the Soviet Union or, therefore, of there being any abatement of the 'threat'. Thus the Cold War was even further prolonged.

In fact, the Central Front force goals of 25 to 30 divisions— whatever they meant in terms of a viable strategy—were virtually attained by the early 1960s. But there were still few countries that actually met their agreed quotas, particularly when reserve requirements were taken into account. This failure occurred for a variety of reasons, chief among which must be accorded the differing perceptions among the Allies of the actual Soviet threat. It was one thing to accept the American view of the Soviet threat almost by default; it was quite another to back this view with money and men, particularly when several European countries had originally thought they were merely bargaining to gain some American protection that would free economic resources for reconstruction and, later on, for economic development.

There were other reasons as well, including an important

strategic one that will be explored on its own in Chapter 4. There was also a process of political bargaining among the various Allies taking place here. This was not just a common effort to solve common problems, but a fundamental approach to the whole question of the role of various countries in the Alliance, what purposes the Alliance should serve, and how political influence should be shared. At its most basic level, this process of bargaining entailed an attempt by each Ally to see which other countries could be induced to carry a greater weight of its own burden.

This was not a one-shot affair, but rather one that extended over the entire life of the Alliance. It was conducted in particular by European nations that attempted to shift the major part of the burden on to the United States. Yet this bargaining has rarely come out into the open, and been dealt with as such. Instead, there has been a series of attempts to arrive at so-called objective standards for determining relative effort. For years, these standards were presented within an exercise called the Annual Review, and have most commonly revolved about some notion of the percentage of each country's gross national product that has been devoted to defence. This standard has never meant very much, and it has impressed few statesmen. To begin with, there has been no corresponding idea of the different returns in terms of security gained by each country. Certainly some countries had more to gain from the existence of NATO than did others. The extremes were perhaps West Germany, on the potential firing-line, and Canada, whose security comes more or less automatically in the United States' providing for its own.

Ever since the Lisbon force goals, however, there has been a regular succession of efforts to induce various countries to live up to their force commitments. At the same time, there have been efforts to revise and adapt these commitments to differing notions of realism, both with regard to the threat and concerning the best strategy for the Alliance. It may be that this was just a way of structuring a bargaining process. Nevertheless, if ever one desires evidence that NATO has been, first, last, and always, only a loose coalition of nations with limited common interests, this bargaining process is the place to look.

In the mid-1960s, the Americans led an attempt to meet this problem in its own terms and to accept that planning for military purposes should be made on the basis of the forces actually made available by member countries, rather than on the mythical goals that everyone knew would never be attained. This was a rational compromise, but it did not last long, before the same old appeals were being renewed for individual states to increase their force contributions. This was a matter that reflected a changing concept of NATO strategy, and will be discussed further in Chapter 4. In addition, the question of force levels became closely involved in a controversy within the Alliance over the best way to prosecute *détente* with the Russians from 1970 onwards, and will be discussed further in Chapter 6.

These issues of force levels, seen in relation to possible strategies for the Alliance, also entailed a dimension of finance that went far beyond debates about actual numbers of forces. This may seem a peripheral topic, since it assumes some common agreement on the best way for the Alliance to meet real or putative threats, but it was really as important as the force level debates. There was simply a shift in the terms of the debates, as they existed at the heart of the NATO Alliance. In particular, questions of finance also related to the gradual evolution of American dominance and to the increasing reactions against this dominance.

Particularly interesting was the process, begun in the mid-1960s, in which the Federal German Republic agreed to make available funds to offset the drain on the balance of payments of the United States and the United Kingdom, owing to military forces stationed in West Germany. This process was all right as far as it went—after all, the West Germans were gaining a good deal of foreign exchange as well as security through the presence of American and British forces. In addition, Washington and London were able to extract significant amounts of money from a West German government which saw these offset payments as premiums on insurance against a future withdrawal of American and British forces from the Continent, while the United States and Britain received help to meet their growing balance of payments difficulties.

The Americans did particularly well, gaining an agreement from the West Germans in 1965 to make offset payments, in one form or another, totalling $1,300 million over a two-year period. Unfortunately, however, the offset talks became a regular feature of NATO activities, and at times seemed to be more important to the Anglo-Saxon Allies than more political or military features of the Alliance. Another such agreement was concluded in 1967, in which the United States agreed to help Britain economically, while West Germany would take steps to ease the balance of payments problems of both. The process was renewed once again in 1970, yet with more serious intent, since the whole matter of the US relationship to Europe was coming increasingly into question. Problems of American dominance were merging with problems of the specific place that America would continue to find for itself in the changing economic and political circumstances of Western Europe.

These efforts illustrated many things. Among them was evidence of the close relationship between the economic strength of the various NATO partners and the bargaining process that went on within the Alliance. Ironically, it was the consistently undervalued West German mark—denominated at a figure arbitrarily set in 1949—that produced patterns of negotiations within NATO that had implications for the way in which other powers looked at the organization's potential as a forum for considering political problems that went beyond the provision of security. This was so because the bargaining on offset costs was conducted on a strictly tripartite basis until the very end of the 1960s. Although the other Allies were kept informed, this bargaining process dramatized the fact that, in practice, only three nations were taking decisions affecting all the Allies, as did the offset agreements of 1967 which entailed the 'redeployment' of US and UK military units back to their home bases, away from the Continent. And a similar judgement can be made concerning the economic factors that helped lead the Allies to accept a modification of NATO's strategy in 1967 (see Chapter 4).

This process, therefore, helped to isolate further the other Allies from negotiations about the basic interests of the Alliance. This was a further indication that, when basic interests of the great powers were involved, the formal 15-nation structure of the Alliance would be conveniently by-passed, especially by the United States; and it was an indication that the West Germans were gaining an ever-increasing importance within the Alliance. The institutional myth of NATO as a consortium of equal Powers was wearing a bit thin.

Of course, there was some logic behind this offset-cost procedure. After all, other European Allies were benefiting less than the West Germans in terms of foreign exchange from having US and British troops on the Continent. But there seemed to be little understanding in this reasoning that those other nations were benefiting significantly in the more fundamental terms of *security*. The Germans alone were saddled with responsibility for helping out the British and American balance of payments and, as part of this process, effectively gained a greater say in making NATO policies—a development that would be especially important when and if it would be time to worry about the priorities to be adopted in seeking a resolution of the division of Europe and the division of Germany.

This lesson was not lost on General de Gaulle (nor apparently on his successor, President Pompidou): at no time did he ask the West Germans for a single franc to offset support costs for the two French divisions that remained in the Federal Republic. This policy both tended to strengthen his hand in Bonn, and to keep him from becoming at all dependent on the West German Economics Minister. This was a policy he also seemed to be pursuing in November 1968, during the crisis over the weakness of the franc, when he ruled out devaluation even though the West Germans would not revalue the mark.

Only in 1969 did the Allies as a whole take account of this problem of offset payments and influence within the Alliance, though without specifically recognizing the problem as such. This happened when the debate was partially shifted from the question of foreign exchange—a trilateral concern of the British, Americans and Germans—to the question of actual budgetary support for those countries supplying forces, a matter that could more logically include all the Allies. At the same time, the changing nature of US perceptions about the world, and of America's role in it, helped to produce a greater degree of common European effort and consultation on the whole question of burden-sharing than had ever been seen before. The 1970 and 1971 submissions of a group of European defence ministers—the so-called 'Euro-group'—were far from being an adequate response either to American fiscal and troop demands or to the need for some greater European common political effort. They did, however, at least broaden the base of NATO decision-making to include all the West European states that were interested in taking part.

In a way, this apparent need in 1970 (and again in 1971) for the European Allies to engage in a joint approach to the United States on burden-sharing could herald the beginning, if not of a concerted European effort to bargain in common with the United States, then at least of a process of consultations that just might help bring more European weight to bear on common deliberations about the way forward in *détente*. This would be something of a political miracle, but it should not be ruled out, despite the current popularity of political agnosticism.

To summarize the foregoing, it can be seen that negotiations amongst the Allies on the civilian side of NATO often came back down to questions of economic strength and the commitment of it to NATO purposes, whether denominated in troop levels, contributions to the US balance of payments, or actual budgetary support. It will also be apparent that these negotiations went far beyond an analysis, through a process of bargaining, of the relative gain by each country in terms of security, or of the relative ability of each country to shift burdens onto others. Far more important, this bargaining effort over the years had a symbolic significance for more fundamental political factors. It was, in effect, a shorthand method of computing the distribution of political influence within the Alliance—insofar as anything as intangible as 'influence' can be measured—according to a standard of willingness and ability to pay.

Of course, there had always been a central weakness inherent in a process of bargaining for influence through the mechanism of contributions made to the Alliance: political 'influence' tends to be distributed on a scale according to quantum jumps rather than on a continuum. Thus, a small power in NATO that was contributing—say—1/20th of the American share of the 'common defence', would only be able to exercise perhaps 1/1000th (if that) of the total political influence in the Alliance. It was very much like America's being a stockholder with a controlling interest of the shares: smaller holdings did not necessarily buy proportionate influence. This situation did not always benefit the Americans, however: it may help to explain why the Alliance never seemed to be able to meet its force goals, with the smaller nations often lagging farther behind the others. It was one thing for the US to have influence for such purposes as arriving at a common strategy or common appreciation of 'threat'; it was quite another to use that influence to stimulate positive efforts to provide money or troops on the part of governments that would not gain proportionate influence for their efforts.

This discussion of political influence within the NATO Alliance may seem a trifle complex. But understanding the way in which the civilian mechanisms of the Alliance helped to shape the relations among disparate nations may help one to understand broader political questions involving crucial

American-European relations through the years. It may also provide some of the historical background needed to explain the discussion in Chapter 6 on the possibilities for *détente* in Europe. In any event, the symbolic importance of these debates taking place within NATO cannot be overstressed. They have been the most effective means for discussing problems of US dominance and the relative importance of European states in NATO, without actually forcing these issues to a direct, and possibly embarrassing, crunch.

But for all the efforts made on the civilian side of NATO, this has really been a secondary part of the Alliance. There have been semi-annual meetings of foreign and defence ministers that attract attention and give an appearance of setting the course for the Alliance. But in actual day-to-day influence, civilian institutions in NATO have paled beside the continuing influence of the military structure of the Alliance, and particularly of Allied Command Europe. After all, this is an institution which actually has had forces on station for more than 20 years. And these are forces that would, in effect (if not in theory), respond to the commands of the integrated force commander, Supreme Allied Commander, Europe (SACEUR).

Yet first and foremost, SACEUR has been a diplomat. And as such he has faced a number of peculiar problems. In particular, he has always been an American officer, partly because of the predominant role that America has played throughout in the Alliance and—after the mid-1950s—partly because of the need to have as commander the only man who could take the necessary order from the American President to use the nuclear weapons in NATO's arsenal. SACEUR has also been the commander of US forces in Europe, and of the US 7th Army. He wears, as the Pentagon would phrase it, 'three hats'. Which one he 'wears' at any one time depends upon his function at the moment, the temper of the man, and the pressures he is under to conform to the wishes of Washington.

General Eisenhower was, above all else, the best man alive

to make appeals to various European countries on matters of contributing forces and money. He did the job as well as any man could, which was moderately well. Whatever skills as a military commander he might have possessed in addition to his diplomatic skills were more or less an unexpected bonus.

The second SACEUR seemed to prove the widely accepted rule about diplomats and politicians who are really military men in training and temperament. General Ridgway was an excellent battlefield commander; but he was a disaster as SACEUR, because he never seemed to understand the rigorous political and diplomatic demands placed on him in this job— as the only man who was in a position to perform the essential function of prising money and men out of 14 nations, including the new Allies, Greece and Turkey. But the next SACEUR, General Gruenther, improved on his predecessor's record: he had, after all, followed the development of NATO as an institution since its beginning and knew the demands placed upon the symbolic leader of the Alliance.

The most extraordinary SACEUR of all was one of America's most extraordinary officers, General Lauris Norstad. It was clear which hat he preferred to wear: that of the naturalized European presiding over a coalition of states in a tradition more appropriate, it might seem, to the 18th century. Indeed, he came so well to reflect the needs and demands of the NATO organization itself—the 'compleat' organization man and a superb politician—that during his tenure the grip of the United States on the Alliance was weakened, and NATO enjoyed its finest hours as a coalition where political problems could also be tentatively advanced, instead of being confined to external bilateral forums. Regrettably, General Norstad's independence from Washington did not go down well with President Kennedy or Mr McNamara, his Secretary of Defense, and Norstad was recalled in 1961, to be replaced by General Lyman Lemnitzer, a man of lesser political skills or independence of mind and temperament. Since then, the relations of the United States with various Alliance members have never been the same, and the problems of reconciling American and collective European interests have increased significantly, though of course for a complex of reasons of which this has been only one, however important. The current incumbent, General Goodpaster, has in many ways been the least conspicuous. This reflects in part a greater sensitivity in Washington about European feelings as well as Goodpaster's earlier training as chief of staff in the Eisenhower White House (though, like his predecessors as integrated force commander, he is willing to broadcast alarums about the Soviet threat). In part, too, the less obvious presence of SACEUR today also reflects the shifting emphasis in Atlantic diplomatic circles away from strictly military considerations at a time of *détente* and expectations for political change. The de-emphasis of SACEUR is also a de-emphasis of NATO, however.

Still, within NATO itself, there is no doubt that SACEUR has been the pre-eminent official throughout the years since 1951. Civilian officials have never approached his institutional standing. And needless to say, other military commanders, whatever their nationality, could never compete with him for authority and influence, either within the American Government or within Allied circles. There were, indeed, other commands: one for the English Channel, which has never had much reality; and one for the Atlantic, with its Headquarters in Norfolk, Virginia, and which has been based largely upon the preponderance of American seapower. As such, Allied Command Atlantic has had even less scope as a forum for Allied consultation and for the bargaining of matters related to the distribution of political influence within the Alliance. In addition, in this command—as in SACEUR'S subordinate Mediterranean command, consisting primarily of the US Sixth Fleet—forces have only been 'earmarked'. This expression means that they only have been set aside in readiness for use by international commanders in time of crisis or of yearly exercises. The forces of Allied Command Europe, on the other hand, have actually been assigned to SACEUR and, as noted above, effectively operate under his general command. Individual nations with forces in Allied Command Europe still retain, in theory, the right to decide whether or not to commit their forces to battle. But the tenuous lines of communication maintained between SHAPE and home capitals (except to the capitals of the principal powers, especially Washington), as well as the difficulties that would be posed by attempts actually to withdraw forces under fire, make this technicality more or less meaningless. Indeed, this was one of the reasons that led the French Government to remove its forces from Allied Command Europe in 1966: in order to give Paris a better chance to decide whether to join in battle. This was, of course, a largely diplomatic exercise, since French ground forces were stationed well back in Germany against the French border, and would not have been engaged in any initial Russian attack anyway. At the same time, French air squadrons would have been involved, come what may, and were accordingly withdrawn from Germany, although for purposes of NATO air *defence*, the French continued to avail themselves of the common system.

This role of the Supreme Allied Commander, Europe, has been pre-eminent, but this has been true only in practice. In theory, he was for most of SHAPE's first 21 years subject to the authority of one of the myriad NATO bodies—actually there were only 291 of them in 1967—the so-called Standing Group of the Military Committee. This small body consisted of the representatives of the Chiefs of Staff of Britain, France and the United States, and was actually stationed in Washington in silent testimony to the dominant role played by the United States. It was technically only a permanent embodiment of the Military Committee, a body which nominally included all the Allies but which effectively had little importance. And even the Standing Group, as the 'superior body responsible for the highest strategic guidance' in the Alliance, was a body of little significance: it ratified the recommendations sent to it by SACEUR and sent them back as their instructions to him.

The Role of Institutions

Even the American government preferred dealing through the clear and direct lines to SACEUR, sometimes to the disgust of the two other members of the Standing Group, especially France (which has always had a strong sense of the difference between the reality and the appearance of power—even though General de Gaulle, too, valued the latter). Not without justification, the French long believed that the United States was arrogating to itself more influence than even its great economic and military importance warranted. Indeed, the proposal made by France in 1958 (and noted above) for the creation of a triumvirate of France, Britain and America to direct all Western activity in the world was designed in part to clarify the ambiguous nature of the Standing Group, and to expose its rule, not as hypocrisy, perhaps, but at least as a casualty of the failure of European states to find some means of countering American dominance.

In 1967, as part of the reorganization of NATO which followed on the 'defection' of France, the Standing Group was abolished: this was an act which was symbolically important as a means of chastising the French for not 'playing the game', but which had no military significance. Instead, there was an effort to 'rationalize' the structure of the Alliance. Policy direction for SACEUR now came straight from the Military Committee effectively composed of 14 nations. This arrangement, of course, was no more significant than having the Standing Group as a means of ratifying decisions taken mainly by the US, and it made it even less likely that there would be any formal, institutional means for representing at SHAPE the very real differences of influence available to the different member states. In terms of institutional programming, the change might have looked like an attempt to produce greater efficiency, but in practical terms it did little if anything to change the pattern of America's domination of the Alliance.

It was only with the semi-official creation of a Euro-group of defence ministers (actually a Euro-dinner, because of the semi-annual circumstances in which they first met) that there

65

developed any institutional forum whereby Europeans could try to develop common positions in the military field for presentation to the United States. But by the late 1960s, when this practice evolved, such a grouping had to be seen for its wider political significance to resolve some particularly knotty problems. Chief among these was the stand that NATO could take on various questions of prosecuting *détente*, while continuing to bind the United States to the psychological support of the Continent (see Chapter 6).

Finally the institutional arrangements of NATO have also served functions different from the formal ones accorded to them, either by the Treaty itself or by later agreements. They have, in particular, helped to bring about a greater willingness among various of the Allied nations to focus attention on their relations with one another, in many cases concentrating attention that would otherwise have been directed towards problems elsewhere in the world. NATO certainly added to the sense of security in Western Europe within which context the relations of these Allied states were further developed—including such ventures as the European Economic Community. This was a very important and complicated process and it will be described in some detail in Chapter 5. Furthermore, the institutions of NATO certainly have given the Americans—as the dominant partner—the opportunity to decide when to deal with their Allies on a bilateral basis, and when to use the forums of NATO for particular purposes, such as applying collective moral pressures to secure financial and troop commitments to the Alliance.

NATO'S institutions have also given the West Germans a greater feeling of participation than they could possibly have attained outside the Alliance. Indeed, this was a conscious policy adopted by the Federal German Chancellor, Dr Adenauer, who postponed any active policy designed to secure reunification of Germany in order to gain respectability and purpose through involvement in NATO. This policy succeeded, although one might argue that the close involvement of West

Germany in the affairs of Western defence actually deferred the time when the Russians and Americans could consider once again the thorny question of the future of Germany.

At the same time, it has been one of NATO's signal functions for seventeen years to provide a mechanism for containing the problem of West Germany, for the benefit of both East and West Europeans (thus the Russians have never been able to abandon all their sense of ambiguity about NATO, and definitely do not wish the United States completely to abandon its involvement in problems of European security). As such, the institution has managed to reconcile and encompass remedies for the two competing forms of anxiety in Europe: about the Russians and about the Germans. This is the real import of the decision to take West Germany into NATO and into Western European Union: these institutional devices provided the means to allay remaining fears of Germany, which were already mere exaggerations by 1955, while gaining for NATO the forces needed to implement the forward strategy. As an institutional solution to a political problem, this conceit has worked wonders, although it has also brought some difficulties as will be seen in Chapter 6.

Regardless, diplomatically and symbolically West Germany has certainly played its part in NATO organs, gaining from this a sense of participation which was essential to what was widely seen as the re-establishment of an idea of national worth. There have been German officers occupying high positions in the military commands—rising to the level of Commander-in-Chief of Allied Forces, Central Europe. And throughout the NATO organization, West Germans have taken their places in a series of military and civilian institutions which were notable for their role in promoting co-operation at the 'working levels' among nations that had relatively little in common beyond the basic goals of the Alliance. Indeed, when General de Gaulle withdrew his contingents from Allied Command Europe and requested the departure of all NATO military commands from France, French officers and civil servants serving with the

Alliance were far less enthusiastic about the change than was their President.

This blending of different nationalities throughout the structure of the NATO organization has been one of its triumphs, as a diplomatic instrument, and one of its weaknesses as an effective political organization. In order for NATO to be effective as an institution, that is, as an organism that is not just the sum of its member states, there had to be efficiency of administration, communications and political bargaining. Nevertheless, this need has rarely been given priority over the sensitive question of the distribution of posts and perquisites among the various nations. Thus the nationalities of the various military commanders have always reflected the relative importance of the member states, with posts being nicely balanced or rotated among nationalities in order to preserve both a common and individual sense of national dignity.

This anxiety to observe the diplomatic niceties has helped to secure domestic support at many sensitive moments—even from national parliaments: 'burden-sharing' problems, for example, would undoubtedly have been much more difficult to resolve than has been the case had it not been for the sense of common involvement and joint responsibility that has been fostered at working levels of administration. Operating with two official languages, but really one unofficial one, i.e. 'American', the NATO institutions have worked remarkably well and have led to a degree of co-operation—especially in the military field— that would have been unthinkable before the establishment of NATO.

Unfortunately, this structure has not been necessarily one that could be relied upon under stress, or one that would at least be amenable to the subtleties which give real force to bureaucracies. There has not been, in effect, the same kind of 'life of its own' in the NATO bureaucracy as one might find in a national bureaucracy, with its procedures for making senior appointments from within a career structure and with its jealously-guarded informal prerogatives.

Officers and civilians have been seconded from outside, and there has been a notion that civilian staff, however 'professional', still remain nationals of different countries. These factors have prevented the NATO bureaucracies—military and civilian—from arrogating to themselves the kind of power that would have made them a true force to be reckoned with in the conclusion of policy. Of course, this problem has been complicated by the isolation of the commands and civilian staffs from individual governments. And, at times, national delegations to the North Atlantic Council have become suspect as far as governments in home capitals have been concerned. This problem is common to diplomatic services everywhere, and is compounded by the institutional framework of NATO that itself creates allegiances—but allegiances that lack their own true sovereignty or constituency.

Finally, these difficulties have been increased somewhat by the need to have a common standard for handling classified information—thereby retarding the flow of information within the Alliance, or at least ensuring that matters of gravest importance would be dealt with in contexts where there is less chance of compromise. For the same reasons, there has also been an outward appearance of NATO aims and goals—shared by all— that has necessarily obscured the real complexities of diplomatic relations and, indeed, may have helped statesmen to overlook the importance of the complaints made by countries like France concerning the issue of political influence exercised by various member states within the Alliance.

It may be concluded, therefore, that the institutions of NATO have served the Alliance well in implementing agreed policies. But they have been unable, perhaps inevitably, to affect seriously the complicated processes of diplomatic bargaining that have been the life-blood of the Alliance and the relations conducted among fifteen nations within that context.

As an institution, the Warsaw Treaty Organization has had a radically different history from that of NATO. This would not be apparent from a simple reading of the two treaties, however, which are remarkably similar. Indeed, the Warsaw Treaty of Friendship, Co-operation and Mutual Assistance (Appendix III) formally embodies a greater concern with general problems of peace and security embracing the entire European Continent than does the North Atlantic Treaty. For example, it provides specifically that a General European Treaty of Collective Security would automatically replace the Warsaw Pact; and it also contains specific references to the 'universal reduction of armaments'. In addition, the Warsaw Pact contains references to co-operative arrangements among the Allied states. These provisions are not unlike Article Two of the North Atlantic Treaty.

On more concrete matters, it provides that 'in the event of armed attack in Europe on one or more of the Parties to the Treaty' there should immediately be decisions by each of the other Parties 'individually or in agreement' to 'come to the assistance of the state or states attacked with all such means as it deems necessary'. There is certainly little difference to be found here between the two Treaties, except in the version of the Warsaw Pact applying to East Germany, which makes its assistance subject to the determination of the states attacked, and in the provision limiting the scope of the Pact to *Europe*— i.e. excluding Russian security problems in Asia. This last-named provision has been the subject of some controversy within the Pact as the Russians have tried to use the East European nations in their struggle, within world Communist debates and without, against China.

Of course, the strength or weakness of institutions lies in their practice, not in their promise. And the Warsaw Treaty Organization has never become a fully-fledged institution like the one facing it to the West across the division of Europe. This is so despite the fact that the Treaty itself provides specifically for a Political Consultative Committee and a Joint Command— while the North Atlantic Treaty provides only for a Council, which could 'set up such subsidiary bodies as may be necessary'. A Permanent Commission on foreign affairs and a Joint

Secretariat were agreed to separately by the Pact members. Yet none of these Warsaw Pact institutions has the significance within the context of Eastern *bloc* security that the North Atlantic Council and Allied Command Europe have had within that of the West.

At least this was clearly the pattern within the Warsaw Pact through the end of the 1950s; indeed, the Political Consultative Committee only met three times during the first five years of the Pact, despite an agreement to meet not less than twice a year; and it was only in October 1961 that the first joint military exercises were held in the East. Furthermore, it was only after the beginning of the 1960s that the Soviet Union began to place any real reliance upon satellite forces, in order to permit reductions in Soviet troops. At first this reliance came during a period of greater Soviet emphasis upon the use of nuclear weapons in any European war, where the limited roles for conventional forces could be played by the satellite states; later the Russians developed even more need for satellite forces as Moscow took tentative steps to downgrade the role of nuclear weapons and to make it possible to fight a European war for a longer time in a non-nuclear phase.

Lastly, so far as is known in the West, there has never been a systematic development of institutions within the Warsaw Pact, entailing, as in NATO, the careful allocation of subsidiary commands or of posts in civilian agencies among competing nationalities. Most of the reins are still held in Soviet hands, with staff planning apparently carried out in Moscow, although from time to time military exercises have been held under the nominal command of satellite officers.

This lack of an institutional structure for coalition politics has not saved the Soviet Union from problems of sharing its influence with its satellite allies, however. In fact, the Russians have come to rely increasingly upon the Warsaw Pact as a channel for influence and as a focus for Eastern *bloc* cohesion— a process that has advanced precisely as the threat of attack from the West has been seen to recede, and tendencies towards polycentrism have emerged in the East. As this has happened, the Russians have looked more to the Warsaw Pact as a means for linking its satellites more firmly within a context of security where, more even than in economic matters that are covered by the Council for Mutual Economic Assistance (COMECON), there can be seen to be a dependence of Eastern European nations upon Russian leadership and support. COMECON, created in 1949 but only really active after about 1955, has until recent years been the principal mechanism to supplement Soviet bilateral treaties with the satellite states and, through a theoretical division of labour, has sought to bind them more closely to the Soviet Union. However, this has apparently not met Russian demands for security in an age of *détente* and increasing East-West economic ties. This definition of security is, of course, far broader and more restricting than any that has developed in the West. Partly as a result of this process, there have begun to develop within the Warsaw Pact some of the same problems that have plagued NATO over a much longer period of time.

Beginning in the middle 1960s, there has been a series of limited challenges to Russian dominance within the Warsaw Pact—led by Roumania, which prepared the way, perhaps as early as 1958 in negotiating the withdrawal of Russian troops from its soil. These challenges began as the institutions of the Pact began to take on more importance for all the nations concerned. In part, this reflected an ambivalence on the part of various East European régimes about the use of Soviet power to put down revolts such as the one in Hungary—a revolt that may be seen as one reason for the Russians' placing an increasing value on the role of the Warsaw Pact in the following years, and for their concluding a number of status of forces agreements with satellite states. In 1968, for example, pressure from other Eastern European régimes certainly contributed to the Russian decision to intervene in Czechoslovakia, lest Czechoslovak 'infection' of liberalism spread elsewhere; but at the same time the co-operation of four Warsaw Pact countries in the actual invasion was undoubtedly designed in Moscow to add legitimacy to Soviet actions, and to play down the purely Soviet character of the political decision and military operations. The use of a Warsaw Pact context to cloak the attack on Czechoslovakia may also reflect Russian anxiety lest the invasion be seen in the West as solely a Soviet venture, thereby having direct, if unclear, implications for Soviet-American *détente*.

But while four Warsaw Pact nations—East Germany, Poland, Hungary, Bulgaria—co-operated in the invasion of Czechoslovakia, the East European governments have still at times demonstrated an ambivalent attitude about the circumstances in which Russian power would be used for purposes inside the Pact, instead of being reserved solely for use against a military attack from the West. In addition, the further away an Eastern *bloc* state is located geographically from the potential front line of hostilities—that is, on the direct axis between West Germany and the Soviet Union—the less enthusiasm it has been able to show for tight institutional arrangements within the Pact itself. Indeed, over the years there has been a popular concept of a dichotomy within the Warsaw Pact, between the so-called Northern Tier states of East Germany, Poland, Hungary and Czechoslovakia—nations which were more politically vulnerable to real or stimulated fears of West German revanchism—and those states further to the east: Bulgaria, Roumania, and Albania. These latter three nations have each had some success at challenging the Soviet Union in one way or another: Bulgaria through a reputed plot of 1965; Roumania by a consistent search for greater national independence; and Albania by effectively withdrawing from the Pact during 1961, and formally doing so in late 1968.

This distinction often made between the two sets of member states in the Warsaw Pact is not really so clear-cut, however. After all, Poland began the first real bid for increased autonomy from the Soviet Union in 1956; Czechoslovakia did move some during 1968 (with unfortunate results, despite all the care taken in prosecution); and even East Germany has moved away from the Soviet Union to some extent since then—albeit in the direction of even less accommodation with the West. It may be that the distinction really lies in the efforts that the Soviet Union makes to contain challenges in the Northern Tier states, because of their greater strategic importance, not because these challenges have not existed in themselves.

The ambivalence felt in several East European countries about the role of Warsaw Pact institutions and the possible uses of Soviet power can be seen in the contrast between Czechoslovakia and Roumania. The former, during its phase of liberalization in 1968, was constrained to reassure the Soviet Union about its loyalty to the Warsaw Pact—thereby hoping to avoid the mistake made by the Hungarian régime of Imre Nagy in denouncing the Pact during the 1956 revolution. But at the same time the Dubček regime in Prague was reluctant to take an active part in Warsaw Pact exercises that would only provide an excuse for the stationing of Russian troops on Czechoslovak soil. There was also some agitation by Prague for a greater say in joint military planning.

Unfortunately, the Czechoslovaks could not reconcile this dilemma within a framework of East European security; indeed the joint invasion in August 1968 was facilitated by Russian communications units left behind in Czechoslovakia, and by Warsaw Pact forces ostensibly on regular manoeuvres near its borders.

For the Roumanians, on the other hand, an ambivalence about institutions has usually led them to challenge, rather than to accept, Soviet views. Lying geographically outside the path of a potential attack from the West, the Roumanians have felt better able to resist Soviet efforts to strengthen the institutional structure of the Warsaw Pact. Of course, the Roumanians have also had little if anything to fear from the West Germans, although since the onset of the Brandt Government's *Ostpolitik* these fears have diminished elsewhere in the Pact as well—a fact that may lead the Russians to be even more wary of apostasy within the Pact and, presumably, to be even more concerned about the role of institutions in fostering loyalty.

Still, over the past five years or so, it has been the régime in Bucharest that has brought to light the growing complexities surrounding the development of Pact institutions, and the growing resentment in Eastern Europe about Russian domination of them. For example, the Roumanians have challenged, unsuccessfully, the practice whereby Warsaw Pact forces are always commanded by a Soviet general.

This is a somewhat different matter from the practice of always allocating the job of Supreme Allied Commander, Europe, to an American general. Within the Warsaw Pact, for example, there is hardly more than a pretence of an integrated command structure with important subordinate posts that could be allocated among the East European allies. Furthermore, there is an even greater reliance in the East on the role of Soviet forces, particularly the role closely connected with the use of nuclear weapons. After all, the Russians have never tried to make the fine distinctions between nuclear and conventional war that have been made by the Americans and their Allies. The Russians have also been under no constraints even to approach the Americans in providing their Allies with nuclear weapons, even under the so-called 'two-key' system, where agreement of both donor and recipient nation is required for their use. In the Warsaw Pact, the Russians have, in recent years, provided short-range missiles to some of their Eastern *bloc* Allies, but there is no evidence that the nuclear warheads for these missiles have been provided to the Allies or that they are even stockpiled outside the Soviet Union.

This last development seems to reflect the existence of a problem somewhat similar to that found within NATO; but there has certainly not been a full-scale nuclear-sharing problem in the Warsaw Pact like that seen in the West. This derives at least in part because of the Russians' reliance in their strategic doctrine upon the use of nuclear weapons at an early stage of conflict. But this is a matter that will bear close attention in the next few years.

In recent years, however, there has been a growing effort by the Soviet Union to provide something like an integrated command structure for the Warsaw Pact. But the relationship between this effort and the provision of increased fighting ability on the part of satellite forces is not clearly established. It is likely that the Soviet Union, having turned to its security pact in some ways as a more reliable instrument than its economic treaty, COMECON, in channelling influence to Eastern Europe, has become more concerned that individual states within the Warsaw Pact should be seen to play a co-operative alliance role. Such a development would, in theory, also provide a context for more effective co-operation *among* the East European Allies, particularly in providing a form of cohesion or discipline within a Soviet concept of security needs.

The Roumanians have consistently opposed this Soviet effort over the years, especially in cases where it has been obvious that the new arrangements would merely work to the Russians' political advantage within the Pact. Where there has seemed a chance that closer co-operation would give satellite governments—meaning Roumania—more influence on Soviet policy and, particularly, on the conditions under which Russian forces would have the right to be stationed or manoeuvre on satellite territory, then the Roumanians have appeared to be more receptive. In any event, following the invasion of Czechoslovakia, the Roumanians modified their lonely stand within the Warsaw Pact, apparently to test the limits of Soviet patience before continuing their effort to define the division of influence within the Alliance. Yet by early 1969 the Roumanians were again attempting to broaden the scope for national action within the context of the Warsaw Pact, although they were a bit more cautious than before in judging the limits placed by the Russians on their definition of security in Europe. In March 1969, the Warsaw Pact Powers 'endorsed' a 'Statute on the

The Role of Institutions

Committee of Defence Ministers'; adopted a new statute on 'Joint Armed Forces and the Integrated Command'; and adopted 'other documents designed to bring about a further improvement in the structure and organs of administration of the defence organization of the Treaty'. But what these cryptic announcements would mean in practical terms was not immediately apparent.

This process of defining relative influence within the institutions of the Warsaw Pact—and in the formal and informal consultative councils—has also introduced the problem known in NATO as burden-sharing. Little is known of the actual division of the costs of alliance among nations within the Warsaw Pact, but a Roumanian diplomatic manoeuvre in May 1966, reflecting once again its long-standing opposition to foreign bases, did indicate that the allied states had been expected to contribute to the financing of Soviet forces stationed in Eastern Europe. To this Roumania was opposed, as a function of the unsettled questions of sovereignty within the Pact and the amount of relative 'influence' gained by the Soviet Union by having forces on the territory of its satellites. Since that time, Poland and even East Germany have given some indications that they are concerned about the costs of joint defence. Like the question of a more closely integrated command structure, this question also does not seem to have yet been resolved satisfactorily by the Warsaw Pact states, although certainly the Roumanians have lost their bid to have the command of Warsaw Pact forces rotate among the member states.

The Russians, clearly, are not yet ready to pay such a high price for an increase in an alliance cohesion that may itself depend largely upon the possibilities of independent Soviet military action within the context of the Warsaw Pact. This is a factor that is very important, for example, in the selection of sites for joint manoeuvres, as was demonstrated by the invasion of Czechoslovakia. And this factor has now been extended by the Russians on their own with the Brezhnev Doctrine on the

77

limited sovereignty of states in the so-called Socialist Common-wealth. The Doctrine has found little response within the Pact nations, for obvious reasons. Yet in Moscow it may seem to be a necessary effort to overcome a structural weakness in the Warsaw Pact itself. So much for the evolution of a common doctrine on the inter-relationship of state interests within the institutions of the Pact itself!

In any event, the Russians' greater reliance upon Warsaw Pact forces in European security has led to a greater elaboration of the Pact's institutional structure, even though the network of bilateral treaties woven by the Russians in the 1940s has mostly been renewed and revised. This began with Czecho-slovakia in 1963, East Germany in 1964 (a new treaty), and Poland in 1965. These bilateral treaties retain their funda-mental importance to Moscow, and, in some cases, entail more binding commitments of mutual alliance than does the Warsaw Pact itself. Yet this process of elaboration, in turn, has gone together with a modernization of Warsaw Pact forces and the development of a greater combat role for them, as opposed to their previous role as a sort of forward air defence for the Soviet Union. These developments, of course, could potentially increase Russian anxieties about the loyalty of individual satellite armies—for example, Czechoslovakia's well-equipped army of more than fourteen divisions—during a period of internal unrest within the Eastern *bloc*. Indeed, the Russian invasion of Czechoslovakia may have derived in part from genuine concerns in Moscow about such loyalty and its impact on Russian security. That is, with the development of more effective Warsaw Pact forces, the Russians may feel a greater need to be assured of the loyalty of individual states and of the strength of interstate cohesion for purposes of discipline within the Pact. Of course, the invasion could not help to make Czechoslovak forces more loyal; but in the short run, it might have helped to minimize the consequences of *disloyalty*, particularly as viewed by Russians with a very narrow and restricted view of the internal changes they would permit within the East. The lesson would be drawn by the other East European states, even if Czechoslovakia were further alienated in the process.

The role played by satellite forces in helping to maintain an internal discipline within the Pact, symbolized by their token co-operation in the Prague invasion, has become all the more important for the Soviet Union, using its extremely broad definition of its own security in an era of *détente* with the United States. There is now a common interest shared by East and West in making sure that the NATO Powers can distinguish between the movement of additional Soviet troops into Eastern Europe for internal uses, as opposed to preparations for attack against the West. In addition, the danger of misperception by the West, which could lead to a mutual process of troop reinforcements and the risk of accidental war, has placed a premium on the Russians' not moving additional forces into Eastern Europe—at least not without the most careful assurances to the NATO nations. These assurances were given in August 1968; and they were accepted by NATO although, as will be discussed in Chapter 6, this process in itself had a disruptive effect on the possibilities for East-West *détente*. Therefore, for the Russians, Eastern *bloc* forces could relieve the Russians of the need to risk a crisis with the West by making conventional reinforcements in Eastern Europe for internal reasons within the Pact. Of course, the presence of satellite forces rather than Russian reinforcements would also inhibit escalation of any crisis with the West, and would be a useful buffer at the outbreak of a European war.

In conclusion, the institutional structure and significance of the Warsaw Pact can be seen as a continuous process of evolution. It has extended from the earliest days of the Pact, when institutions existed only on paper, and when the Pact was more a propaganda counter to West Germany's entering NATO than anything else, until now. This is a time when some real problems have emerged—problems of cohesion, of command structure, of burden-sharing. These have emerged as a function of the greater elaboration of the Pact and reliance of the Soviet Union on it for security, both against any threat from the West, and against erosion of the Russian position of influence within the Eastern *bloc* itself.

But for all the similarities of this process with problems evident in NATO's institutions, major differences caution one against seeing NATO and the Warsaw Pact as complementary institutions, except in the most fundamental terms of the super-power guarantees to the military security of the Continent, and the symbiotic relationship imposed upon alliances in confrontation. The Warsaw Pact has only lately begun to take on aspects of a forum for channelling influence back *to* the super-power, as the Roumanians have succeeded from time to time in thwarting Russia's plans for strengthening the Pact as a vehicle for its own influence in Eastern Europe.

These developments are still tentative, but the Soviet Union is clearly in need of the Pact, in which decisions are reached by unanimous vote. Paradoxically, therefore, the Brezhnev Doctrine may represent in part a Soviet attempt to minimize the consequences of accommodating the East European demands, and particularly to establish an alternative source of discipline during the progress of West Germany's *Ostpolitik*. At the same time, the Russians have established the principle that, in the main, the 'road from Bonn to (say) Prague lies through Moscow'—about which more will be said in Chapter 6. Yet they have at least shown a willingness in theory to support East European interest in those aspects of a European Security Conference that would permit greater East-West contact, although this has not so far come to fruition.

In general, however, the Warsaw Pact has still not paralleled NATO as a means for individual member states to influence significantly the policies of the Soviet Union.

Furthermore, the Pact has not been as successful as NATO in the West in co-ordinating the military effort of the Eastern *bloc* states, and it certainly has never become the focus for grander efforts by the Eastern European states, themselves, to proceed to more elaborate forms of functional integration. Indeed, in the late 1940s, the Russians blocked movements towards integration among the Balkan states, in order to preserve unimpaired their own bilateral lines of influence. Insofar as roles of co-ordination and integration have been played at all by institutions in the East, they have taken place more within the context of COMECON.

Even more important, however, in distinguishing NATO from the Warsaw Pact as an institution, has been the sense of assurance within the NATO Alliance (possibly excepting France) concerning its basic, though limited, political purposes, despite some increasing disagreement in an era of *détente* about the kind of Europe each country would like to see in the future, and the ways of attaining it. There is also a basic acceptance of the concern of the United States for the political and economic growth of Western Europe. In the Warsaw Pact, on the other hand, there has been no such sense of assurance, since it has rarely been clear whether or in what manner the Soviet Union would accommodate itself to the needs and interests of its East European Allies. This difference between the two Alliances is partly reflected in the process of their creation: NATO was largely a European creation that co-opted the United States; the Warsaw Pact was essentially a function of Russian foreign policy from the beginning. Of course, in part this reflects the difference in the power each super-power actually possessed to determine the behaviour of its allies. The United States could never have duplicated in the West the degree of Russian control in the East even if it had wanted to do so. This is a standard problem of international relations: a perception of national ambitions can never be separated from an analysis of the power to attain them.

A useful comparison for the United States has existed in the Organization of American States, where for most of the last 20 years Washington was in a better position to dominate its Allies than it was in NATO. At the same time, however, it also had a lesser interest in actually getting its Latin American

Allies to act in positive ways (such as creating military forces); and the United States did not as a rule exercise the same degree of political hegemony that the Russians developed in East Europe.

Still, these observations indicate that a comparison of the *political* purposes of the two Alliances must be made very carefully indeed, and with a host of qualifications borne in mind.

Finally, there are certain facts of geography that have prevented there being a symmetry of relationship between the Americans and NATO, on the one hand, and the Russians and the Warsaw Pact on the other. The most important of these facts, of course, is the close proximity of the Soviet Union to all its European Allies, and the overshadowing of Eastern Europe by Soviet military power, of whatever form—a fact that certainly helps to reduce the chances of a crisis of confidence in the Warsaw Pact (a problem of 'credibility') concerning Soviet military involvement in East Europe's defence. There was some apprehension in East Europe during the Six-Day War, when the Soviet Union retired early from the crisis, but this apprehension has never attained the dimensions of the debate over the credibility of the American commitment that has taken place in West Europe.

Despite all these qualifications, however, it is certain that over the last few years the importance of the Warsaw Pact as an institution in the development of European security has become more important, first as a focus of super-power influence; second as an element of stability for the whole Continent; and third as a source of problems among the Pact allies. As such, it deserves to be given even more attention in the future in any study of the problems of European security.

Chapter 4

Strategy

Histories of NATO are usually written in terms of the strategic problems that faced the Allies, and of the steps they took—successfully or not—to solve them. This study cannot ignore these problems, as boring as they may be in themselves. Above all, understanding strategic problems is important because of their impact upon politics, and the ways in which they have helped shape political relations, not only within the Alliance, but also as between East and West.

The strategic doctrine of NATO began, as noted in an earlier chapter, with the so-called 'forward strategy', a political doctrine designed to protect the nations of Western Europe against a putative threat as far forward geographically in Central Europe as possible: that is, in West Germany itself. And, as discussed before, the adoption of this doctrine meant that German forces would have to be involved if it were to be at all viable.

It took many years to implement the forward strategy; indeed, it was not until the 1960s that the conventional component of the strategy came to be realized. Throughout the early years, there were repeated efforts, primarily by the United States, to stimulate the Allies to meet the ideal force levels agreed at the Lisbon meeting of the North Atlantic Council in February 1952—i.e. 25 to 30 divisions on the Central Front as opposed to the 15 there were at the time. But for a variety of reasons, achieving these goals continued to elude the military planners. Of course, there was still no real consensus within the Alliance about the practical nature and extent of the Soviet threat, though there was a general sort of agreement in theory. These failures to meet force quotas were good indications of the true feelings that member countries had about their supposedly parlous state. Still, there were certain advantages to be had from adopting verbal forms of concern. Chief among these advantages was the securing of a continuing US commitment to the future of Europe.

Of course, from the beginning of the Alliance not all the NATO nations were actually involved in providing forces, and as time went on, many of them never really became deeply involved in this effort. Portugal, for example, has never contributed troops to Allied Command Europe; Iceland has had no forces at all (and has, therefore, been represented on the Military Committee of the Alliance by a civilian). And, throughout the years, Norway has never allowed Allied troops to be stationed permanently on her soil, except for short periods of time for the purpose of training exercises. Finally, neither Norway nor Denmark has allowed nuclear weapons to be based on her territory.

These are illuminating facts, in view of the tremendous uproar that occurred, particularly in the United States, when France withdrew from Allied Command Europe in 1966, as the final act in a three-stage withdrawal from the Allied military commands (the first two stages entailed withdrawal of the French fleets from their earmarked status in the commands covering the Atlantic Ocean and Mediterranean Sea, respectively). French forces and territory, of course, constituted an important part of the defence structure of the vital Central Front, and there was at least a marginal case for believing that French force withdrawals from Allied Command Europe would affect NATO strategy.

But in reality, these withdrawals—as well as those undertaken by Canada in 1969—had their most significant effect in *appearing* to affect NATO strategy, or, at least, to affect the sense of common purpose, or cohesion, upon which planners had long based the credibility of the conventional component of the NATO deterrent. It had been this way throughout the history of NATO—i.e. the appearance of a viable strategy often came to stand for reality, if not in Russian eyes (and we do not yet know what the Russians thought of NATO's changes in strategy over the years), then at least in the eyes of NATO beholders themselves. It little mattered that NATO's actual strategic posture on the ground contributed to Soviet inactivity during all those years. The continuing gap between that posture and the ideal laid down as the basis for inter-Allied bargaining about the sharing of common burdens still helped to focus attention on the half-empty bottle, not the half-full one. In effect, there was no real frame of reference that encompassed both the strategic posture of NATO and what was going on in terms of threat on the other side of confrontation in Europe, at least not a frame of reference that could be translated into Alliance politics, let alone break the continuing context of military confrontation that was imposing a logic of its own. The strategy of NATO, like its institutions, acquired a personality that had to be fulfilled, almost without reference to the causes that had brought it into being in the first place.

As the 1950s wore on, so did the debates about NATO's strategic posture. 1954–55, the Year of Maximum Danger, came and went, without anyone's saying that the danger had then diminished. The troop goals were still not fulfilled. Of course, throughout this time, NATO's strategy was not based entirely on ground troops and fighter aircraft. Since at least 1948, the United States had been providing a form of nuclear deterrent for Europe, first with B-29s ostentatiously based in England during the Berlin blockade—although it now seems clear that these bombers did not actually carry nuclear weapons at first and were more of symbolic significance than of anything else. Later, this deterrent was centred on a great complex of bomber bases strung out around the world. Therefore, from the first, the American nuclear arsenal was implicitly a part of NATO strategy. Indeed, if there had been a major Russian attack on Western Europe, America would have been expected at some point to unleash its bombers. After all, the United

States was until the late 1950s practically invulnerable to Russian nuclear attack, and could make this pledge to her Allies with relative impunity.

As the decade progressed, Europeans put increasing reliance on this American nuclear guarantee, partly from economic motives, since this guarantee would, in theory, relieve them of the need to provide all the conventional forces demanded by the ideal strategy of conventional defence and the force goals adopted at Lisbon in 1952. But European behaviour stemmed only partly from economic motives, or even from the sense that war was really most unlikely. It also soon became obvious that no Western European country that might be a battlefield in a Third World War had much to look forward to in a conventional defence; the destruction would be catastrophic, even if the Allies eventually prevailed. Not surprisingly, this argument appealed with strongest force to people in West Germany, a country which had been a major battlefield of the Second World War and promised to be one in the Third, whether or not nuclear weapons were ever used. The emergence of this attitude helps to explain some of the special problems that arose in the Alliance when the West Germans were admitted; indeed, along with the Americans, the Germans were always most willing to take seriously the consequences that might ensue from underestimating the Russians' ability or willingness to attack the NATO nations.

This chain of reasoning meant that there was considerable appeal in Western Europe for policies designed to *deter* Russian attack, even if the response to this attack had to be largely confined in practice to nuclear weapons. Of course, the chief means for accomplishing this strategy, whether of deterrence or of defence following the failure of deterrence, rested on the American nuclear arsenal.

As a result of a growing concern in Europe for policies of nuclear deterrence instead of conventional defence, an Allied debate took place between January 1954 and December 1956 on a single question: should NATO planning be based on the making available of relatively small nuclear weapons that the Americans had developed but had not so far chosen to base in Europe? According to the theory, these weapons would be used soon after combat began and, if their use against enemy forces and communications did not stop the Russians and force them to think again about aggression, then the Strategic Air Command would be brought into play. For reasons of simplicity, these small weapons were called tactical—a word that seemed to be an unfortunate misnomer. Indeed, the NATO debate on their use took place without anyone's having been able to explain adequately (either then or since) how it would be possible in densely-populated Europe to use a weapon roughly of the size of those used at Hiroshima and Nagasaki and yet talk of tactical instead of strategic destruction. This point has not been lost on many Europeans over the years.

In any event, after a long, boring, and esoteric debate, the North Atlantic Council late in 1956 adopted a new strategy which really did little more than to formalize existing attitudes, and to accept, finally, the concept implicit in a Council decision of December 1954. This was for NATO to plan on the basis that nuclear weapons would be available for use, whether or not the enemy used them first. According to this concept, the Allies would only try to mount a conventional defence of Western Europe for a very short time, and then would rely upon the United States to introduce nuclear weapons, presumably leading up to a major nuclear war if need be. The only reason for having conventional weapons at all was to serve—as the jargon went—as a trip-wire or plate glass window that would signal the start of the tactical phase of the nuclear war.

This somewhat macabre idea seemed to many observers to be a sound strategy, particularly since it was being adopted in a period when the American massive retaliation doctrine still prevailed. At that time, the Americans were placing much emphasis on the potency and viability of their nuclear arsenal, particularly since the United States appeared to be effectively invulnerable to direct Soviet attack.

In political terms, however, the adoption of the new NATO strategy marked the beginning of an era in which the relationship of the United States to its Allies in Europe came increasingly to be debated in terms of nuclear strategy. Indeed, if there had ever been any prospect of developing a real division of military labour as between the United States and her Allies—a division of labour which could have had some meaning in terms of the sharing of political influence—then that time was now passing, never to be recaptured. The Europeans now came to accept that only the United States could implement the necessary strategy for the Continent, not just in terms of psychological support that an American guarantee would provide, but also in hard practical terms as well. For good or ill, the viability of a nuclear strategy came to symbolize the underlying health of the US commitment to Europe and, with it, of the entire Atlantic Alliance itself.

It was not entirely a coincidence that this period also marked the beginning of a process in which the Allies began thinking about means for broadening the scope of the Alliance. They wished to build upon the common military effort and escape the conclusion that they were so centrally dependent on the US. And if the Europeans were to be even more dependent upon the Americans than before, then there might at least be some means for spreading the influence available within the Alliance into other fields in which the Americans did not have such an obvious monopoly of the symbols of power. Some of the Allies therefore put emphasis on the so-called non-military uses of NATO—a subject to be described at length in Chapter 5; others—mainly France—meanwhile put more emphasis on the symbols, as France did by pressing forward with the development of nuclear weapons.

Before long, however, this carefully thought-out NATO strategy of rapid nuclear escalation was itself under review. Significantly, the review began in Europe at the end of 1956, under the sponsorship of the new Supreme Allied Commander, Europe, General Lauris Norstad. In 1957, the Military Committee of NATO adopted a major study that, although designed to implement decisions concerning the use of tactical nuclear weapons, actually outlined a new form of strategic and political relationship between conventional and nuclear arms. Implicitly, the proposals made in this study—the so-called MC-70—undermined the basic assumptions of the strategy that had only just been decided upon. According to MC-70, there should no longer be merely a plate glass window or trip-wire, but rather, once again, a significant level of conventional forces (a shield). Yet these forces would be designed, not for the purpose of fighting a truly conventional war (with all the destruction that this implied for the forward countries). Instead, they would merely serve to force the enemy to pause after the initial stages of an attack, and think again whether the advantages of continuing the conflict outweighed the risks. After that, according to the theory, the enemy might still press on, but at least he would be fully aware that the US was prepared to unleash its nuclear arsenal in response, with all the obvious consequences this would entail for everyone.

This new strategy reflected an important new change in Allied attitudes. Indeed, a new era was beginning. No longer were the Russians to be regarded in official NATO thinking— that is, predominantly in American thinking—as infallible giants whose first probing attack could reasonably be taken to mean a necessarily successful all-out drive to the English Channel. Rather, they might only try to make limited intrusions into NATO territory. What would happen, the European allies began to ask, if the Russians did not believe that the United States would use nuclear weapons, thereby starting a world-wide nuclear war, just for the defence of a small corner of NATO territory? Surely, the reasoning went, the Russians should be given an opportunity to consider their error in starting a conventional attack, before the world was blown up? Or what if there were an accident, or simply miscalculation? Shouldn't there be a second chance? Indeed (though this idea was rarely expressed in public) few Europeans were really anxious to face the prospect of sudden escalation to nuclear war, despite the comfort they derived from believing that the Americans were prepared to take the fateful decision if it ever proved necessary. Mounting a strategy of deterrence instead of defence had its appeal, but there was still a limit to the price most people would be willing to pay for it.

The new doctrine therefore seemed to make eminent sense, although it had the unfortunate implication of requiring more conventional forces than had originally been planned under the trip-wire doctrine. It also led the Americans to put more pressure on their European Allies to build up levels of conventional forces on the Continent—a phenomenon that is still with us, today. But at least a pause doctrine introduced more sanity into NATO strategy and reduced the likelihood that a nuclear war could happen as the outgrowth of a process based on logic but not on politics. Already the strategists who thought in terms of systems rather than politics or psychology were being challenged by thoughtful people. A mechanical approach was not enough. There must be the possibility of responses that lay between suicide or surrender, as well as some provision for second thoughts and sheer human fallibility.

But most important, by urging a revised strategy, this report of the Military Committee permitted real glimmerings of an attitude of *détente* to appear—at least as viewed in the West. The NATO Allies were finally able to comprehend the probable nature of conflict in Europe as it would actually transpire, and not as they had chosen to imagine it. Even more, the Allies accepted the need to find a way out of the terrible dilemmas created by the cataclysmic doctrines which had evolved during a time when there seemed to be, especially in America, an implacable Soviet military threat to Western Europe. By confronting these dilemmas, the Allies were able to foster attitudes that could permit some relaxation of tensions and that, eventually, could underpin a broader awareness of *détente*.

Be that as it may, the development of a pause doctrine, and its interaction with the role envisaged for the American nuclear deterrent, then entered a phase that entailed the most subtle political and strategic interchanges in the history of the Alliance. These interchanges demonstrated time after time the dependence of the Europeans on the Americans, and repeatedly strained relations across the Atlantic. This is not to say that perceptions of the problem were accurate—that either a strategic response based on pause or one based on early first use of nuclear weapons was the proper one to deter a Soviet attack. After all, there was still little attempt to relate NATO strategy to a concept of Soviet threat that was unclouded by the context of conflict which had solidified at the beginning of the 1950s. But even if this strategic problem were largely an exercise in self-deception (a moot point), it served as a convenient focus for the debate that ensued.

This debate began soon after an important development—one of the most important in changing the whole Atlantic relationship in terms of politics and strategy. This development took place during the period 1956–58, as it became obvious to all that the United States had lost its invulnerability to Soviet nuclear attack. For a short time of course, the Soviet Union had been capable of launching a bomber attack against the United States; but suddenly, after the launching of *Sputnik* in October 1957, America began to appear genuinely vulnerable. Not only did this promise difficulties for the Alliance. The Americans themselves began to think seriously about the structure of their nuclear power. In the process, the civilians finally took over the lead from the military thinkers on the subject, and began to worry about constructing a system of deterrence that could survive any Soviet attack and remain viable. In practice, this meant building invulnerable missiles underground (*Minuteman*) and under water (*Polaris*). In time, these new weapons would enable the United States to survive anything the Russians could do, and still retaliate in force. Thus would deterrence of attack against the United States be preserved.

In Europe, however, a new crisis was brewing. Since the United States was now seen to be directly vulnerable to Soviet attack, how could one believe that the Americans would risk their own destruction in order to preserve the security from Soviet attack of America's European Allies? This was a line of reasoning pursued by the Gaullists with increasing persistence over the years. Thus was ushered in a long period of fundamental uncertainty and a complex political process within the Alliance which became known as the 'nuclear sharing' problem.

There have always been at least two elements to this problem: first, how could the United States convince the Russians that threats of nuclear retaliation against Russian conventional attack in Europe were credible—i.e. that Europe was of such political worth to the United States that any risk would be justified? Second, how could the Americans convince their Allies of the same thing? Throughout the years in which this issue has been important it has proved far easier to accomplish the first of these tasks than the second—for perhaps a simple reason: the Russians had only to calculate the risks of *gaining* political objectives—while the West Europeans were concerned about *losing* political values, as well as defining a fundamental political relationship to the United States.

It has been perhaps one of the greatest political miracles of the twentieth century that America's Allies in Europe have continued to believe her commitment to defend them with nuclear weapons for as long as they have. In 1966, for example, General de Gaulle put together a very logical case for withdrawing his forces from Allied Command Europe. The risks of being drawn into a nuclear war because of some American misadventure elsewhere had gone up, he argued; and the credibility of the American nuclear guarantee had gone down as the Americans had become increasingly vulnerable to Russian nuclear attack. Such was his case; and in many respects it was a compelling one. But few Europeans have ever agreed with him. And that fact speaks, perhaps, of an American diplomatic triumph achieved through a period that included perhaps the most incredible series of American diplomatic blunders in the history of the North Atlantic Treaty Organization.

To understand this process, one must examine more closely a major event in the development of NATO strategy: a highly controversial speech made by the then American Secretary of Defense, Mr Robert McNamara, to the North Atlantic Council in May of 1962. The speech itself has never been made public, but what was reputed to be a reasonable facsimile of it was contained in a speech delivered at Ann Arbor, Michigan, that summer. Immediately, it was clear that something was seriously amiss in US—European relations, and a great hullabaloo went up in Allied capitals. What did Mr McNamara say that aroused such consternation among America's European Allies? And why had he chosen to put the cat among the pigeons at this particular moment?

The answers to these questions can best be explained indirectly within the context of the intricacies of nuclear strategy, and that unpredictable quantity known as the diplomatic confidence of one nation in another. Quite simply, in 1962 the United States was facing some hard choices with regard to her own relations with the Soviet Union—relations that contained elements of the more abstruse strategic doctrines—and with regard to her relations with the European members of NATO. Almost imperceptibly, some of the basic interests of the US and European members of the Alliance were drifting apart.

And most importantly, the Americans were beginning to define a relationship with the Russians that did not always centre on the chief prize in their Cold War relationship—namely Europe. Since the Russians could attack the United States directly, so the reasoning went, the Americans must be able to manage their nuclear relations directly, in order to ensure that a nuclear war between the two powers would be as unlikely as possible. In the process, however, America's relations with Europe might have to be readjusted to the larger and more immediate need.

What happened? Basically, the Americans were becoming increasingly concerned about the problems of controlling a nuclear war if for any reason one should begin. This concern was most evident on the part of the US Defense Secretary, a man with a lucid, logical and quite unpolitical mind. And not surprisingly, this concern was also a logical extension of the thinking surrounding the pause doctrine itself. How could a nuclear war be brought effectively under control? How could destruction be limited? How, indeed, could a nuclear war be conducted, so as not to become just one long spasm of nuclear explosions from its beginning to the end of the world? Under the massive retaliation doctrine of John Foster Dulles, the former US Secretary of State, these questions were not even asked. Under the new Administration, however, they had both to be asked and answered, even though it was doubtful that the answers would ever be needed and, as it turned out, even though they would create political difficulty for the Atlantic Alliance in the process.

The answers to these questions were slowly evolved in the American Defense Department, in one of the more abstruse elaborations of doctrine that have marked the development of the whole depressing—and arguably insane—subject of nuclear strategy: the calculus of Armageddon. According to the theory that was devised, there should be an attempt to spare the enemy's cities—in this case Russian cities—in the first nuclear exchange of a nuclear war, in order to give leaders in the Kremlin an incentive not to strike American cities. Ideally, the battle would be fought by firing nuclear missiles against nuclear missiles and bombers, with a chance that the madness that would characterize any nuclear war could be brought to a halt before many people were killed. Each side would be given time to come to its senses.

Unfortunately, there was a basic flaw in this proposition: at that time the US had such a superiority in nuclear weaponry that the Soviet Union could never survive a contest in which America destroyed all of Russia's missiles and bombers, yet had some of her own left over to hold Russian cities hostage. And, indeed, the Russians never agreed to play the game as it was conceived in the Pentagon. Even today, the Russians reject American efforts to maintain a margin of superiority in any class of nuclear weapons, even as they contend they do not want this superiority for themselves. Despite a decade of experience, however, the American Government—or at least the Nixon Administration—still pursues the chimera of somehow gaining political advantage from impressing the Russians with their inferiority.

Be that as it may, the idea of a war fought out in terms of attacks on opposing nuclear forces seemed attractive to the Americans in the early 1960s, and this so-called no-cities or counterforce doctrine gained currency. But here the United States had to reckon on yet another factor that had a direct impact on the NATO Alliance: the emergence of other nuclear deterrent forces owned by NATO Allies. There were two: one British—already in being—and one French that was still several years from readiness. Neither of them seemed to have much value, strategically, when compared with the overwhelming strategic might of the Americans and Russians. Indeed, both the British and French deterrents were planned before the formal elaboration of a doctrine that could give them some value. This was the so-called doctrine of proportional deterrence—that is, the idea that nothing that an enemy could gain from the utter destruction of, say, Britain could possibly be worth the loss of those few of its cities that the British V-Bomber force (later *Polaris* missiles) could always be sure of destroying.

Nevertheless, the existence of the British force, and the development of a French one that was then conceived as part of the coin of great-power status, did pose some real problems for the United States in controlling its problematic nuclear war, to say nothing of the incentive these forces might create for further nuclear proliferation. After all, in order to bring a nuclear war to a halt, the American theory required central direction of diplomatic interchanges and, even more important, central control of the use made of *all* nuclear weapons on each side of the possible nuclear confrontation. The Russians, of course, have never relaxed their grip on the satellite nations of Eastern Europe to the point that any of them could consider acquiring nuclear weapons of its own. As a result, Moscow has never had to face this problem of Allies who could not be seen to be under firm control of their dominant partner.

But the Americans had not exercised such firm control of their Allies. In addition, there was a possibility that use of the European deterrent forces could actually start a nuclear war on its own—a so-called 'catalytic war'—thereby involving the Americans in a nuclear war with the Soviet Union whether either super-power wanted one or not. The Americans them-selves also thought that the Russians would be concerned that one of these smaller nuclear arsenals could go off by accident or miscalculation, and would therefore be more jittery.

They had not thought through the viewpoint of the Euro-peans, however. For them there was a certain value—a psychological value of confidence—in having the ability to involve the US in a nuclear war on behalf of Europe even if the US President proved reluctant in the event. After all, were not the US troops in Germany really only serving as hostages to the Europeans in order to demonstrate the US nuclear commit-ment? Therefore, American efforts to minimize the importance of nuclear weapons and discourage their production led to the raising of a number of eyebrows on the Continent.

This, then, was the context within which we must view Mr McNamara's speech and the enunciation of the famous McNamara Doctrine. To begin with, he reviewed some of the less controversial aspects of the debate then going on in the United States. For example, he downgraded the special nature of nuclear weapons, and argued that they should be used primarily for attacks on enemy forces, not on enemy cities, at least in the first instance after a nuclear war had begun.

As discussed above, the Europeans were already uneasy about the credibility of the US deterrent. But there was even more to the McNamara speech to concern the Europeans: the US Defense Secretary also minimized the importance of European deterrents, and stressed the need for central control. As far as he was concerned, this was a strategic problem, to be solved logically, not a political problem to be resolved through negotiation, and in which national sensibilities would be involved. In passing, of course, he tried to reassure the Allies that American nuclear guarantees to Europe were firm; but very shortly thereafter he undermined this point by suggesting that deterrence of Soviet attack in Europe would actually be enhanced by having more conventional forces on the ground— an idea to be vaguely termed flexible response.

These comments touched an old nerve. For years the Europeans had been uncertain how best to balance two conflicting needs: of committing the US to the nuclear defence of Europe (few troops, rapid escalation), and of delaying the awful onset of nuclear war (more troops, and a pause). Now this issue was being decided for them in the worst possible way—in the midst of a unilateral American declaration of strategy affecting the whole Alliance. Yet there was more to come. The Secretary then committed the most cardinal sin: he suggested that a conventional defence of Europe was actually becoming possible!

Pandemonium broke loose in Europe—largely among people who had no understanding of the complexities of nuclear problems (a category which has always included almost everyone), as well as among people who did. But this reaction stemmed not so much from the content of the McNamara Doctrine as it was enunciated, as it did from the psychological overtones of the whole process. Here, suddenly, the United States seemed to be backing away from the unequivocal nature of its commitment to NATO—a commitment that had remained credible despite the fact that the United States was growing directly vulnerable to Russian nuclear attack. It was true, of course, that the new doctrine might actually have made these guarantees more credible to the Russians by the strict logic of deterrence—that is, by not threatening the end of the world over the loss of a small parcel of Western European territory. But the two facets, the problem of preserving credibility with the Russians on the one hand and the European Allies on the other, came into direct conflict. As usual, it was the need to reassure the Allies that caused the Americans the greater headaches.

It was almost entirely a psychological problem. The American nuclear guarantee had rested upon a promise—and blind faith on the part of Europeans. America, once Fortress America, had renounced her isolation in order to participate in the defence of Europe. This commitment therefore had to be complete, whole, and not subject to a moment's doubt. But suddenly the illusion of certainty was being shattered; whatever the intentions of the American government or the merits of the strategic arguments, the purity of the American commitment was compromised. And no one was more surprised to learn of this than the Americans themselves, who had believed they were meeting a straightforward and logical problem with a straightforward and logical solution.

The capstone to all this concern was the emphasis Mr McNamara had placed upon European conventional arms. This was already a shibboleth—or, better, a sort of standing joke—in which the Americans asked and never succeeded in getting the Europeans to match the agreed force goals. But at the beginning of the 1960s, as suggested above, it was seen in Europe actually to be dangerous to have too many conventional forces in being. This was so not just because such a situation might turn a country like Germany into a devastated battleground before the American President took his decision to use nuclear weapons, but that he might not take that decision at all. This fear, of course, was based on a logical deduction that was really nonsense in view of the obvious—if irrational—willingness of successive American governments and the American people to risk all on Europe's behalf.

But now, with the McNamara speech, the problem was firmly thrust upon the Alliance. And Mr McNamara had made the problem about as bad as he could possibly have done by appearing to talk about an actual conventional defence of the Continent. No matter that this might actually now be within the realm of possibility, given the almost unnoticed build-up of NATO forces over the years despite the failure to meet goals; no matter that Western perceptions of the Soviet threat were being radically reduced from what had appeared in 1950 to be 175 divisions—but even then had been substantially mythical. The impact of the McNamara speech derived from the new doubts sown about the commitment—the fundamental psychological commitment—of the United States. As a result, the problem was suddenly much worse than the remedy Mr McNamara was prescribing for possible Allied doubts. By trying to reassure Europeans about US intentions, through the elaboration of a means to make the US commitment more credible in Russian eyes, he had only watered the seeds of European worry. For the Allies, US calculation was no substitute for US blind loyalty.

The ensuing period of consternation also stemmed in part from the symbolic role that strategic issues played in the politics of the Alliance. Indeed, competitions for influence within the Alliance were largely fought out in terms of the kind of strategy that was to be adopted along with the way in which the burdens of implementing the strategy should be shared. And here was the United States enunciating a new strategy, and making it very clear where the preponderance of political clout lay.

On this occasion, however, the Americans did not get their way. Perhaps this was so because the McNamara Doctrine had been put forward in such a ham-fisted way; more likely it was so because the psychological shock to the Europeans helped to upset the orderly process of discussion. That is, for once the Europeans showed they could agree among themselves on a vital issue affecting their relations with the United States. This was a first indication that the Europeans might not always be so tractable in future. As a result, the whole set of new propositions was quietly put aside within a short time.

The Doctrine was not dead, however. Five years later, in a time of *détente*, the flexible response doctrine was formally adopted under another name by NATO's Defence Planning Committee. This time, there was little fuss or bother. But even this Doctrine was only a modified version of the McNamara strategy; under it NATO would respond to any attack with a level of force appropriate to deal with it. But there was no question that this form of flexible response ruled out the use of tactical or strategic nuclear weapons. A large-scale conventional war was still not acceptable. And, most important, it was no longer as evident that debate on this doctrine represented a test of strength between the United States and its European Allies: a war simply was not going to happen, and strategic issues, generally, were being taken far less seriously.

Earlier, at the beginning of the decade, European concern with the scope of American influence in the Alliance had also appeared in other ways, some of which were related to strategy. In addition to the McNamara speech, the Europeans also felt some distress at the apparent insensitivity of the US Government to West European attitudes in general. This insensitivity was particularly evident after the Kennedy Administration was inaugurated and General Lemnitzer was sent to SHAPE as a mouthpiece of American policy to replace General Norstad, the man who had been more European than American. From then on, there were a whole series of incidents that might earlier have passed with relatively little notice. Now they seemed to dramatize both the strains of European confidence in the United States that were growing in the Alliance, and the potentially divergent interests separating the partners in the Alliance on opposite sides of the Atlantic. These factors were reinforced by the working-out of the context of conflict, and the arising of new issues concerning the future—particularly issues related to the securing of a stable peace throughout Europe.

In the autumn of 1962, for example, there occurred what came to be known as the *Skybolt* incident. As the British tell the story, the United States rather unceremoniously informed London that the *Skybolt* missile would have to be cancelled. This was a missile being built by the Americans, both to diversify the American arsenal, and to serve as the next generation of the British deterrent. The Americans cited rapidly rising costs, and the lack of successful flight tests of this ballistic missile that was designed to be launched from strategic bombers. From the point of view of the Americans, this decision to cancel *Skybolt* was a logical one: they no longer needed the missile for their own arsenal, and were therefore abandoning it. But there was obviously little or no consideration for the feelings of the British Government, which still wished to maintain a viable nuclear arsenal—an independent deterrent—if only, as the phrase went, to get Britain a seat at the top table in diplomatic negotiations. There was a simple failure of diplomatic communications somewhere which was quickly seen as symptomatic of the Kennedy Administration's attitude towards Alliance consultations and co-operation.

To make matters worse, there was a hastily called diplomatic gathering between President Kennedy and the British Prime Minister at Nassau, at the end of which—for reasons that remain obscure—the British were offered missiles and related equipment which would enable Britain to build and maintain *Polaris*-type submarines. Thus the British independent deterrent was to be preserved yet a while longer.

However, apparently no one had thought of the repercussions that this decision would have within the rest of the Alliance, particularly in those countries which were growing more sensitive about the problem of America's seeming divergence from the rest of the Alliance on matters of nuclear policy and of dealing diplomatically with the Russians. France, in particular, had some reason for annoyance, and President de Gaulle made a point of ignoring a similar offer of *Polaris* missiles without the warheads that the British were then capable of building for themselves—an offer made to him after the Nassau Conference. He had not been consulted; clearly this was unacceptable. And, if one thinks of this problem in terms of Alliance politics, he was right. Whether he really felt that way or not, he used this incident as one reason for excluding Britain from the Common Market in January 1963 on the grounds that the British were too closely tied in with the Americans to be —as the slogan went—good Europeans: a good ironic touch.

But the most important evidence of the strains developing within the Alliance was provided in October 1962 during the Cuban Missile Crisis. Here was a real testing ground for the viability of Alliance consultations and the sharing of influence. There seemed to be a simple question: in time of peril—that is, when the safety of the world seemed to be at stake—would the Alliance serve as a focus for reaching vital decisions, or would the United States act in the name of all, with potentially the same consequences (including nuclear war) for all?

The United States chose the latter course. This was not un-reasonable, considering the gravity of the situation, and the narrow margin by which disaster was averted. Or at least so it seemed in retrospect. Indeed, one would have expected little complaint from the Europeans. Yet this incident fell within the ambit of the growing problem centred on the conflict between America's relations with the Russians, and America's relations with her European Allies. Would the United States ever take her Allies completely into her confidence? Would there ever be any form of common decision on these matters of life and death? And, even more importantly, might the Americans some day deal behind the backs of the Europeans in order to further the cause of American-Soviet understanding at the expense of European interests? These were serious questions that were made worse by President Kennedy's making it very pointedly clear that he had *not* consulted his Allies. Indeed, this problem has only grown in magnitude, and was the chief motive for President Nixon's rather hasty—if hardly eventful—visit to Western Europe at the very beginning of his Administration: namely, to reassure the West Europeans that essential US negotiations with the Russians on vital matters of arms control, which would affect the future security of all concerned, would not be conducted at the expense either of West European interests or of NATO Alliance co-operation. He has repeated this gesture twice, as the problem itself has become more acute since the beginning of the Strategic Arms Limitation Talks (SALT) between Russia and America. These talks are potentially very divisive of the Alliance, both because the US deterrent remains the cornerstone of NATO nuclear policy— and a symbol of political influence—and because the talks must inevitably touch on issues of national nuclear forces in Western Europe, Soviet medium-range missiles targeted against that part of the Continent, and the place of American tactical aircraft assigned to NATO but capable of strategic bombing in the Soviet Union.

Over the years, the problems raised by differences of strategic interest as between the US and its Allies have been the basis for a number of projects designed to demonstrate what is usually called crisis management or consultation. However— except for the rather special circumstances surrounding the Berlin crisis of 1958–61; the establishment of a Nuclear Planning Group and Nuclear Defence Affairs Committee; and a set of deliberations on the policy for using tactical nuclear weapons—these procedures have never proved much of a practical proposition. It is still too early to tell whether America's consultations with its Allies over the SALT talks will be adequate over the long term. The first real test was expected in early 1972, with a first major US-Soviet agreement. Yet this agreement was likely to be so general that it would leave until later the knotty problems outlined above.

At the time of the Cuban Missile Crisis in October 1962,

Dean Acheson, the former Secretary of State, was sent to Europe to explain the situation. In a famous confrontation with General de Gaulle, Acheson was asked whether he was seeking French advice or merely informing about US plans. 'Informing' was the honest reply. 'Good,' the General is reputed to have answered, 'I believe in independent decisions.' And from that moment, perhaps, one can date the full awareness in de Gaulle's policy of the need for France to be able to make its *own* independent decisions, if the Americans' prerogative of doing so could obviously compromise the interests of Europe in general and of France in particular.

Thus, formally, began a period in which American governments searched for some way out of the central dilemma of reconciling US-Soviet interests with US-West European relations. In part, the Americans' dilemma was of their own making, since it contained all the complicated issues they had raised of confidence and trust—issues that were basically matters of psychology.

But for a time American attitudes to Western Europe continued to reflect a misinterpretation of this essential political element in US strategic policy-making. It was conceived in Washington that Europeans needed a greater role in making the decisions governing the use of nuclear weapons, in order to quiet fears that the United States would abandon the Continent in a crisis. This was a view that accorded well with much thinking on the Continent, particularly in West Germany, where the prospect of losing the American nuclear guarantee was most frightening.

However, in the American approach to the problem, emphasis was placed, not so much on reaching a new political understanding with the West Europeans, as on prescribing the creation of actual weapons that the Europeans could have, and thereby feel that they were taking part in the West's nuclear deterrent. In theory, the credibility of the US nuclear deterrent would be enhanced in the eyes of the European Allies if the latter had some say in Western nuclear policy. Independent deterrents, of course, were still suspect in Washington: they were too small, too vulnerable, and too likely to frighten the Russians into doing something rash.

The so-called hardware solution to the so-called nuclear sharing problem was a fascinating exercise in diplomatic gymnastics. It began rather early, with a proposal in December 1960 by the Eisenhower Administration to earmark US *Polaris* submarines for NATO. And this proposal was put into practice in 1963 when three of the US submarines were assigned to NATO for planning purposes. Of course, the conceit was transparent: the nuclear warheads would never be fired without the permission of SACEUR. He, in turn, had to receive the necessary command, not from the North Atlantic Council or any of its agencies, but rather from the President of the United States. Indeed, this was also true for nearly all of NATO's nuclear weapons, including US tactical and so-called interdiction weapons stationed with Allied forces. Only the small British strategic arsenal was technically exempt.

This was not the only American effort to resolve the problem of nuclear 'credibility'—an effort that no European for a moment took seriously. There has also been an arrangement since 1963 whereby a certain number of NATO officers have been permitted to take part in the planning process of the Americans at the headquarters of the Strategic Air Command in Omaha, Nebraska, where targets for nuclear attack are selected. But equally, this step involves no influence for Europeans on the use of the weapons themselves.

This step was little noted at the time, but seems in retrospect to have had more merit than was granted to it—at least in terms of creating patterns of political co-operation. This will become clear in the following discussion of the Nuclear Planning Group.

But the big effort by the Americans to resolve their dilemma was to follow, in a proposal that lived and died at least twice. This was a proposal for a fleet of ships equipped with *Polaris* missiles. The ships were to be under the command of SACEUR and manned by men from as many NATO countries as wished to take part. The overall proposal was dubbed the Multilateral Force—or farce, as some Europeans put it. It was the most ludicrous of a host of NATO eccentricities, and was the product of a small group of men in the American State and Navy Departments who were once referred to as 'a tidy-minded group of fanatics', because of their failure to reconcile the logic of their case with the facts of European political and psychological attitudes.

In any event, this group of supporters for the MLF, as the project came to be called, won the day from time to time within the American government; and over a period of more than two years, West European governments were submitted to varying degrees of pressure to adopt the proposal. Many did, though largely because of this pressure from Washington, which was not the way in which the project had been conceived at all. The idea had been that Europeans should be reassured by the MLF, not dragooned into accepting it as a way of showing their loyalty to American leadership of the Western Alliance. Plans were drawn up; a ship was commissioned; it was filled with a multi-national crew. Special cooks and foods were provided, facilities for separate religious observance were laid on, and a great show was made of the value of mixed-manning.

But the central issue was continually evaded. Who would be able to fire the missiles with their nuclear warheads? And how important would the MLF be in the Western deterrent strategy since it was Lilliputian in comparison with the American strategic arsenal? The answers were clear: the Americans would retain custody of the nuclear warheads, and the force would really be rather insignificant. Yet the Americans made a promise, which reflected still another underlying characteristic of the whole history of NATO: if the Europeans somehow managed to forge among themselves a measure of *political* unity, then control of the MLF warheads could be turned over to them. This promise was conceived to be part of the so-called twin pillars, or dumb-bell approach to the concept of Atlantic

Partnership, in which Europe and America would represent two strong but united poles of Allied cooperation spanning the Atlantic. The subject of this Atlantic Partnership is worthy of extended discussion, particularly since the American penchant for European political unity has had such an important role in the shaping of NATO and preparations now under way for the exploitation of *détente*. This discussion will follow in Chapter 5.

Of course, for the simple reason that West European unity was premature at best and visionary at worst, the American offer to transfer control of the nuclear warheads for the MLF was never taken up by the Europeans, and the whole project fell into increasing disrepute. Even those countries which had agreed to participate felt somehow that a mechanical approach was no way to solve the *political* problems of consultation and confidence within an Alliance. But the point was not appreciated in Washington, nor the hardware approach abandoned, until damage had been done to relations among the Allies. Ironically, American domination of the Alliance was most apparent at the very moment—and through the very agency—that the Americans were using to try to cope with the problem of that dominance.

As with the earlier dilemma posed by the need for rearmament of West Germany, which had led to the proposal for a Western European Union in 1954, the British Government provided a way out of the MLF debate. In the autumn of 1964, the new Labour Government proposed an alternative to the MLF. It was to be called the Atlantic Nuclear Force (ANF), and was a scheme designed to be based on existing deterrents. Suddenly the context of debate was broadened from the old one requiring a stand either for or against the MLF, and other nations were given scope to try ending the whole search for a hardware solution to political problems. By this time, of course, the prophecy made by the supporters of the MLF had largely been fulfilled and there had indeed emerged a German nuclear problem—that is, a growing desire in the Federal Republic for greater assurances concerning the US nuclear guarantee. Of course, as with any historical problem, it is impossible to tell whether there would have been such a problem, anyway. But President Johnson rightly concluded that the MLF was not the right road to anywhere, and quietly buried the project.

So, with the demise of the MLF, the Alliance was faced with a true dilemma; there appeared to be a real need for some means of solving the problems of nuclear sharing, and especially to establish West Germany's place in it. Yet there was no obvious approach to make that did not raise as many problems as it solved.

In the event, the solution proved to be relatively simple: at Mr McNamara's suggestion, the interested nations of Western Europe joined together in discussions that gave the Allies a real sense of participation, not in any hardware solution to the sharing of nuclear weapons, but rather in working through the actual problems faced by the Americans as principal custodians of the NATO nuclear deterrent. Out of this process there developed in December 1966 a Nuclear Defence Affairs Committee and a Nuclear Planning Group (NPG) of 7 nations[1] that almost miraculously seemed to put the nuclear sharing problems more or less to rest. All at once, the issue of the decade had largely evaporated—an issue which had taken the Allies through the agonizing boredom of the MLF debates. Of course, these debates themselves showed that the Alliance was stronger than often believed, since it survived this shock largely intact in political terms. The NPG was the lesson derived from the three-year-old practice of sending NATO officers to Omaha. It seemed to work for the Alliance as a whole.

Yet this explanation is all rather too simple. Again, one must look at the development of events outside the limited NATO context. Following the Cuban Missile Crisis of 1962—one might even say following the last of the Berlin crises in 1961, and the

---

[1] Membership rotates among the Allies, but in practice West Germany, the United Kingdom, and the United States are always members, while Greece and Turkey alternate in sharing one of the other seats.

building of the mutually convenient Berlin Wall—the political air began to clear throughout Europe and in Russian-American relations. The awful risks taken by both nations over Cuba became obvious to all; it was equally clear that such risks were intolerable for so little potential gain.

Almost immediately, the political climate between East and West improved; and in August 1963, a treaty was signed at last to end the testing of nuclear weapons in the air, underwater, and in outer space. Of course, there were many factors working towards this new spirit of *détente*—factors that will be discussed in more detail in a final chapter. They included the onset of strategic stability that entailed the mutual acquisition of second-strike deterrents; the recognition that the borders of Europe had remained stable for 15 years; and the psychological impact of the Cuban Missile Crisis itself.

But within Europe, the most important effect of this process was the gradual recognition that the context of military confrontation, begun so many years before, had just about worked out its own internal logic. To begin with, NATO was widely believed to be relatively equal in terms of military power with the nations of the Warsaw Pact—although, as noted earlier, the perception of this development depended on certain specific assumptions about the nature of warfare in Europe. In addition, there was a clearly recognized strategic division of the Continent which could serve as a basis on which to conduct a form of bargaining between East and West. These facts were well understood; and because they were, it became possible to see that there was less to fear than in the past, when it had seemed that only a rigid military structure conferred any certainty of security in Europe. Gradually, it now became possible for governments to raise their heads above the parapets, and see how the world had changed. Down at NATO Headquarters, bureaucrats and military officers still viewed matters within the same logic of their narrow context—and many still do as this book is written in 1971; but outside these narrow confines and those, perhaps, obtaining within the military structure of the Warsaw Pact, there appeared to be some scope for looking beyond the limits of Cold War. One could appreciate the possibilities of actually *changing* patterns of confrontation—and patterns of economic and political behaviour—throughout the Continent.

The debate over the MLF ended at just about the same time that the new spirit in Europe—the new basis for the relaxing of tensions—was becoming truly apparent. Therefore, when the Nuclear Planning Group was proposed, it proved to be the political effort that was needed more or less to solve the problem of nuclear sharing. After all, within the new context of relaxed tensions (*détente*), where the prospect of war was seen to be receding further every day, there seemed to be less urgency in considering the actual fighting of wars, or even of being certain about the process of deterring them. For most Europeans, including many West Germans and Americans, the prospect was not of war, but of a more or less permanent peace and the possibility of changes in existing patterns of confrontation in Europe. It was as though the MLF were the last exercise in which many of the Allies were willing to bury their heads in the sands of the old context of military confrontation, and in doing so, to abide by the rules of that limited game. Now, quite rapidly, the game was changing, and presented a wide range of new possibilities.

Therefore, as the context of conflict seemed to change, however slightly, so did the strategy of the Western Alliance. Some observers also detected changes in Warsaw Pact strategy, as well, leading to a gradual modification of the central role to be played by nuclear weapons in any European conflict. In the East, too, the prospect of cataclysm no longer seemed to be inevitable in war and, as a result, was no longer the exclusive focus of planning.

In the West, changes in Alliance strategy waited for the not very subtle work of France. In February 1966, the major change in French attitudes was presented in one of the well-rehearsed press conferences of President de Gaulle. In the first place, he emphasised his view that the external threat to the Alliance had decreased rapidly. The accuracy of this observation undoubtedly was a basic reason for his making it, whatever more political motives the General might have had in mind; but this particular motive was more or less lost on those Alliance members who were struggling to maintain the cohesive facade of the Alliance. Because of their urgent institutional pre-occupation, they were prone to ignore the profound changes then taking place on the Continent: i.e. changes in the direction of a gradual dissolution of at least the non-military aspects of confrontation.

It was in this context that de Gaulle noted the classic argument about American vulnerability to Soviet nuclear attack—discussed earlier—and said that the use of American nuclear weapons on Europe's behalf had become uncertain (see Appendix IV). This, for France, had removed the justification there had been for continuing with the integration of French military forces within Allied Command Europe. But the General was careful to stress that there was still a need for the Alliance itself. Characteristically, few outsiders listened to this qualification. Nor did they give much credence to the other half of his argument: that integration also meant that conflicts involving the US in other parts of the world might draw Europe auto-matically into a wider conflict. The emphasis was on the idea of automatic involvement; and it was certainly true that the integration of forces within NATO was such as to erode the right of national decision in the event of an actual war. There-fore, the costs of alliance had gone up, at the very moment that the benefits had gone down. And, furthermore, France was in the process of acquiring atomic bombs, and had a new-found opportunity—as well as the will—to be responsible for her own destiny.

The practical consequences of this act—which in de Gaulle's words re-established a 'normal situation of sovereignty'—were not long in coming: the Allied Commands were required to depart from the soil of France, as were all American and

Canadian forces stationed there. French forces were withdrawn from Allied Command Europe—although, in a special agreement concluded with the West Germans, France's two divisions remained on station in the German Federal Republic. The Germans, apparently, were less inclined to be purists about the sanctity of the NATO integrated command than they were about their relations with France.

Then the acrimony began, with the Americans revealing several previously secret treaties about the stationing of forces, which France was supposed to be violating by its *démarche*. France was told bluntly that she would have to pay for the whole move and for the real estate being left behind. The French Government refused. And some rather strange ideas were touted, including a proposal to place a communications satellite high over the NATO area, thereby supposedly eliminating France's physical importance to NATO communications!

At the same time, the Allies prepared for the move from France, and immediately saw this as an opportunity to streamline Allied Command Europe, in order to make it conform to the ideal principles of the way a command structure should be run. This streamlining was accomplished with dispatch, and the two expelled military commands were relocated in the Netherlands (Allied Forces Central Europe) and at Casteau, in Belgium (SHAPE). Within a year, France's formal links with the integrated command structure of NATO had been effectively dissolved.

At first, the blow struck by the French at the fabric of the Alliance and of its strategy seemed a severe one. But subsequently a cooler view prevailed. It soon appeared that, in actual combat terms, the loss of the two French divisions hardly mattered at all to Allied Command Europe. Quite simply, NATO strategy would require an escalation to a nuclear phase of warfare before these French troops, lying well back from the Czechoslovak frontier, were even engaged in combat. French attack aircraft were lost to SACEUR, but French air defences continued to be integrated with those of the rest of the Allies.

Supply lines had to be re-routed away from France, and became more vulnerable to enemy attack, and air space over France was no longer automatically available for training purposes. But all in all, there was very little strategic loss to Allied Command Europe occasioned by the departure of the French contingents from SACEUR's command.

Why, then, was there all the fuss, particularly at a time when there was a gradual loosening of NATO ties as more governments perceived a radical reduction in the Soviet threat? The answer lies in the problems that the Allies were having in trying to construct something more out of the Alliance than just an expedient mechanism for combating a specific threat.

There was, quite simply, no clear idea of how to convert the process of confrontation in Europe—the logic of which was rapidly working itself through to a conclusion—into something else in which NATO and the Warsaw Pact did not occupy the central positions in ordering strategic relations among European nations. And, faced with this prospect, most of the NATO Allies found that preserving an existing security arrangement was essential to the process of developing alternative arrangements, as well as being necessary to preserve the appearance in the meantime that the NATO Alliance was as viable strategically and politically as it had ever been.

Strategically, therefore, in 1966 de Gaulle really did little *to* the Alliance. But he did much *for* it politically: he focused attention on the difficulties and the strains involved in changing the pattern of confrontation across the whole of Europe. (Most of these strains, of course, related to the problem of American dominance.) De Gaulle was, in effect, requiring NATO's officials and national leaders to come to terms with the problems that they had been unable or unwilling to handle; and he did it in circumstances that dramatized that need, and perhaps even overdid it.

The further development of this point really relates to the specific problems of *détente*, which will be discussed in the final chapter. Yet it is worth noting here the intimate connection between NATO's strategic posture and the political relations within the Alliance at every period in the Alliance's history. In 1966 de Gaulle at least *seemed* to change some of the strategic understandings of the Alliance. He thus began a process of strategic change within the Alliance. Many Allies complained with some justification that it had been delayed by French intransigence. But at least this process began to come to grips with some of the changes taking place in the problems of European confrontation and security. And these changes had been delayed since the last Berlin crisis of 1961, and the Cuban Missile Crisis of 1962.

Within months of the final adjustments brought about by the French *démarche*, the strategy of the NATO Alliance was changed in noticeable ways. At the same time, the Allies removed the North Atlantic Council from Paris—unasked—on the grounds that close co-ordination was needed between it and SHAPE, despite the fact that this step had the effect of isolating France further within the Alliance. The Allies also reactivated the Defence Planning Committee (DPC) of the North Atlantic Council in order to keep France from being privy to military secrets that would otherwise have been shared in common in the Council.

But more importantly, the Allies began to take some decisions that reflected that they, too, were able to act on the perceptions that had already occurred to the French. This was most evident in May 1967, when the DPC gave new 'political, strategic, and economic guidance' to NATO's military planners. This meant two important changes in NATO's strategy. In the first place, the final adjustment was made on the long-standing political debate whether to plan NATO's defences on the basis of Soviet military *capabilities* as opposed to their political *intentions*. In 1967, the Allies decided that interpretations of the latter could be given much greater weight. They did this in view of an obvious reduction in the Soviet threat—a reduction occasioned by *détente* and the perception that the confrontation across the Continent had now become genuinely stable. This was, in effect, an admission that war in Europe was unlikely, and that the retention of NATO in its present form depended as much upon failure to find ways of providing alternative means of European security, as on anything else. There was some modification of this view following the Soviet invasion of Czechoslovakia in August 1968, but the distinction between Soviet intentions and capabilities was even then not again entirely blurred.

Still, in 1970–71 there was much greater attention paid in NATO to conventional force levels than had been true for several years. Indeed, following its December meeting, the Defence Planning Committee stressed the need for NATO to 'maintain a sufficient level of conventional and nuclear strength for defence as well as for deterrence'. Since this statement was coupled with a discussion of improvements taking place in Warsaw Pact forces, there was a clear implication that the balance struck between Soviet intentions and capabilities, as factors in NATO planning, was shifting back toward the latter. Of course, this new emphasis on forces was conceived as part of maintaining the military posture needed for successful negotiations with the Warsaw Pact nations on a range of issues arising in the prosecution of *détente*. This is a line of reasoning that Mr Laird, the American Defense Secretary, pressed strongly. Indeed, in December 1971 he announced that 20,000 US troops, withdrawn from Europe because of Vietnam, were being returned to NATO. Most important of these issues was the goal of eventually achieving Mutual and Balanced Force Reductions (MBFR). Ironically, the prospect of being able to *change* patterns of confrontation has led the Allies to take more seriously their actual strategic capabilities than they did when there was a more palpable Soviet threat. Again, the reliance upon military instruments to express the state of a diplomatic balance is imposing requirements of its own that go beyond any real perception of defence or deterrent needs.

These developments in 1970–71 also related to a decision

taken in 1967, along with that concerning the issue of intentions versus capabilities. The Allies had also agreed that war would not come in Europe without political warning time adequate to permit Allied defences to be brought up to the level required to cope with any plausible threat, at least on the Central Front. This change was even more profound than the one relating to the issue of intentions versus capabilities: it not only indicated the fact that sophisticated means were available to detect troop movements in Eastern Europe. It also meant that the West was accepting, philosophically, the existence of an intimate connection between political conflict and military threat.

The adoption of the concept of political warning time was, therefore, a fundamental indication of the progress of *détente*. It meant equally that there was a narrowing of the gap in what could be called a philosophy of conflict as between the Russians and the Americans. As discussed earlier, in this philosophy the Americans have long tended to place most emphasis in their perceptions of threat on military capabilities, rather than on the nature of political conflict. The Russians, on the other hand, have tended to argue that the size of military forces is not terribly important, provided efforts are made to sort out political problems. By mid-decade, however, the Americans were beginning to realize that forces, alone, did not confer threat, while the Russians were beginning to understand that there could be no political progress without steps towards the control of arms. With the NATO decisions in 1967, therefore, the gap had apparently narrowed so significantly as to make possible real political understandings between East and West, despite the continued but less important context of military confrontation on the Continent.

These changes in attitude within NATO reflected more than just changes in the perception of Soviet political attitudes; as with all of NATO's strategic problems, the acceptance of political warning time reflected the economic needs of member states. Of course, one might argue that the willingness of nations to undertake expenditures on defence is at least one clue to judging their real belief about the nature of the potential threat, whatever the political rhetoric of their statesmen. In this case, balance of payments difficulties, especially in Britain and America, increased the domestic pressures on governments to re-examine and minimize the Soviet threat, and, with it, NATO's response. The long discussions within NATO on offset-cost payments (discussed in Chapter 3) influenced official perceptions of threat and response. Indeed, as discussed earlier, by the beginning of 1968 the Americans were even able to contend that NATO commanders on the Central Front actually had more forces available to them than were available to Warsaw Pact commanders. Of course, this contention did not go uncontradicted, and it depended both on a definition of those forces required in an actual conflict, and on an assumption that no war would last long enough for there to be major reinforcements from the Soviet Union. But it was still significant that the Americans chose to see NATO as being able to implement its newly adopted doctrine of a form of flexible response.

It was even more significant that the NATO Allies (less France) had agreed to accept the criterion of intentions as well as that of capabilities for determining threat and response, and to accept the existence of political warning time. These agreements meant that a number of troops could be withdrawn from the Central Front. 5,000 men were returned home to the United Kingdom, and 35,000 to the United States. In theory, these troops were only being redeployed—that is, they could be returned to Europe in the event of a crisis. In actual fact, they represented real troop reductions which, taken together, potentially had a greater strategic impact on the Alliance than did the withdrawal of France's two divisions from Allied Command Europe—French divisions which, of course, were not withdrawn from the Federal Republic of Germany itself.

Significantly, there was no outcry on the Continent about all these moves; no anxiety that fewer troops would mean a weakening of the American nuclear commitment and no onset of a new nuclear sharing problem. Thus *détente* reduced still further the strategic problems facing the Allies, and, with it, the political rationale for keeping the Alliance together. This development was recognized, and the results—culminating in the so-called Harmel Study—will be discussed in Chapter 5. Of course, it would have been rash at any time to discount a recurrence of some of these pre-*détente* problems within the NATO Alliance. Indeed, some of these problems have re-appeared, although in slightly different guise and with far less sense of menace to NATO's ability to meet any possible military threat.

The first problem arose in August 1968. Then, following long deliberations within NATO about further steps in pursuit of *détente* and even proposals from the Eastern bloc about finding ways of dissolving both NATO and the Warsaw Pact—there came the invasion of Czechoslovakia by the Soviet Union.

Many observers reacted initially by saying that the strategic balance had been altered in Europe. This was the view put forward by the American Secretary of State, perhaps less because of considered judgement than because he wanted to obscure the real basis of *détente* as he had understood it. This was the tacit acceptance of spheres of influence in Europe, despite their unacceptability within the terms of American political rhetoric (see Chapter 6). In fact, it was quickly accepted that the presence of extra Soviet divisions on NATO's eastern boundary did not seem to upset the actual strategic balance in Europe, since these troops faced mountains in South Germany that were secured primarily by US forces. The really vulnerable areas on NATO's Central Front remained those embracing the northern plains; and the Russians had clearly acquired a number of strategic liabilities with their alienation of the whole nation of Czechoslovakia—at the very least, none of the more than 14 Czech divisions could any longer effectively be counted in the Warsaw Pact Order of Battle.

But the truly remarkable phenomenon was the limited reaction on the part of the NATO Allies after they had had time to consider the situation; even at the time, NATO forces did not go on alert status. There was later some pressure to increase troops levels of West European states—pressures exerted largely by the Americans—as well as token increases by Great Britain and one or two lesser Allies. But beyond these half-hearted measures there were no radical transformations. Even more remarkable, perhaps, was the fact that, in all the new talk about force levels, the so-called nuclear question was only reintroduced obliquely by the British Defence Secretary, and even then there has been no wide-scale revival of the pressing anxieties in Europe about the US nuclear guarantee. This was so even though no one but the Americans argued that NATO had the forces needed actually to put into operation its official (though obscure) doctrine of a form of flexible response.

Détente was definitely impaired, at least from the standpoint of the Western Europeans. But in the process, there was no automatic re-establishment of a rigid context of military confrontation. It was as though, once the period of anxiety of the Cold War had passed, it could not return. The mould had been broken. Indeed, it was clear that the understandings reached with the East over the years on strategic matters would not disappear in spite of violations of certain rules of thumb on more political and economic matters—e.g. the increasingly free relations between Eastern and Western European countries. This was definitely a firm sign that the end of military confrontation was at hand, provided that some means could be found to convert confrontation into an alternative means of providing security. At the present time, no such scheme has gained widespread acceptance, although many have been canvassed (see Chapter 6).

Finally, it is important to understand the special uses made of strategy within the Alliance, as more direct steps are taken to prepare for specific moves in *détente*. But first it is important to note that, during this period, considerations of strategy, in and of itself, have really concentrated on matters extraneous to the problems of fighting a war on the Central Front. There have been minor exceptions. The French, for example, have tried to define an independent role within the general context of NATO, and have shown some interest in strategic problems surrounding the *force de dissuasion* and the concept of proportional deterrence. More recently, the French have taken a less rigid position *vis à vis* the formal military organizations of NATO, although there is still no question of their rejoining these institutions. From France's point of view, NATO's military institutions do not require its strategic support and are mainly important because of the role they will play in the prosecution of *détente*.

At the same time, there has been some revival of British interest in strategic problems—including some old chestnuts—but this interest has largely reflected concern on the part of the British to be seen as good Europeans, during their recent (successful) bid to be accepted by the European Community. Only in Germany is there found any real enthusiasm for European strategic problems, largely, it seems, as a way for the Germans to demonstrate that they are ready for some leadership in West Europe and the Alliance.

In terms of actual strategic problems, however, Allied concern has been limited to other matters. For example, will the Russians be tempted to achieve a *fait accompli* in the northern reaches of Norway (Finnmark) or the eastern lands of Turkey? This question is more psychological than strategic. But the NATO Allies have been genuinely concerned lest the increasing Soviet fleet in the Mediterranean should provide strategic—as well as political—problems. This concern has been particularly acute when measured in terms of threats to the flank areas and the question of Alliance cohesion (see Chapter 5). Indeed, in November 1968, the Allies established a new command to keep watch over the Soviet Mediterranean fleet—Maritime Air Forces Mediterranean; earlier in the year the British had agreed to commit some extra ships to the

Mediterranean; and even the French seemed interested in the problem.

This Allied concern for the Mediterranean became even more acute during the Middle East crisis of 1970, when the Americans became convinced that the Soviet fleet would in some way threaten Western interests unless the US Sixth Fleet made a show of force. Some European states, particularly on the Mediterranean littoral, did become more anxious, but even they did little in a practical way to show they believed there to be a major strategic problem for the Alliance as a whole. Yugoslavia, alone of the Mediterranean powers, was truly concerned by the strategic problems posed by Soviet naval activity. Yet because Yugoslavia is not a member of NATO, despite the importance of its security to East-West understandings of the European strategic balance, NATO did not consider this situation, at least not formally.

With these limited exceptions, therefore, the strategic interests of the NATO Allies seemed to be concentrated, not so much on actual military threats, as on the strategic implications of specific steps proposed for transforming the pattern of military confrontation, or otherwise furthering *détente*. In particular, the focus was concentrated on the increasingly divergent interests of America and her European Allies. To begin with, these issues involved the question of whether or not the United States would be able to proceed to reach limited understandings with the Soviet Union over the heads of her Allies. For example, there was considerable concern about the negotiation of the nuclear Non-Proliferation Treaty (NPT). Not without reason, many Europeans chose to see this treaty in the light of US-Soviet and US-Western European relations. There was a specific German problem here, too. But it was not one of the Bonn Government's needing nuclear weapons or even guarantees for defence and deterrence. Rather the West Germans wanted to have a veto on possible US-Soviet arrangements for Europe. This was, in effect, a form of Gaullism, and a recognition that these political-strategic matters also centrally influence the distribution of power within the NATO Alliance.

The same factors obtain with regard to the Strategic Arms Limitation Talks. As noted above, these SALT talks are also potentially very divisive of the Alliance. They touch on matters that could affect, not only the familiar modes as opposed to the basic facts of security, but also the growing determination of Europeans to have more influence on matters affecting their future. Indeed, it is this symbolic factor that makes the whole question of arms limitations such a delicate one.

Even today a strategic debate in NATO cannot be politically neutral. Whatever country or group of countries is able to make its will felt scores a gain that goes far beyond the merits of the issue being considered. In addition, the mere fact that strategic issues have become so central to this process means that it is very hard to put them aside, as attempts are made to readjust influence within the Alliance. Indeed, the political function of strategic questions within the Alliance may even help retard progress towards agreements with the East that will require changes in Western strategy—for example, force reductions and the concepts underpinning the use of those that remain.

This interaction between strategy and political influence within the Alliance threatens to pose real problems for the Alliance for one additional reason: the impending reduction of US conventional forces on the Continent. The fact of these reductions is now clear; the only questions remaining are 'when?' and 'how much?' During 1970, President Nixon gave his assurances that there would be no reductions before 1973; but no one can promise anything beyond that, or even guarantee that the Congress will not take action sooner.

In terms of strategy, it is easy to exaggerate the impact on NATO that a reduction of American forces would have. Of course, the doctrine of flexible response might then have far less meaning. But if there is not going to be a war anyway— and if the nuclear deterrent remains sound—why should there be a problem? After all, NATO strategy worked in deterring conflict during earlier periods with fewer forces, and that was before *détente* reduced perceptions of threat to new low levels.

The problem lies first with the nuclear deterrent: will it remain credible if there are fewer American hostage forces on the ground in Europe? But this question is only part of a deeper concern that relates to America's experience in Vietnam and the general unpopularity in the United States of far-flung commitments abroad. It may be that the NATO commitment would be the last to be eroded, if ever. But Europeans still are concerned that a new form of American isolationism could leave them without the protection they might need on some future day—however hypothetical.

So far, there has not re-emerged a real nuclear sharing problem like that of the 1950s, even though much of the rhetoric of NATO discussion by early 1971 contained the echoes of earlier debates. But the whole process of concern in Europe is truly remarkable, because it indicates once again that strategic issues can be debated, not for what they could mean in themselves, but as symbols of deeper concerns. In this case, it is the concern with America's overall commitment to Europe's future—a future going beyond confrontation—and its willingness to share influence with its Allies in decisions affecting either symbols or substance. It is therefore most unfortunate that strategic problems have become so symbolically important. It means that even discussions in America about reducing troop levels have a far greater political impact in Europe than they could ever merit on their own in an age of *détente*. And it means that the Europeans are thrown back on old debates and old arguments about strategy as a way of expressing anxieties about America's more basic involvement in Europe's future. Fortunately, because the mould of the Cold War has been broken, none of these anxieties threatens Europe with a return to the strategic insecurities of the past.

But there is a danger of increasing the political strains within the Alliance, and of making it more difficult for the Allies to agree on specific steps in *détente*, without illuminating the very real differences of outlook that exist, because of this habitual preoccupation with strategic symbols. In 1970, for example, NATO reaffirmed its collective belief that the prevailing level of US forces in Europe—about 310,000 men—is essential to the political strength of the Alliance. This was an absurd position to take, in part because it is not tenable in the long run. A later reduction in US forces will therefore cause more psychological problems than if the magic number had never been adopted.

In response to the American agreement to maintain this level of forces, ten European Allies agreed in December 1970 to a special European Defence Improvement Programme (EDIP). This programme included promises by the Allies to spend about $1,000 million over five years in ways to help ease the financial burden of the United States of supporting troops on the Continent. And one year later, the ten European states agreed to increase their collective defence, spending a further $1,000 million during 1972. At that time, West Germany also agreed to help offset US troop costs by $2,034 million over two years. This included $184 million in a novel kind of support: the modernization of living quarters for US troops in Germany.

Once again, burden sharing became a central focus of NATO concern, instead of the emerging problems and possibilities in *détente*. Once again the United States was applying pressure—though in a more subtle fashion than in the past—to get the Allies to increase the level of their conventional forces. Of course, there would also be no real force goals so there could be no real failure to achieve them—a nice conceit. But most interesting, this time there was no outcry that increases in levels of conventional forces will erode the nuclear deterrent. Again, the ending of the Cold War has left these developments with little strategic significance. They threatened, unnecessarily, to increase the resentment of Parliaments asked to spend more money on unwanted and unneeded defence.

The arguments that lay beneath these efforts to bolster

NATO's conventional capabilities were straightforward enough: mainly, to preserve a sense of Allied unity during a process of negotiations with the Eastern states. It would not do to reduce forces in the West, and then expect the Warsaw Pact forces to follow suit. There must be Mutual and Balanced Force Reductions (MBFR), or none at all. However, this argument missed an essential point: quite simply, the strength of the Western Alliance in negotiating with the East does not lie in numbers of forces, but rather in a sense of common Allied purpose. In fact, this sense of common purpose might be secured, in the military field, with a third as many American troops; and, if the Allies still appeared to be united, the Warsaw Pact states might then decide to secure economic advantages by reducing their own forces, especially if US reductions took place in parallel with talks on Mutual and Balanced Force Reductions. This possibility is at least as likely to happen as the alternative: that the Soviet Union would try to exploit Western military inferiority on the ground—though not weakness in nuclear weapons.

For the Western Allies, the big mistake has rested in not adopting a process of special consultations, throughout the Alliance, that would pave the way for future US force reductions that would not be divisive. Instead, by reaffirming the same old and untenable magic number of American forces, they have decided to tempt fate. Of course, the so-called Euro-group of ten Defence Ministers has begun a process of European consultations that can help, particularly in countering American dominance within the Alliance. This development is essential if the Alliance is to survive. But its first effort—the European Defence Improvement Programme—was potentially a step in the wrong direction. The symbol of strategy continued to get in the way of the substance of politics.

In addition, the symbolic role of strategy is complicating the issue of holding a European Security Conference as part of *détente*. One issue either at such a conference or on its own must be troop reductions. And they must someday be a part of *détente.* But the United States, in particular, has insisted on placing Mutual and Balanced Force Reductions high on the list of objectives to be achieved before other efforts in *détente* can be pursued. To an extent, this has been a reasonable position: it is better to seek mutual force reductions before they take place in the West alone. Until recently, however (see Chapter 6), there was another factor militating against this position: by concentrating upon such a radical step at the outset, the Alliance risked decreasing the chances that the political process of *détente* would flourish, and did not recognize that MBFR is more likely to come as a late step in this process instead of as an early one (see Appendix VIII).

Even more important, MBFR became a central issue in NATO's official view of *détente* because of the failure by the Allies to find other political objectives in *détente* around which they could coalesce. Once again, the place occupied in NATO by strategic issues, as political symbols, made it difficult for the Alliance to meet present-day circumstances in their own terms. Once again, the Allies had to fall back in their deliberations on patterns of the past that were familiar to them, even if this meant that they would focus on issues that were no longer important to the strength of the Alliance or to the maintenance of deterrence.

Despite these factors, in the spring of 1971 MBFR began to seem a live possibility, following a proposal for talks by the General Secretary of the Soviet Communist Party, Mr Brezhnev. At time of writing, NATO is busy following through on the response it decided upon at the May 1971 meeting of the North Atlantic Council and reaffirmed in December 1971.

Yet the points made above are still not invalid, particularly since the Soviet Union began backing away from MBFR negotiations in late 1971, and the Warsaw Pact Powers essentially ignored the issue at their January 1972 meeting. And even if this stalling is only temporary, it is a long way, after all, between today's concentration on beginning MBFR negotiations and an actual agreement. And substantial troop reductions are even farther off. The current diplomatic effort is really an attempt to have the best of two worlds: to concentrate on troop levels—a subject which the NATO Allies have a history of being able to discuss (if not always agree upon)—and to have the process of *détente* continue and be expanded to include a multilateral forum as well as a series of bilateral acts. This last-named objective—a multilateral forum—is becoming important as a way of ensuring, among other things, that West Germany does not get too far removed from its other Allies with *Ostpolitik*.

As a diplomatic effort such as described here, the MBFR negotiations promise more symbol than substance, and will likely become a continuing forum, like the SALT talks. In balancing SALT—where only the superpowers are present—MBFR negotiations will help America's Allies to think that they, too, are involved in deciding vital questions of strategic importance. These negotiations thus will become a bridge between competing objectives, by seeming to reconcile the US goal of putting force reductions first with the European goal of gaining some movement in political aspects of *détente*. Of course, this bridging will take place at some risk: namely, that military issues will be given much too much emphasis, and will tend to lead, again, to a restoring of the outdated and divisive symbolic importance of strategy. This is particularly true within the Atlantic Alliance, where there will be concern about working out bargaining positions down to the smallest detail, thus shining a bright light on all the inconsistencies that exist in the theory of Western strategy. There will be a further concentration on the fact that Soviet forces would only have to withdraw a few hundred miles from Eastern Europe, while American forces would have to withdraw 3,000.

This built-in asymmetry can be a major stumbling-block to arms control in Central Europe, if the asymmetry becomes a dominant issue. Unfortunately, by its very nature, a process of trying to negotiate MBFR that comes this early in *détente* will tend to focus on problems like this one, thereby distracting attention from the more important political climate and possible understandings that are the real stuff of *détente*. This type of thinking has already appeared in the SALT talks. There, a preoccupation with the technical details of excessive firepower—firepower that neither side needs anyway—has made these talks more a cloak for further massive armaments buildups than a way of creeping towards greater Soviet-American understanding on their broader political need to prevent the arms race from continuing.

In addition, talks on the reduction of forces that come this early in *détente* may simply lead many European states to reduce their contributions to defence still further, in anticipation of a successful outcome of negotiations. Or they might see them largely as a US effort to obscure a decreasing concern with Europe's future. In either case, the lack of an *orderly* process of change within the Alliance could cause trouble, and opportunities for the Soviet Union, without corresponding benefit for the West.

Furthermore, the Allies—and particularly the Americans—will stress the bargaining element of MBFR negotiations, just as the US Government has done at SALT, to everyone's cost. Initially, at least, the process of negotiating MBFR is thus destined to go the way of SALT: to require more forces, not less. This was the import of the US government's actually adding 20,000 troops in late 1971 to reach the nominal role of 310,000 instead of accepting a *de facto* cut. Again, too keen an approach to bargaining and strategy will get in the way of the politics at issue.

Instead, these negotiations should be seen as a process of coordinating between East and West on mutually acceptable terms that will give all nations concerned greater confidence about the political understandings that are being sought—understandings, especially, about the need to preserve the climate of acceptance for the strategic *status quo*, despite a lower level of forces. These understandings can include an initial discussion of principles and preliminary agreements on subjects like force ceilings, limitations on force movements, exchange of information, posting of observers on both sides, and perhaps even the old idea of nuclear-free zones (the Rapacki Plan). Most important in these discussions, however, the military tail must not be allowed to wag the political dog.

Finally, of course, a process of negotiating MBFR will require the Allies to work out a viable strategy for the period after troop reductions take place. Because of the difficulties of doing this—coupled with the tough problem of insuring that the West German *Bundeswehr* is not left as the only major military formation in West Europe after reductions take place—the US and West Germany, in particular, do not favour major reductions, even though the US still prefers talks on MBFR to broader ones at a European Security Conference. Thus the natural tendency to focus on post-reduction strategy will, in the West as well as in East-West relations, increase the prominence of dying questions of strategy that most Europeans would rather just see 'wither away'. (More will be said on this subject in Chapter 6.)

As part of this process of considering MBFR within the Alliance, there has also been a revival of interest in Western Europe concerning a West European defence organization and nuclear deterrent. In part this interest is an outgrowth of developments taking place in the European Community. It also reflects uncertainty about America's future role in Europe, the recognition that there must always be some form of institution to preserve security in Europe, and a desire to balance US influence in Atlantic Alliance discussions. But like NATO's concentration on conventional force levels, a movement towards a European Defence Community would divert attention away from *détente* and the political problems of Alliance, and towards the nuts and bolts of threat, forces, and strategy. In addition, the Europeans would be unlikely to build much of a defence community with conventional forces, and would tend to fall back on nuclear weapons—not because they needed them, but rather because of the force of a military 'logic' once that logic were adopted. Needless to say, the prospect of a European nuclear force, in which West Germany would inevitably play some part (if only to contribute to it financially at first) would be to no one's liking. The fear of such a development would be enough to cause serious difficulties for all parties interested in European security.

Furthermore, by concentrating on a defence community, the West Europeans would be likely to delay the exploitation of what opportunities do exist in *détente* to dispense someday with these strategic problems more or less altogether. Once again, therefore, an over-emphasis on strategy in an age of *détente* could prove self-defeating.

This last-named issue provides one of the strongest arguments for proceeding with a process of negotiating Mutual and Balanced Force Reductions—however long it takes—at this time rather than later, as proposed above. Ironically, starting this process now may be the only effective way to head off the emergence of a move towards a fully-fledged European Defence Community, which would have all of the drawbacks listed here for *détente* and for getting away from strategic pre-occupations. Even with all the problems of negotiating MBFR, noted earlier, seeing the Europeans create a new security community is potentially worse.

With Britain's impending entry into the European Community, London seems to have stimulated some French interest (and Paris some British interest) in having such a defence community, especially one that has some place for the nuclear forces of the two countries. Thus defence issues would be used to serve a political purpose in Anglo-European relations: a politics of opportunity, despite the strong arguments against Europe's focusing on the paraphernalia of strategy in a potentially 'post-strategic' era on the Continent. Of course, it would also be far better to deal with problems of influence within the Atlantic Alliance in non-military forums or, to the extent that military questions still must intrude, through consultations in the Euro-group that would not raise all the many and unneeded questions of a Defence Community. Some day, perhaps, there would be value in having a European Community that had technical responsibility for all the traditional functions of a sovereign state, including foreign policy and defence. But there is a difference between proceeding in that direction now, with the problems noted above, and doing so later, when strategy is even less important in European politics, and some form of force reductions has taken place.

This has been a cursory analysis of the strategic problems facing the North Atlantic Alliance over the years. These are not all the strategic problems that are usually discussed—such as the infinitely boring and virtually irrelevant debates on tactical nuclear weapons. But they are the essential problems that illuminate the manner in which strategy has affected politics within the Alliance. This construction is used deliberately, instead of the one that would seem to be important—i.e. the relations between East and West. For over the years, the strategic problems of NATO seem to have related more directly to the processes of bargaining within NATO—and to adjustments in internal influence—than to changes in the actual pattern of confrontation with the Soviet Union. Of course, there were significant changes in that confrontation. But how many of them were real? In particular, on several occasions the West changed its view of Soviet intentions and capabilities. Did these changes actually take place, or had the threat been exaggerated in the first place? So, too, the West saw many changes in its relations with the East. Were these based on information that can be verified? Or were they based, both in East and West, on new expectations—a kind of wish fulfilment? Finally, to what extent did the establishment of a military context of confrontation impose a logic that had to be worked through and, only then, permit radical reappraisals to be made of the conditions that were believed to have established the context in the first place?

Some of these questions have been answered, at least in part, in the course of this discussion. At least we can certainly see the way in which strategic debates and the political climate within the NATO Alliance interacted with one another. But other aspects of the same phenomenon must also be examined. There were, for example, a number of functions not related directly to military confrontation that were either proposed for or adopted by NATO. How did they affect the development of the Alliance? And how much bearing did they have on questions of security in Europe? Similar questions, of course, need to be raised about the Warsaw Pact.

Chapter 5

Non-Military Roles of the Alliances

In order to understand the progress of European security since the Second World War, we must go far beyond a simple analysis of the construction and operation of NATO; beyond an analysis of threats and responses; beyond a discussion of strategy; and beyond a consideration of the role of the Warsaw Pact in Eastern Europe. There must also be some discussion of the non-military aspects of Alliances. This is particularly so with regard to NATO, where the dominance of the Alliance's super-power (the United States) has been most clearly evident in the way the military institution has functioned.

From the very beginning of the Cold War, important non-security matters were involved in the formation of a Western security institution. These matters had profound significance, not only for the nature of security, but also for the political and economic future of Western Europe, of US-European relations, and of the prospects for altering the basic pattern of East-West confrontation.

To begin with, in January 1948 the British Foreign Secretary, Ernest Bevin, proposed the formation of an alliance of several West European states, beginning with Britain, France and the Benelux states. This would be a Western Union. At that time there were strong feelings, particularly among people and statesmen on the Continent, that this approach should be used to form the basis of more comprehensive political and economic arrangements. As a result, the Brussels Treaty Organization, which was established in March 1948 to embody the institutional aspects of this Western Union, carried considerable political and economic potential. Indeed, for at least the four Continental members of Western Union, these aspects were as important as those military ones which gained so much attention following the Czechoslovak *coup* and the beginning of the Berlin blockade.

This European interest in political and economic co-operation was reflected in the nature of the organization set up under the treaty—even though the treaty was largely negotiated after the *coup* in Prague. Among other things, it established a Consultative Council that, in practice, involved consultations among national finance ministers as well as among those responsible for military and foreign political affairs. The finance ministers interpreted their brief in very broad terms. In their deliberations, they covered issues going far beyond what would be expected in a traditional military alliance and, indeed, far beyond what came to be the practice in NATO itself.

This was understandable. After all, these European nations were in the midst of a complex process of forming a comprehensive set of institutions among themselves to cover matters such as customs unions. At the beginning of 1948, for example, the Benelux Union was becoming a reality, with the establishment of a customs union and the unification of external tariffs. At the same time, the French were actively engaged in negotiations with Italy to establish a customs union of their own. Within the year, active discussions were also on foot concerning a merger of the two schemes, to be called by the unattractive term 'Fritilux', while to the north the Scandinavian states began talking of a similar project, to be called 'Danosve'.

Partly because of their interest in these projects of economic co-operation, the European nations in Western Union were concerned to keep their new venture tightly-knit and free from competing focuses of attention. They were anxious to preserve the potential benefits Western Union could provide in moving all of them in the direction of greater European integration.

As we know now, the flaw lay in the attitude of Great Britain. In 1948 the British Foreign Secretary had managed to give his new European allies the impression that the British

Government was also interested in matters of political and economic co-operation, if not integration. This impression was further reinforced by Winston Churchill's leadership in Britain of the European Unity Movement.

It is not the purpose of this study to demonstrate whether or not subsequent British aloofness from involvement in Continental moves towards political and economic integration was foreordained as early as 1948. But there was certainly a considerable display of unhappiness by Continental statesmen when the British later showed themselves to be less than 'good Europeans'—as they were regarded to be by terms of this political shibboleth of the 1950s and early 1960s. At the same time, the British themselves were presented with a series of difficult dilemmas, as they attempted to reconcile their involvements on the Continent both with their commitments to the Commonwealth and with their hankering to establish and maintain a 'special relationship' with their giant neighbour across the Atlantic.

Soon after Western Union came into being, however, it became apparent that the attitude of the British was moving towards Atlantic ties. Later, these were widely seen on the Continent to be, almost by their very nature, incompatible with the most profound of European involvements—namely, full political union. Accordingly, during the period of discussion leading up to the establishment of an Atlantic Pact, British attention swung round to the possibility of getting the best of all possible worlds: America, Europe, and the Commonwealth. This was the so-called three circles policy that was pursued in different forms by several British Governments for more than a decade. Britain, therefore, was not a wholehearted supporter of moves towards close co-operation with the Continent on matters vitally affecting national sovereignty.

These considerations were all important in the development both of European security arrangements and of relations across the emerging division between East and West. As we shall see, this was so because the character of Western European political and economic interests played a significant role in the whole history of NATO's development, not only as a security organization, but also as a focus of efforts to achieve European integration.

This process had for a long time the strong support of various United States Administrations and the Congress. Americans saw a United States of Europe as possibly the best means of avoiding further fratricidal conflicts on the Continent, like the wars of 1914–18 and 1939–45 in which the Americans had reluctantly been led to take part. Indeed, the establishment of a Western Union in the first place owed much to the American Government's desire that the Europeans take concrete steps towards political and economic integration before Marshall aid came flowing across the Atlantic. Thus, partly in the interest of advancing European integration, the Brussels Treaty Organization was brought into being. In turn, it helped to institutionalize the Cold War and to bring into sharper relief both the division of Europe and the concrete forms of this division, including Russia's network of bilateral treaties in Eastern Europe.

There was concern among the four West European members of Western Union to protect their efforts at achieving economic and political integration from being dissipated; this concern was reflected in the process of forming the wider alliance, NATO. The basic question was this: which other nations should be invited to take part? The Western Union countries felt strongly that the new Alliance designed to bridge the Atlantic should be limited to the original five countries, plus the United States and Canada; at least these limits should be fixed until the Brussels Treaty Organization was assured of preserving its integrity. There would be guarantees from across the Atlantic to provide a foundation for economic recovery, while Western Union would be preserved as a basis for further political and economic efforts. Nor was this an idle concept; after all, this period in European development—from 1948 to about 1952—was one of the most creative periods in the

Continent's history, when viewed from the standpoint of new institutions and new approaches to solve old problems. From its inception, Western Union was widely seen to be a central part of this process, and it was thought to be worth preserving, however great the need to gain firm commitments from the Americans and possibly also their direct involvement in Continental affairs.

Almost immediately, there appeared a conflict of interests, one which had significant implications for the structure of confrontation as well as for the political and economic development of Western Europe. The American Government's enthusiasm for European integration led it to tie together virtually every step towards providing aid and security, beginning with the Marshall Plan, with political developments on the Continent. The Americans—including the Secretary of State and Senate leaders—wanted some grand conception to be based upon the 16 Marshall Plan countries. For this reason, as well as to provide security on an efficient and co-ordinated basis, the Americans favoured a broadening of the North Atlantic concept. For example, there was considerable reluctance in Washington to see the Nordic powers in Scandinavia develop a form of security organization on their own, separate from the one which the Americans envisaged in Western Europe. Washington saw the prospect of a Nordic Pact as diminishing the prospects for wider West European integration, as, indeed, would have been the case. As a result, the Americans put some pressure on these countries to join the new, wider Alliance, by declaring that no pact of which the US was not a member— i.e. any but the emerging Atlantic Pact—would receive the military aid that the others could expect.

From the American point of view, this stand made some sense, as it also did when viewed from the standpoint of running an efficient system of foreign aid and of forging a strong bulwark in Western Europe to meet the Soviet threat as the Americans interpreted it. But both of these views presupposed that an immutable confrontation already existed; that it had to be seen in military terms; and that the best way of dealing with it was to eliminate all traces of ambiguity throughout Western Europe. Consequently, the Swedes found it necessary to abandon consideration of any form of Scandinavian security organization. They wished to preserve what, for them, was an ambiguity more essential and valuable for their defence than could be any guarantee from the Americans or any participation in a North Atlantic Alliance. Ironically, the Swedes had actively considered joining Western Union and had been impressed by its economic and political possibilities as opposed to the military ones that eventually came to dominate it.

A similar view obtained in Norway, but the Norwegians did eventually join the discussions that led to the formation of a North Atlantic Treaty. They did so after the Russians provided Oslo with a convenient rationale by putting diplomatic pressure on the Norwegian Government to stand aloof. This was just another example of Soviet obtuseness, helping to produce the opposite result from that intended; and yet the West continued to credit the Russians with perfection in intrigue and in the manoeuvres of diplomacy!

Three years later, a development took place in NATO that was similar to the American pressure on the Scandinavians to join the wider Alliance. In 1952, Greece and Turkey joined the twelve-member Alliance, not so much because there was any strategic rationale for their doing so—they were hardly linked to the European Central Front—but rather because this step helped them to share in the common sense of cohesion and purpose. It may be argued that bilateral American guarantees to these latter two countries would have been more effective—as would, perhaps, even a Mediterranean-American security pact. But at the same time there was a strong sense in the United States that the Soviet threat should be regarded as indivisible: if any one 'Western' nation were attacked, all would be at risk.

In both these cases—US pressure *against* a Nordic Pact and

for a pact including the eastern Mediterranean powers—the process itself helped to solidify the East-West division and formalize the military nature of confrontation. And in this process considerable room was lost for diplomatic manoeuvre and for excluding some areas from the scope of confrontation— as happened with Sweden then and later with Austria. Of course, this view assumes that there did indeed exist some room for diplomatic manoeuvre in 1949: a moot point.

But as the Atlantic Treaty was being discussed in early 1949, the process of including outside states went even further, partly for parochial reasons. Since the integrity of Western Union was to be breached at the outset, so the reasoning went, then France wanted Italy to be included, largely in view of Franco-Italian rapprochement and the discussions on a customs union. This request was granted, even though it entailed some real compromises for the new Alliance in view of Italy's status as a defeated Axis Power. Similarly, Britain wanted Norway to be included, partly because of the close ties evolved long before the Second World War. Britain also wanted Portugal, the nation linked to her by the ancient and honourable treaty of 1373—the oldest surviving treaty of alliance in Britain's collection.

The inclusion of Italy suited the Americans, who had already made some pledges concerning Italy's defence that could be more easily redeemed within a broader alliance rather than on a bilateral basis. They were also pleased with the prospect of having Portugal, in order to use the air bases established in the Azores during the war, although the Americans did agree that no troops would be stationed there in time of peace.

Should there be more? Indeed there should: Denmark decided to join, partly at least, in order to regain some control over portions of Greenland that the Americans had been using since the war as bases. By placing these agreements within the broader context of a multilateral alliance, the Danes ran less of a risk of trouble in coping with a super-Ally. And Iceland joined, also partly, at least, because of the anomalous status of foreign forces which had to all intents and purposes occupied the island during the war.

Two countries, however, were left out—to say nothing of the Western part of Germany, which was still in a particularly uncertain position in Europe. These were Ireland and Spain. The former offered to join if Britain were excluded. Not surprisingly, practical politics prevailed over the sentiments of Irish-Americans. As for Spain, the Americans argued loud and long for its inclusion—over the bitter opposition of the rest of the Allies—until President Truman himself intervened on the side of the liberal Democrats in Congress. But Spain was later admitted to NATO by the back door, as it were, in the form of bilateral agreements made with Washington and with the provision of enough economic aid and payments for the rental on US bases in Spain to underwrite its economic development. And even today, Washington favours Spain's formal inclusion in the Alliance.

Thus NATO became, not a seven-nation alliance, but a twelve-nation one, and would eventually become one of fifteen. The nature of confrontation was broadened, and those ambiguities remaining in Europe were discounted for the sake of efficiency and a better chance to have a real defence and system of guarantees. This was not necessarily a bad choice, although it proved somewhat limiting diplomatically in later years. And this says nothing of the problems of maintaining Alliance cohesion, of finding ways to co-ordinate Alliance policies on *détente*, and of reassuring outlying Allies—Norway and Turkey—against a possible Russian snatch and grab attack. These problems were all exacerbated by the size of the Alliance.

Despite its size, however, the Brussels Treaty Powers tried to preserve the sense of their own organization until, at least, the British found Atlantic ties to be more desirable than the prospect of submerging their sovereignty in some wild and woolly European venture. Indeed, the Western Union Defence Organization and all of its appurtenances were not completely subsumed under NATO until the end of 1951, and even then the semblance of political organization was retained. It was even broadened to become the Western European Union (WEU) after the Germans and Italians acceded to the Brussels Treaty in late 1954. Indeed, well past the 20th anniversary of NATO, there was still talk of using this framework of WEU to co-ordinate the policies arrived at with the United States. This was an approach that was also implicit in the idea of a European Caucus within NATO, and of the attempt to achieve some co-ordination of defence policies within a Euro-group of Defence Ministers.

But in 1949 the rudimentary structure of Western Union was unable to retain its zest in the face of the overriding demands imposed by the developing relationship with America, and in face of the new Alliance's heavy emphasis on military matters. In consequence, soon after NATO came into being the Continental members of Western Union began to follow other courses toward integration. These began with the Schuman Plan for a European Coal and Steel Community (ECSC). For reasons alluded to above, the British did not accede to the ECSC as it was set up in 1950-2, but there were six countries to take part: these were the nucleus of Western Union (which included France and the three Benelux countries), plus Italy and West Germany. This was a significant list. In part, it was a recognition that the division of Europe (and of Germany) had been institutionalized to such an extent that there was little to be lost in terms of future diplomatic movement with the Russians on the issue of Germany. This was so because the Federal Republic was being included in an economic scheme which was envisaged merely as the first step towards functional integration—i.e. integration proceeding area by area—and eventual political and economic union.

But there was another, more strategic, significance behind the ECSC and the European Movement in general. This process also indicated that the Americans and, to an extent, the British, had not taken seriously enough the real fears felt by the four Continental members of Western Union that there could be a resurgence of military threat from a revived Germany. In theory, the ECSC would make war impossible by tying up the basic resources of war—iron, coal and steel—in a supranational context that would give no single nation the power to launch another major European conflict. In the nuclear age, such an assumption may be inadequate. But at least this rationale did indicate the widespread fears that remained about Germany's future behaviour. Indeed, it is interesting to note that the Russians never opposed this move towards Western European integration to the same degree that they opposed either the less encompassing Marshall Plan, the inclusion of West Germany in NATO, or the defensive component of West European integration—namely, the ill-fated European Defence Community (EDC). As far as the Russians were concerned, the major point at issue in all these efforts was the possibility of a revived German threat. Moves towards what was clearly West European integration therefore set the Russians a problem of conflicting objectives: they were against further progress towards consolidating and strengthening Western Europe, but they were also in favour of containing German power.

It was the next step in European integration after the ECSC that brought the strategic problems to the fore. This was also in part an effort to find a place for Germany that would settle fears about her behaviour. It reflected the complex issue that centred on the best way of raising West German forces to implement NATO's forward strategy, but without creating a truly national West German Army.

The solution seemed to lie in the Pleven Plan advanced by France. It proposed an extension of the concept of functional integration into the realm of defence. By implication, this concept would extend eventually into the strictly political realm through a politically unified European community. West Germany would take part in this new European Defence Community (EDC) as an equal partner with the other five members, and would be allowed to rearm; but there would be no question of re-establishing a German General Staff, or of permitting German units to operate on their own. Within European parliaments, there was some debate about the size of units that should be permitted to be all-German, above which point all commands would be organized on a supranational basis. But the principle was clear: no independent fighting capability should be returned to Germany, and her troops were to be firmly subordinated to an international command. This arrangement, in turn, was to be made an adjunct of NATO, and thereby would be firmly committed to it.

Needless to say, this proposal for an EDC brought the stiffest opposition from the Russians, although it was undoubtedly less provocative to them than, say, Germany's admission to NATO. Indeed, Moscow apparently realized this later, as evidenced by its reactions during the period of discussion on the EDC as compared with its reaction later when West Germany joined NATO. Then, the Russians threatened to establish a military Alliance of their own in Eastern Europe if the latter step were taken; and they duly carried out their threat.

The debate on the EDC continued until August 1954, and led to the signing of the treaty and its ratification by five of the six signatories. But then the French National Assembly rejected the agreement, and it collapsed. There were many reasons for this. One, perhaps, was decisive. For the French, the problem lay less in the failure of Britain to adhere to EDC, than in a growing reaction within France against the pace of European integration and the necessary merging of sovereignties that that process entailed. The establishment of common sovereignty in the crucial sphere of defence, as opposed to the limited economic sphere of coal and steel, was just going a bit too fast for the French. It should be noted, of course, that the emergence of this feeling at that time undercuts some of the attempts made to place French opposition to European integration during the 1960s on the shoulders of General de Gaulle

143

alone. French caution and reservations have a far longer history than that, and, in their context, they are the counterpart to British reservations.

This point about French rejection of the EDC is borne out in a number of ways, not least by the French acceptance of West German rearmament in principle as early as 1950. In addition, the next time the six nations returned to their search for integration, they concentrated on far less ambitious projects, in so far as these projects involved national merging of sovereignty. These were the Treaties of Rome providing for customs union, economic union, and peacetime development of nuclear power. And the six partners in these ventures proceeded to develop their new communities one careful step at a time.

But even more important in indicating that France's real objections were to the supranational characteristics of EDC were the immediate steps taken in the area of security. Only a few short weeks after the EDC treaty was rejected by the French National Assembly, the five Western Union countries agreed to broaden their organization to include West Germany and Italy, and took steps to provide for the raising of German forces. In the process, the Germans were subjected to even fewer controls on their armed forces. They were to have complete national divisions, although still no independent General Staff; and the French agreed to arrangements under which they had even less ability to dominate the use of these West German forces than they would have had under the EDC.

Significantly, the WEU agreements were proposed by the British—who also wished to stand aloof from integration in Europe, even more than did the French. Yet the British Government recognized that the American desire for German troops had to be met. Indeed, Mr Dulles, the American Secretary of State, had spoken of an 'agonizing reappraisal' if these demands were not met. Britain was therefore able, with little risk to her own independence from Europe, to satisfy this demand and gain some credit for resolving an impending crisis. Britain also pledged to keep four divisions (the British Army of the Rhine) and a tactical air force on the Continent, in theory until 1998. And she agreed not to withdraw them except with the permission of a majority of WEU powers in the event of 'an acute overseas emergency'. This was an effort to pacify European opinion about German rearmament. Yet the British began withdrawing these forces almost immediately, partly because of the Suez Crisis and financial pressures, and partly because the potential threat from West German troops seemed increasingly remote as the West Germans showed a marked and continuing reluctance to regain an army.

By this device—WEU—West German forces were brought into the structure of Western defence, and West Germany was brought into NATO. It did have to accept some inhibitions— such as the famous one against the manufacture of atomic, biological, and chemical weapons 'in its territory'. But for all intents and purposes the West Germans became full allies, and Dr Adenauer achieved his objective of making Germany respectable again.

The problem for European security lay in the impact that the entry of West Germany into WEU and NATO had on the Soviet Union. For these steps finally formalized the process of West Germany's increasing integration into a concept of Western defence, and formalized the division of that country into two parts.

Still, it was not until about 1957 that the Soviet Union dropped all pretence of flexibility on the issue of the division or reunification of Germany. By then, however, the possibilities for ambiguity were exhausted. Henceforth, the Russians adopted a hard and consistent line of confrontation. There would be no new offers by the Russians to 'join NATO'; and no new approaches to resolve Germany's division through negotiation. Germany was finally divided in the sense that really counted—i.e. from the standpoint of whether a diplomatic effort were feasible in order to change that position. Whatever the prospects had been before, they were now dead.

Until the logic of military confrontation worked itself out, there could be no real effort on either side to explore the possibilities of establishing security in Europe on any basis other than the simple formulation of two armed camps poised and ready to defend themselves against one another.

It is possible to argue that this integration of West Germany into NATO was one of the factors that led to the series of crises over the status of West Berlin between 1958 and 1961. These crises were, at least in part, an effort by Khruschev to clarify the position of the two Germanies. In other words, this was an effort to create a basis of understanding that the existence of two Germanies had to be accepted as the start of any diplomatic process to change the pattern of confrontation in Europe. It is true that Khruschev wanted this clarification to take place at the expense of West Berlin's ties with West Germany. But at least there seemed here to be an effort to find a basis—of which recognition of East Germany by the West was the most important element—on which the anomalous position of a Germany not officially divided would no longer dominate the perspectives of the major powers on European security. Therefore, this position of Germany would no longer be a barrier to strengthening, preserving and extending security on the understanding that Germany was divided.

Insofar as this is an accurate assessment of Soviet motivations, it illustrates the complications that were introduced into the process of achieving stability in Europe—as both a political goal and a security interest—by West Germany's formal entry into NATO. The difficulty lay with what might be called a problem of logic. The West had West Germany in NATO, but at the same time did not recognize East Germany. Of course, in the context of NATO politics, this double standard was adopted for understandable reasons, in view of the West Germans' desire for reunification. But now the issue of Germany's division had become part of the formal structure of military confrontation, as opposed to being merely an outstanding political problem. Therefore, the working out of the logic of confrontation came to include the need for mutual acceptance of a political and strategic *status quo* that recognized the formal division of Germany. And only when this acceptance was broadened to include the tacit acquiescence of America and Russia did *détente* begin in Europe.

Within months of West Germany's entry into NATO, the Soviet Union constituted a military pact of its own in the East, through a treaty signed in Warsaw on May 14, 1955. As discussed in Chapter 3, Russia and its seven satellites in Eastern Europe were brought together for the first time in a joint military venture. Previously, military relations between the Soviet Union and each of its seven satellite Allies were conducted on a bilateral basis that formed the pattern of security in the Eastern *bloc*. Indeed, this situation continued for at least the six years following, after which the Pact began to hold joint military exercises. But after the entry of West Germany into NATO, the Russians suddenly stood to gain some benefits from a formal military organization that stood in direct confrontation with NATO.

To begin with, there was no longer any need for the Russians to maintain the fiction that Eastern *bloc* relations were less formalized than those of the West. In what appeared to be the Russian view, there would be no diplomatic movement anyway, and therefore no need to worry about future difficulties of dismantling formal institutions—institutions which would tend to focus attention along clear and rigid lines. Second, a formal organization might at least give an appearance of a more formidable opposition to NATO—particularly a NATO containing West Germany—than mere bilateral defence pacts on their own. Third, the existence of the Warsaw Pact also gave the Soviet Union a parallel position to the United States during the Geneva Conference of 1955; and it permitted the Soviet Union to begin urging the abolition of both NATO and the Warsaw Pact. Militarily, as well, the existence of the Pact helped the Soviet Union to accept the Austrian State Treaty, by giving it clear lines of access to

Czechoslovakia and Hungary that had been provided for Russia as a Power occupying Austria.

But most important, the entry of West Germany into NATO gave the Russians something they had very much needed: a convincing rationale for keeping the Eastern European countries wedded to the Soviet concept of security in Europe. Indeed, as early as the proposals for Western Union in 1948, the Russians had reacted by calling this a ruse to permit the establishment of an independent West German state. In 1955, the threat posed by the United States to Eastern Europe might have seemed remote; but the threat of West Germany was very near indeed—always a major concern of those states that had suffered most in the Second World War. With the Federal Republic now directly integrated into NATO, a greater rationale existed in Eastern *bloc* countries, and especially in Poland, for making an active military effort. East Germany also feared pressures in the Federal Republic towards reunification. Then the possibility arose that a multilateral alliance would permit these countries to reinforce one another's perceptions of the threat. They would thus bind themselves even more closely to the Soviet view of West Germany and European security than they would do with only the simple bilateral relations they had with the Soviet Union and with one another.

As discussed in Chapter 3, however, it was not until after 1961 that the Russians began to rely in a serious way on the Warsaw Pact. This was after the break-up of the Sino-Soviet Alliance, the defection of Albania to the Chinese camp, the arms build-up by the United States, the worries culminating in the building of the Berlin Wall, and the arms reductions at the beginning of the 1960s in Russia. Through this greater Soviet reliance on the Warsaw Pact, there emerged a greater correspondence between the Warsaw Pact and NATO than there had been before. There were joint manoeuvres, and even some Eastern European (mostly Roumanian) discontent with Russian domination of the military organs.

But the most significant point is one made earlier: that to

take a simple view of these two security organizations, as though they were even remotely comparable in their relations and functions, does not do justice to the complexity of events in Europe as they really were. In short, the working out of a logic of military confrontation has depended far less upon the development of relations between NATO and the Warsaw Pact, than upon two other factors. These were the development of relations between America and its NATO Allies on the one hand and, on the other, the Soviet Union's much more predominant strategic and political influence over its own Allies. This latter factor became particularly important after the formal creation and later elaboration of a military pact in the East as part, initially, of Russia's own attitudes towards the German problem. Both in the West and the East, it was the stabilization of relations *within* the contending *blocs* that permitted some end to military logic, in the knowledge that a decrease in threat perceived by each side would not ravel the whole structure of each military Alliance.

Thus relations between East and West were made even more concrete and static by the entry of West Germany into NATO, and by the resulting inauguration of the Warsaw Pact. But there have been other ways in which the development of the security institutions—particularly of NATO—have affected patterns of influence and confrontation.

To begin with, there has been the question whether NATO could serve as the focus for any kind of Atlantic relations—or even European ones—that would go beyond the scope of purely military affairs. It has already been argued (Chapter 3) that the fundamental common interests of the Allies over the years can be reduced to two: namely, to preserve whatever level of defence might from time to time be thought necessary; and to keep the Americans committed to European security—particularly to preserve their nuclear guarantee.

This may seem a rather narrow definition—or even one that is unkind, in view of the tremendous efforts made to preserve Alliance unity and that ineffable substance called cohesion.

But it is still largely true, as we will see by taking a closer look at efforts made over the years to broaden the scope of NATO. Indeed, cohesion within the Alliance has only been possible when there has been a high degree of mutual appreciation among the Allies that there is at least some military threat from the Russians. And there has had to be widespread agreement as to the potential target of this threat. In other words, there has had to be agreement to keep the focus of the Alliance at its most narrow.

But having in mind questions of European integration and Atlantic relations, the framers of the North Atlantic treaty did include an article that dealt (in the most general and vague terms) with problems of political understanding and—more precisely—economic relations. This was Article 2, which provided, in part, that member states should 'seek to eliminate conflict in their international economic relations and will encourage economic collaboration between any or all of them'. (See Appendix II.) Ever since, there has been a continuing question: can anything concrete be made of these provisions? Nothing of substance ever has been, however. This has been so partly because the very size of the NATO organization has prevented the emergence of a definition of sufficient common interest that could serve as the focus of economic or other co-operative ventures. Instead, these ventures have been centred on the European Economic Community, the European Free Trade Association, the General Agreement on Tariffs and Trade (with a membership even wider than NATO's, but dealing with very specific problems) or the Group of Ten. The Council of Europe, on the other hand, with its broader focus but more limited mandate, has been a dismal failure at achieving anything at all significant: even it seems to include too many nations with diverging political and economic interests. As we shall see at the end of this chapter, however, there is now a new need to make some form of wider Atlantic co-operation a reality, as a condition of preserving European security in its broadest sense.

This is not to say that there have not been efforts over the years to turn NATO into something more than a mutual security pact. Indeed, there has been a succession of trials and failures well past the 20th anniversary of the organization. The most important of these efforts began in 1956, with the report of a special committee of the North Atlantic Council, composed of Sr Marino from Italy, Mr Lange from Norway, and Mr Pearson from Canada. They were called the three wise men, and were actually NATO's second set, the first having put together the Lisbon Force Goals in 1951–52. The wise men of 1956 proposed a broadening of the Alliance to include increased co-operation in economic, scientific, political and cultural affairs. In particular, there were to be greater efforts on the part of the Allies to settle their differences inside the NATO context instead of outside it.

It is significant that the Committee of Three and its sponsors reflected the opinion largely of the smaller powers of NATO. They saw in the new arrangements for consultation a chance to dilute some of the preponderant influence of the larger powers, meaning in particular the influence of the United States. And because of the idealistic nature of the proposals, the major powers concurred in their adoption.

The new purposes even met with some success. For example, in the Cyprus crisis of 1958, in which three NATO Allies were involved (Britain, Greece and Turkey), the good offices of NATO did play some part in the resolution of the crisis on a more-or-less amicable basis. Significantly, in the later Cyprus crisis of 1964–65, after this NATO consultative process had been allowed to decay, NATO's influence in settling the dispute was much less marked. And, again in 1958, the NATO forum helped to resolve a dispute between Britain and Iceland over fishing rights.

But it was still difficult for any of the major Allies to see NATO as a forum for resolving disputes that went beyond the limited liabilities imposed by the North Atlantic Treaty. For that matter, it was also difficult for many of the minor Allies, whether or not they had outside interests (as in early disputes on residual colonial problems). In particular, as will be developed below, NATO proved woefully inadequate—almost by common consent—in dealing with problems that arose outside the NATO treaty area itself.

Yet there was still some limited effort towards conducting political consultations within a NATO context on matters that could prove contentious among various Allies. In time, however, even that process broke down, largely because of the attitude towards NATO adopted by the Kennedy Administration which came to power in 1961. It was not so much a new attitude; rather, it was perhaps a more aggressive (i.e. less diplomatic) assertion of the potential of American influence that had always been present. Fundamentally, the idea of submitting American problems located outside the treaty area (e.g. Indochina) to the Council did not appeal to the new Administration, and the Allies allowed the procedures for consultation on a regular basis quietly to fall into disuse. In later years, there have been some joint efforts at consulting Allies, or at least informing them of decisions reached by national governments, but these efforts have never recaptured the tenuous yet tangible quality of Allied political consultations during the years 1956–1961. By no coincidence, these also happened to be the years when General Lauris Norstad was in command at Supreme Headquarters, Allied Powers Europe.

Thus ended the grand experiment with Article 2. Still, ten years after the report of the Committee of Three, there were celebrations in NATO about the forward-looking and idealistic character of this effort.

But this experiment was significant, if only because it illustrated the very narrow basis of common interest on which the NATO Alliance has been based. It also presaged the difficulties that would be encountered if ever the Alliance were to be used as a forum for discussing ways of recasting political confrontation in Europe—indeed, of finding any way to change the existing pattern of confrontation. Each member nation, in fact, has had certain interests which it prefers to pursue on its own, or at least on a strictly bilateral basis with one or another Ally. The patina of Alliance unity (cohesion) has rarely been permitted to obscure the pursuit of these interests.

From time to time, there has even been some measure of resentment at efforts by Allies to use the Alliance for what others have termed extraneous purposes. Some American efforts to stimulate greater European political integration (as through the Multilateral Force) met with resistance almost as much because of the attempt to channel much of the effort through NATO as for the nature of the pressure itself.

From the point of view of overall European security, however, this failure of the NATO Allies may have had salutary benefits (if failure is even an appropriate word to describe a process that has been so little grounded in practical politics). After all, despite the increased difficulties that would be posed by Allied consultations on problems of changing patterns of European confrontation, the lack of a broad political base for the Alliance has also meant that change across the East-West division has remained a greater possibility than might otherwise have been the case. Lacking certain elements of greater political or economic integration, NATO, as a forum, would have less to dismantle if ever the prospect arose of ending the military confrontation and bridging the gap, politically or economically, between East and West Europe. This is a dilemma for NATO, today. If the Allies are able to agree on the way to bring about change—that is, if they are more cohesive—then there is also likely to be a more rigid apparatus that, itself, will be resistant to change.

This dilemma becomes clearer when we observe that there has been a basic formula throughout all these years for observing what has often been called the cohesion of the Alliance—cohesion being, in effect, the willingness of the Allies to accommodate to one another on matters that have not pertained directly to the most important matters of mutual security. As mentioned earlier, when there has appeared to be a high degree of Soviet threat, there has been a greater sense of cohesion—i.e. of willingness to work together; and when that threat has diminished, so has cohesion. But this has not been entirely a matter of laziness in the face of a reduced threat. For as suggested above, an increase in cohesion within the Alliance would also mean a more formalized division of the Continent, and fewer prospects for change of a political, economic, or other nature. And many European states resist the use of cohesion when there is reduced threat, if this would inhibit approaches to the East.

Therefore, the appearance of threat from the Russians—in whatever form—has been not so much a signal that defences have had to be increased, as it has been that the prospects for change have once more receded. And it is in this context—and in this one alone—that the Russian invasion of Czechoslovakia in 1968 may be said to represent an increased Soviet threat to European security, as opposed to a threat emanating from the very existence of military *blocs* (see Chapter 6).

This also helps to explain why, during times of tension, American requests for increased troop levels in Europe have so often been received on the Continent with such bad grace. Of course, this has been partly a matter of Europeans' worrying about the credibility of the American nuclear guarantee if conventional forces were to be increased (see Chapter 4). But it has also been true that many Europeans have regarded the appearance of cohesion merely as the political alternative to accommodating US demands for increased troop levels, at times when hopes for change have been proving unrealistic. This was what happened in the autumn of 1968, when the Soviet invasion of Czechoslovakia signalled the postponement of prospects for change in Europe. The invasion therefore helped to increase the political cohesion of the Alliance. This was true not so much because there was any belief in an increased military threat to Western Europe. Even the small force increases were really only of diplomatic significance in indicating Western displeasure. Rather there was an awareness of the need to take political steps to make *détente* in Europe possible once again. If a warning to the Russians were required, in order to establish, once again, the conditions for *détente* and later for change, then so be it: the Russians would be shown— through increased cohesion in the West—that they had to pay a price for *détente* with the West by exercising restraint in the East.

But at least the Allies at times have agreed to make an effort to find some means of co-ordinating opinion. The most important of these efforts was undertaken officially through a study commissioned for the North Atlantic Council in 1967 (the Harmel Report). It was presented to the Council at the end of that year. Despite the fanfare with which it was launched, the Harmel Report (Appendix VII) once again demonstrated the almost impossible nature of the task of co-ordinating Alliance policy for the future. Indeed, it can be argued that it would have been better not to advertise the difficulties obviously facing the Alliance as it tried to cope with the future. The Allies were, in effect, worrying about the cohesion of the Alliance and the integrity, for political purposes, of Allied Command Europe. But what was the purpose of doing that if the Allies were simply going to proclaim that they could not really find ways to reconcile their differences in exploiting *détente*, or in going beyond this to *entente* or engagement?

There were platitudes in the Harmel Report, of course, but little that was concrete. All that *was* concrete was still to be found in policies pursued by individual nations, such as the United States, which has been searching simultaneously for a way to deal with a Soviet-American *détente*, with its pledges to West Germany about German reunification, and with the perennial problems of trying to hold the Western Alliance together. In fact, the Americans have so far been unable to reconcile these different objectives, and their dilemma has become even more apparent since the Czech invasion (see Chapter 6).

But it has been the French, at least under President de

Gaulle, who have seen most clearly the dangers in cohesion pursued for its own sake, so long as the Alliance is unable to define criteria for turning *détente* into something more positive. It is not that criteria cannot be discovered—that proposition has yet to be proved—but that they have eluded Alliance statesmen. For the French under de Gaulle, therefore, the alternative was relatively simple. They should prepare for the exploitation of *détente* on their own. And so they did, with General de Gaulle's series of *démarches* to the Alliance in 1966. By dropping the pretence that cohesion in the Alliance had any value outside a situation of real threat, General de Gaulle appeared to believe that he could gain greater flexibility in dealing with the Russians.

In the event, the realities of America's predominance in Western Europe led this policy to misfire (though not entirely to fail). It became clear that France could obtain nothing in the direction of change in European confrontation without American acquiescence. But at least the French were looking in that direction, and they succeeded in hastening the search among the rest of the Western Allies for ways to change the patterns of confrontation in Europe.

With the Russian invasion of Czechoslovakia, the French made some changes in their position. As noted in Chapter 4, they did not rejoin the integrated military structure of NATO, but rather edged diplomatically closer to their Allies. At the same time, the French began to co-operate with the Allies in their surveillance of Russian naval activities in the Mediterranean. As with the Allied reaction, itself, the new French position can be seen as an effort to demonstrate to the Russians that the pursuit of *détente* requires Russian restraint in Eastern Europe—as well as toleration of change in the Eastern *bloc* that, in itself, does not affect Russian security in any real sense—if *détente* is to be mutually beneficial.

Thus, the French modified their separate position, adopted to gain flexibility, simply to preserve the conditions under which they could continue to act for *détente*. And they have continued to play a unique role within NATO with regard to *détente*. Despite the death of de Gaulle, they still have not returned to the fold of Allied Command Europe.

At this point, it will be clear that the problem of getting agreement among the 15 Allies—or even a portion of them—has proved difficult in matters directly relating to Europe (such as the best manner for bringing about a change in the pattern of European confrontation). But it has proved almost impossible where questions outside the NATO treaty area have been concerned.

There has been no lack of trying. From the beginning of the Alliance, one Ally or another has tried to use the Alliance for its own national purposes outside the carefully delimited geographical limits of the Alliance's guarantees. In the first place, there was a question of the scope of the treaty's purview. Did it, even in a philosophical sense, embrace all the Western interests in the world? Not surprisingly, this question entered into the process of burden-sharing. What element of a nation's defence expenditures could be included? Just those spent directly in the defence of Europe, or all of them, wherever spent?

As indicated in Chapter 3, this problem has been settled throughout most of NATO's history by a crude process of bargaining. There has also been competition (particularly among European powers) to see which country could default the most on its commitments without endangering the Alliance structure. But some issues have been brought into the open. For one thing, several of the Allies had colonial possessions when the Treaty was signed—namely, the Netherlands, Britain, France, Portugal, Belgium. Each of them claimed special dispensation for the forces required to maintain overseas garrisons. And, of course, the United States indirectly claimed such dispensation every time the general standard of percentage of gross national product spent on defence was introduced as a criterion for assessing 'fair shares'. As argued earlier, perhaps it has been appropriate that the United States, on balance over the whole period, has borne the brunt of NATO financing wherever it has taken place. After all, the United States has clearly received the greatest share of influence and security for its investments elsewhere. Of course, this proposition begs a question: who benefits most, if at all, in the European context from military efforts outside the treaty area? But it does, at least, illustrate the problem of relating American global involvements to the more limited involvements of even the most widely involved European ally. And it also illustrates how difficult it is for the Allies to decide which external involvements of, say, the United States, relate to European security itself.

These problems are difficult enough. But there is another one that has had even more direct relevance to the development of Alliance relations. This is the problem of the role to be played by NATO itself in areas outside the treaty area. There have been specific conflicts and problems that have led various Allies to ask for outside aid. There have been instances in which colonial powers have demanded the support of their Allies—culminating in the fulminations of Prime Minister Salazar in 1966 about the failure of NATO to give adequate support to Portugese colonial policies in Angola and Mozambique. There was, of course, the extraordinary row within NATO over the Suez war, when the Americans thwarted the efforts of the British and French. At one time the French wanted NATO's support for their policies in Algeria; at others the Americans have tried to keep Britain involved east of Suez; and there was the long-standing American effort to link NATO with the war in Vietnam. Ironically, it was the French who first tried to get support from the Allies in Southeast Asia; and they received certain verbal assurances in the form of resolutions. But when the Americans tried it, they got even less, time after time, no matter how hard their spokesmen tried to present that war as an extension of the defence of Western Europe.

Throughout the history of NATO, therefore, these efforts to involve the Alliance elsewhere in the world have met with almost total failure. This was so largely for the basic reason of narrow common interests: it was difficult enough to get 15 nations to agree at any one time on the nature of the Soviet threat in Europe (if there ever were agreement); it was infinitely more difficult to get any one of the Allies, except where bilateral commitments were concerned, to agree to help another Ally in need outside the area.

This remained true even in 1958 when the French tried to restructure both the Alliance and all commitments of the major Western Powers. Each of the three major Powers—Britain, France, and the United States—was to oversee the defence of separate areas of the world. Not without considerable justification, the Americans at the time merely noted that 'it was simply not possible to establish an organic directorate either over NATO or the rest of the world'. Yet this event demonstrated a central problem that has plagued NATO and would certainly plague any larger organization or more broadly-based Alliance: namely, the tremendous difficulties of establishing patterns of influence among different countries, where the partial merging of sovereignties comes up against divergences of political interest. This holds true even in so limited a venture as NATO. In the NATO context, these divergences of political interest would be more inhibiting as they became more profound and deviated further from the limited goal of providing a common defence against a common and palpable threat.

This issue related to an objective of the Harmel Report in 1967—and another of its conspicuous failures: namely, the attempt to gain some common basis for co-ordinating the activities of individual NATO nations in the outside world. But there simply was no basis for working together where there was no common threat to perceived interests, nor much chance of finding an effective mechanism for the adequate sharing of influence—that most evanescent, yet most troublesome, of all the elements of the NATO Alliance.

This situation was not necessarily to be regretted when seen from the standpoint of the NATO-Warsaw Pact pattern of military confrontation. Was there a possibility of extending it beyond the confines of Europe? By keeping the scope of NATO limited to Europe, the Allies reduced the chance of spreading the context of confrontation to other areas of the world. During the 1950s, to be sure, the nature of the US-Soviet relationship came to mean that virtually any new area in which one super-power found itself involved almost surely attracted the other as well. The confrontation was regarded as global (at least by Dulles and his ilk), and in a sense it became indivisible.

It was difficult enough, in terms of keeping separate various spheres of possible confrontation, to have 15 nations belonging to NATO; it would have been even more difficult if the NATO Alliance had become a seamless web, stretching throughout the range of Western interests. How then could there have been accommodation between East and West anywhere, without the most profound consequences for the structure of the overall super-Alliance, and for the problem of cohesion? The United States would do well to bear this problem in mind as it attempts to introduce the concept of 'linkage' into its relations with the Soviet Union. In the Middle East, for example, the Americans have on several occasions attempted to argue that Soviet involvement *necessarily* affects US-Soviet understandings in Europe, whether or not there is any direct political or military relationship between the two problems. Fortunately, America's European Allies have been reluctant to involve NATO in this foolish diplomatic exercise.

This question of seeing East-West confrontation as indivisible also has direct significance when seen in relationship to other American-sponsored or supported security alliances. These were conceived during the early 1950s, and extend from the Central Treaty Organization (CENTO—an outgrowth of the Baghdad Pact), to the ANZUS Treaty and the South-east Asia Treaty Organization (SEATO). As we have learned, the more nations that have their security bound up within the same institutionalized context of confrontation, the more difficult it is to see that context transformed into a phase of accommodation. There could even be added impediments placed in the way of settling outstanding political problems. Settlement of a problem, for example, might be of compelling interest to nations at one end of an Alliance, but be of relatively little concern to those at the other. After all, what real interest have the West Germans had—much less the Danes—in possible conflicts of interest between the Russians and the Turks? Therefore, beyond the need to preserve some semblance of cohesion (almost for its own sake), being concerned with Turkey offers little to Governments in Bonn or Copenhagen that are contemplating the prospects for pursuing the position and role of *détente* across the Central Front of Europe itself.

CENTO is particularly instructive in this regard—i.e. in considering the political functions that can be performed by an alliance—political functions that go beyond the simple guarantees of security, however broadly defined, that are implicit in its basic agreement. CENTO is particularly worth a brief comparison since, for one country in the local area—namely Turkey—there has been overlapping membership with NATO.

Despite the existence of CENTO as a formal alliance, there have rarely been any ideas put forward for transforming it into an institution to further political integration among its three local members—Turkey, Iran and Pakistan: three states which have seldom even been able to agree on the nature or even the existence of any Soviet 'threat' to their interests. In the case of Pakistan, in particular, the CENTO Alliance has in recent years been seen to be of almost no 'security value' at all. United States support for CENTO after all, is organized through a series of bilateral agreements, and is specifically limited to threats emanating from communist sources. The US commitment also provides no support at all to Pakistan in its dispute with India over Kashmir and, more recently, strife in Bangladesh (East Pakistan)—security issues that are far more real for the Government in Islamabad.

Indeed, for some time there has been a process among CENTO nations of resolving conflicts with the Soviet Union, largely over local issues that antedate the Soviet-American competition in Europe. Since that time, the significance that CENTO has retained has been in the field of economics. But even this effort has not been conceived, as in Western Europe, as a functional approach to integration; instead it is a limited effort to approach common economic problems of developing nations through joint efforts. These are supported by Britain, the only outside member of CENTO, and by the United States, the more or less affiliated partner. In pursuing these limited goals, Iran, Pakistan and Turkey set up a Regional Co-operation for Development (RCD) in 1964, and deliberately kept it outside the framework in CENTO. This Regional Co-operation for Development provides what impetus there remains to hold CENTO together; yet the RCD has stimulated pressures neither in America nor elsewhere for converting this into functional integration. Nor has it especially aroused American anxieties about future security requirements in this area along the southern borders of the Soviet Union—security requirements that were seen to be of such importance in the late 1940s, during the formulation of the Truman Doctrine. Even increasing contact by each of the three local CENTO Powers with the Soviet Union has not, as yet at least, caused the US undue alarm. This is so even though, in the case of Iran, this development has led to trade with the Soviet Union, including the supply by the Russians of certain types of armaments, and flow of Iranian natural gas to the Russian neighbour. These relations can be expected to develop even further.

The Western partners of CENTO clearly have different attitudes to developments in that region, in contrast to the US attitude towards the integrity of the NATO Alliance. This difference is not so much the result of a greater sense of stability in the CENTO region, *vis-à-vis* the Soviet Union. In fact, there is certainly a good deal less security there in terms of the possible success of a Soviet military venture. Neither do the same kinds of political and strategic understandings exist between the two super-powers, as obtain across the Central

Front of Europe, (although, of course, there is some tacit, if uneasy, sharing of influence by the two super-powers in the local CENTO nations). Nor can the less vital importance of the CENTO region entirely explain this difference in attitude concerning the effective collapse of CENTO as a collective pact for security, on the one hand, and, on the other, the political anxieties expressed for the future of NATO. Indeed, in the case of NATO, these anxieties were given a kind of concrete form in the very commissioning of a Harmel Report on the Future Tasks of the Alliance, and other later efforts.

The answer to this apparent puzzle lies more in the non-military functions being served by the two Alliances. In the case of CENTO, little is expected by the United States of the local Powers. For example, they have not been subjected to the same concerted and public pressures to support US policy in Vietnam.

They, in turn, expect little from the United States beyond a measure of economic assistance and a residual commitment against an undefined and almost unspoken possible threat to their political interests that could re-emerge from the Soviet Union. There is a partial exception to this pattern in the case of Turkey. But the significant point here is that Turkey has chosen to express its security anxieties within the context of NATO, not that of CENTO. It is true that in NATO a greater sense of American commitment has been generated, but for Turkey's purposes this is a commitment that derives at least in part from the high value placed by the Americans, in particular, on the question of Alliance cohesion. And this is to say nothing of the value that this cohesion has acquired as an end in itself within the NATO Alliance, almost without reference to any functional uses to which cohesion may be put.

Turkey, therefore, is more likely to achieve its security objectives (which largely take the form of an American guarantee) within the scope of the NATO Alliance than through CENTO or even on a bilateral basis. It has, in effect, succeeded in posing as a European power. And the seriousness with which

NATO councils study Turkish claims for 'nuclear land mines', for example, seems to indicate that this approach has merit for the Turks, put in terms of the integrity of the entire NATO Alliance. The merit of this approach has also been demonstrated in the creation of the ACE (Allied Command Europe) Mobile Force, a small military force designed at least in part with Turkey in mind, and in general almost entirely as a political device to promote the elusive political cohesion in the outlying areas of the Alliance.

But the comparison between CENTO and NATO, made within the context of the non-military uses of an Alliance, can be taken even further. As argued above, the process of change in patterns of confrontation is vitally affected by the number of nations with interests in the outcome of this process.

The more nations involved, the more difficult it will prove to use, say, NATO, as an effective instrument for settling on common future political objectives virtually anywhere within the compass of the North Atlantic Treaty area, *vis-à-vis* Soviet political and security interests as defined in Moscow. Within CENTO, no such process is envisaged: there is, for a start, no outstanding problem of a divided Germany. Nor is there any legacy of fearing a former dominant power whose reunification is still widely seen in terms of the stereotypes of 1939, a time when today's two super-powers remained aloof from European security problems.

Again, there is in the CENTO Alliance no significant institutional framework, including a peace-time military command structure and actual forces under Allied command. Hence, there is not the same sense of a military logic of confrontation that has had to be worked through between the United States and the Soviety Union in the CENTO region as there has been in central Europe itself. Nor is there any elaborate apparatus that must be dismantled, and seen to be dismantled, as the Americans and Russians pursue a limited form of political accommodation in the CENTO region that fully exploits the political ambiguities that exist there. Indeed, this political accommodation has apparently been judged by both sides to be worth more than the certainties that derive from a frozen and sterile military confrontation.

But most important, perhaps, there is again the whole question of the role played by NATO over the years for bargaining out the relationship between the United States and its Western European Allies—a process (or rather an interlocking series of processes) that the United States has never really channelled to Turkey, Iran and Pakistan through the CENTO organization as such. Within NATO, this is a process of bargaining out a relationship that is becoming of critical importance where the pursuit of *détente* has become the dominant focus and concern of the NATO Alliance and of competing American and Western European interests. This is so whether *détente* is pursued by the United States directly with the Soviet Union for their common interest (on such matters as arms control), or by West Europeans dealing with the East on Continental matters.

As a result, the end of the old context of military confrontation as between NATO and the Warsaw Pact—the working out of the logic—contains a lesson which argues strongly that the process of bargaining within the West on matters of *détente* be limited to as few nations as possible. This is particularly so with regard to reconciling those divergent American and Western European interests that have been made quite evident since the Soviet invasion of Czechoslovakia.

Indeed, the process of changing patterns of confrontation in Europe, as opposed to maintaining the strength of those patterns, is more likely to succeed where issues can be isolated within contexts where there can be mutual agreement by both East and West. This is why recent increases in Soviet fleet deployments in the Mediterranean, beginning about 1964, have really been so disturbing to some members of NATO: they could appear to pose new threats of a limited nature to more outlying areas of the Alliance, as well as to Italy. This is a nation which has come to be seen as part of the Central

Front, however unjustified this view may be in terms of genuine European security problems. These new threats, followed by an appeal for Alliance cohesion, also come at a time when progress towards solving problems across the Central Front with the nations of the Warsaw Pact could well be retarded as a result.

It is arguable that a new context should be considered for structuring American guarantees to the Eastern Mediterranean countries in NATO. At least the guarantees to Turkey (if not also to Greece) should be treated in this way, because of the greater significance of neighbouring Yugoslavia to the West in terms of the prospects for *détente* in Central Europe following the invasion of Czechoslovakia. A Balkan Pact (Treaty of Ankara) was concluded between Greece, Turkey and Yugoslavia in 1953, and developed into a full defensive alliance in 1954, although it has meant very little since then. Still it is just conceivable that this pact might provide a focus for indirect or surrogate US participation in the Eastern Mediterranean that would leave the rest of Western Europe free for recasting the context of confrontation with the Warsaw Pact. This would depend, of course, on both Russian and Yugoslav attitudes towards something of a lessening of the ambiguities surrounding the position of Yugoslavia. At present, this would pose a particular dilemma for Yugoslavia, which is experiencing a great sense of anxiety about the Soviet Union (and its Mediterranean squadron) since the Brezhnev Doctrine was announced, yet relies to a great extent on the implicit support of the US Sixth Fleet.

Alternatively, the US could give bilateral guarantees to Greece and Turkey—guarantees that would enable the United States to bring its commitments to these countries more properly into line with a structure that is capable of taking care of them without encountering the stifling problems of cohesion within the NATO Alliance. In any event, the US will need to keep the Sixth Fleet up to strength, especially if there are force reductions on the Central Front in Europe.

These are really matters of *détente* and properly belong in a discussion of that particular subject. But there are at least two other matters that cannot be ignored in a discussion of the non-military functions of the NATO Alliance—hidden political problems and the possible role of NATO in *détente*. First, to what extent has the very structuring of an Alliance, and of East-West confrontation, driven underground some of the residual political problems that exist in a muted form within Europe? In other words, are there problems and conflicts that would tend to re-emerge if there were ever a resolution of the central conflict dividing the Continent? These questions may apply especially to traditional enmities among nations of southeast Europe, whether Greek-Turkish disputes that have not been entirely submerged by the overriding need for cohesion as it has been expressed within the context of NATO, or disputes among Balkan countries within or adjoining the Warsaw Pact. But there is also the more pressing problem of the relations between Germany—however structured—and its neighbours. The fundamental dictum of French policy on this issue since the Second World War—*rapprochement*—will be made no easier by the approach of real chances to change existing patterns of European confrontation. Indeed, this central problem of Germany will probably become more difficult to resolve —or at least it will become of more immediate concern to all its neighbours, who, again, may operate with outdated stereotypes, if and when the issue of reunification becomes again one of central importance and discussion. This problem may be muted somewhat by the progressive development of the European Community, which continues to find a place for West Germany in a strictly Western venture. But the issue of reunification, with all its emotional overtones, is still not dead. Indeed, West German *Ostpolitik* ensures that the issue will be kept alive.

Finally, introduction of this subject of Germany brings the discussion in the latter part of this chapter back to the basic question posed, and hardly answered, by the Harmel Report.

That question remains whether NATO could be a forum for pursuing *détente*, and for carrying it beyond to *entente* and engagement.

As indicated above, experience so far does not provide much room for optimism that NATO will provide the necessary forum for decisions within the Western Alliances on these questions of *détente* and beyond. Of course, the Allies are still proceeding on the assumption that NATO can be effective. Preliminary efforts leading to negotiations on Mutual and Balanced Force Reductions are being conducted through NATO. There was a Deputy Foreign Ministers' meeting in October 1971, and Sr Manlio Brosio, the retiring Secretary-General, was appointed 'Explorer' to the Soviet Union. As of the time of writing, however, the Russians have studiously spurned his advances.

This use of NATO as a forum for *détente*, and the selection of MBFR as the way of creating a multilateral framework, were not coincidental. Indeed, the lack of an alternative Alliance forum for discussing *détente* issues helps to lock the Allies into a focus on these military questions, with the potentially adverse impact on progress in *détente* that was forecast at the end of Chapter 4.

Perhaps there is no forum in the West for dealing with broad political issues in *détente* on a multilateral basis, and no real way to go beyond today's patterns of confrontation, except on a haphazard and piecemeal basis. This scepticism is founded largely on the diverse interests of the various Allies in what happens now. These differences divide nations on either side of the Atlantic, but they also appear among the European Allies themselves. West Germany, of course, remains the central figure in this discussion. Its concern to become at long last a fully accepted member of Europe may lead it to take steps in the prosecution of *détente* that are not always fully acceptable to its Allies. Some steps in *Ostpolitik* have been accompanied by latent fears in some European hearts of another Rapallo agreement between Germany and Russia.

These steps, therefore, have not always received universal applause.

Even if there is no ideal forum in the West to serve for discussion and resolution of problems of *détente*, however, there are some comments that can be made. In the first place, the United States needs to take more seriously the concerns of its Allies that some means be found for prosecuting *détente* with the East in an institutional manner. Here, the Americans have been dilatory on several counts, in part because of (understandable) fears that the process will get out of hand. What cohesion is left within the NATO Alliance might then be jeopardized, or the East might gain what is called a propaganda victory, without the West's achieving tangible results.

This American anxiety has sometimes appeared to Europeans to lead away from avenues that are available, however. For example, during a time when Europeans were most concerned with the Brezhnev Doctrine on limited sovereignty within the socialist camp, the United States proposed to set up a Committee on the Challenges of Modern Society. This committee, which deals with common problems of threats to the environment, may be worthy in itself (see Appendix VIII), but it is certainly not the 'third dimension' that the Americans represented it to be. In addition, since Europeans had more important things on their minds, it struck many of them as another example of American inability or unwillingness to understand what was happening on the Continent. Instead of *détente*, pollution: in a way, this is Article 2 run wild.

Yet at the same time, there is at least one valuable process of consultations taking place within the Alliance that is centrally linked to a problem of *détente*. These are the informal consultations on the Strategic Arms Limitation Talks (SALT) which began in November 1969. As discussed in Chapter 4, these talks are potentially divisive of the Western Alliance. This is so partly because they throw into stark contrast the American interest in stabilizing the arms race with the Soviet Union, while West Europeans are more interested in securing better Soviet behaviour in East Europe. Of course, the West Europeans will gain whatever benefits emerge from the SALT talks in any event, and have at first glance no price to pay for it. At the moment of writing, however, there is one matter at the SALT talks that could exact a price from the West Europeans, but which has not been raised in any systematic way within NATO forums. This is the question of so-called forward based systems (FBS)—those US aircraft and missiles stationed with NATO that could deliver a nuclear attack against the Soviet Union. The Russians obviously want them included in any comprehensive arms control agreement with the United States that goes beyond broad outlines of total force levels. This issue will be joined probably in the second stage of the SALT talks, after a first major agreement expected in early 1972.

It is equally obvious that the United States will find it difficult to allow these missiles and aircraft to become the subject of discussions at the SALT talks—a bilateral forum. If they do so, they will unsettle their European Allies. Of course, it is possible that the simultaneous conduct of the SALT talks and negotiations on Mutual and Balanced Force Reductions could help to solve this problem. Then, the forward based systems could be the focus of attention at either set of negotiations, with firm connections to the other. With luck, the issue could be settled amicably, because the European Allies would be assured of a full role in all deliberations on these tactical nuclear weapons.

Nevertheless, as noted in Chapter 4, there has still so far been no apparent attempt within NATO to evolve a process of consultations that would allow the whole question of the US nuclear guarantee to Europe to be discussed in a rational and amicable way. This question of the nuclear guarantee, of course, must include the character and number of US weapons actually committed to NATO, even if this is only a matter of psychology. Furthermore, the question of forward based systems, as part of the process of arms control negotiations, is also intimately linked to the problem of the US troop commitment to NATO Europe (see Chapter 4). Regular consultations on the SALT talks themselves do not appear to be adequate for dealing with these potentially explosive issues.

These are areas in which NATO as an institution does have a positive role to play in preparing the Allies to take advantage of *détente*. These are non-military roles to be played by the Alliance. But there are other factors emerging that carry the debate far beyond conventional lines. There is, in effect, a need for the philosophy of Article 2 on non-military co-operation to become a prime focus rather than just an adjunct to the Atlantic Alliance. This is true even if NATO, itself, is not the forum to make Article 2 effective. There are several factors leading to this judgment, the most important of which is the diminishing importance of military questions in determining effective security in Europe. This is a complicated point, but it grows out of the success of NATO and the Warsaw Pact, and the understandings on European Security reached between East and West. These understandings limit what is permissible in order to bring about political changes. Clearly, the use of military force across the line of confrontation in Europe is no longer considered legitimate by any nation party to European security.

Therefore, it is no longer as valid as it once was for the United States to try channelling its influence to Europe through the military organ. The questions being raised there are simply not the crucial ones affecting the health of the Alliance. The growing economic strength of the European Community nations is now seriously rivalling the dominance of the United States in important matters that have a major political element, and in fact, the health of the Atlantic Alliance is coming to depend less upon military relations, and more upon economic ones.

During the 1950s and 1960s, when the US was the economic giant of the Western Alliance, it was possible to place these economic questions in the second rank. Today, it is no longer possible. Already we have seen the prospect of an Atlantic trade war, occasioned by possible passage (during 1972) of restrictive legislation in the United States and by protectionist policies on the part of the European Community. This issue became even more acute following the decision of the US government in August 1971 to end conversion of the dollar into gold and to impose a 10 per cent additional tariff on manufactured imports. Such a trade war, or other failure to resolve the international economic crisis, could do more to undermine confidence across the Atlantic than maintenance of the full complement of US troops on the ground in Europe could do to sustain it. In December 1971, the Allies gained temporary relief through an agreement to devalue the dollar, but the problem of economic co-operation is still pressing—even more so than problems of troop levels in Europe.

Indeed, there is a host of other economic matters to be worked out as between the United States and its European partners. In addition to the construction of some modification of the Bretton Woods Agreements on international monetary co-operation, including new exchange parities, these matters include the harmonization of business and tax laws, and the regulation of the activities of multinational corporations. This is indeed where the real health of the Atlantic Alliance will be determined in future: namely, by the willingness of the various Allies to solve these problems in an amicable fashion. There will also be no giant among a bunch of pigmies: rather, there will be a greater sense of economic and (potentially) political equality—or a growing breach between the two halves of the Alliance.

It is no longer enough, therefore, for the United States to express its commitment to the future of Europe through the military organ, NATO. It is now necessary to do so in other ways, and through other organizations, such as the OECD and the Group of Ten. These institutions include non-NATO powers, such as Japan. Yet in a world that is becoming increasingly interdependent economically, the role of Japan is becoming tied up with the basic 'security' of North Atlantic relations. In June 1971, the US Secretary of State paid his first-ever visit to an OECD meeting. In future, this practice will gradually come to be more important than his attendance at semi-annual Ministerial Meetings of the North Atlantic Council.

In a strange way, these economic institutions are beginning to relate to the most crucial matters of security in a time of potential change. The most crucial matter is, of course, the sense of Western co-operation while some means is found to discuss matters more directly pertaining to *détente*. This, again, is a matter of cohesion. But it is no longer one of *degree*, varying inversely with the Soviet threat, but rather one of *kind* and of *forum*. A lack of economic anxiety (outside NATO) is beginning to be substituted for military commitment (within NATO) as a test of the cohesion needed to preserve an Atlantic Alliance during the process of *détente*. This economic goal is also a test of America's ability to share influence in the area emerging of greatest competition between the two halves of the Alliance.

What cohesion still remains in the Atlantic Alliance, therefore, is facing challenge most directly in this economic realm; so it is there that some of the answers must be found, especially regarding US commitments to Europe's future, both now and following any process of *détente* that is even reasonably successful. Coupled with consultations on troop levels, economic consultations and harmonization thus become a chief focus of security efforts in the Atlantic Alliance. Indeed, if an organized process of troop reductions takes place in the West while economic consultations proceed, then these will provide even less scope for Soviet mischief making. The Allies will then be still better placed to find a new magic number of US troops without eliminating the Soviet Union's incentives to reduce its own forces, as well (see chapter 4).

It can be seen, therefore, that, beyond its role in consultations on matters like the SALT talks, there is little in NATO's history or promise to justify the hope that it could be an effective instrument of *détente*. This judgment, which may even apply to the use of NATO as a way of controlling negotiations on Mutual and Balanced Force Reductions, is not just based on the poor record of consultations within NATO—partly because of the great disparity in power among the Allies and the failure of American efforts to create a politically unified equal in Europe for the Atlantic Partnership. But there are also what appear to be the radically different political interests of the several Allies in a world in which they are not confronted with a simplistic and one-dimensional Soviet military threat across Central Europe. Indeed, the failure of the Harmel Report to produce anything more than promises to try finding answers further indicates that it is nearly impossible to find in NATO an adequate forum for handling these problems—or to handle them in joint diplomatic efforts by NATO and the Warsaw Pact. Furthermore, letting NATO dominate the diplomatic process leading up to negotiations on Mutual and Balanced Force Reductions will only emphasize military factors at the expense of the political ones that are essential in this step towards *détente*.

Of course, the Warsaw Pact may prove equally inadequate as a forum for consultation, if such a time is ever reached that the Soviet Union will consider changes in patterns of European confrontation that will be acceptable to East and West Europeans alike. This may be so, even though, since the invasion of Czechoslovakia, there has been an increase of bargaining within the Pact.

But there is still much that has to be said about the nature of *détente* in Europe, about its impact on the continuing problems of European security, and about the possible character of a new pattern of confrontation. These topics need to be explored, even if there is no clear way of transforming the patterns of 1949–71 into those postulated for the future.

Chapter 6

The Development of *Détente*

The process commonly known as *détente* has had many sources, both in direct US-Soviet relations and in political developments taking place on the Continent. Some of these sources have already been presented here, but they are worth recapitulating. In the first place, the ability of anyone to *relax* (the literal meaning of *détente*) depended on the beginning of a form of strategic stability as between the Soviet Union and the United States. And indeed, by 1962–63, it was becoming apparent that the development of new weapons would insure that each country could survive any attack by the other, and retaliate with devastating consequences. Second, both superpowers began to see by the end of 1962 that the Cuban Missile Crisis had taken the world uncomfortably near the brink of nuclear war, over issues that were not politically worth such a threat to end the world. From then on, they each began to see that the concept of a generalized global competition in power between themselves could have destructive consequences for them both, unless they could clarify what was, and what was not, important to them in terms of intrinsic political and economic interests.

In fact, from then on, both the Americans and the Russians began to conduct their affairs with a great deal more caution than they had exercised before. By the late 1960s, therefore, the two superpowers developed an extraordinary ability to segregate out and compartmentalize the various areas of their political disagreements. Arms control and related issues, for example, came to occupy one package of attributes and decisions, while Europe came to occupy another that could be seen as largely separate and distinct. Even efforts by the

Nixon Administration to restore a sense of interrelation, or linkage, among all aspects of US-Soviet relations has not succeeded in making this connection. In addition, there were other factors that led to *détente* in Europe. These included the Sino-Soviet split and the spiralling costs of the arms race. Together, these developments implied the need for the superpowers to exercise greater restraint in their behaviour towards one another.

Finally, there were internal developments taking place on the Continent that made *détente* possible. In particular, most real doubts had vanished that continued pressure from either the East or the West was fundamentally going to change the political organization of the one or the other. There would be no 'roll back' of communist power in Eastern Europe; and neither the pressures nor the blandishments of the Soviet Union were going to prevent West European states—at sixes and sevens in the Common Market and Free Trade Area—from advancing their own economic and political experiments. These developments had been foreshadowed as early as 1955, with West Germany's entry into NATO and the formation of the Warsaw Pact. By 1962, they were emerging as facts in the psychology of European security in every country but one—as we shall see. As such, these growing political certainties within the East and West supported other factors underpinning a genuine *détente* across Europe.

Within the context of Europe, therefore, as distinct from that solely of the superpowers, the most important factor making for *détente* was the acceptance in both East and West of a single proposition. Both recognized that there was no longer much to be gained, and considerable risks to be run, in attempting to alter the pattern of confrontation to the advantage of one side or the other. This was basically a strategic proposition. But it also had important political aspects, as outlined above.

This view had been shared by most Europeans, in both NATO and the Warsaw Pact, for many years. But there had to be a real effort by the superpowers before there emerged the climate of acceptance needed to develop this view into a real relaxation of tensions. The superpowers, too, had to realize that their own best interests lay in ending the recurring crises, such as those over Berlin, that had prevented the strategic *status quo* from being permanently formalized. Only by being formalized, after all, could the *status quo* become a firm basis for negotiation on the future of Europe.

But despite the long-standing realization throughout the Continent that it was necessary to accept at least the strategic division of Europe, in 1962 there remained the problem of Germany. This problem was defined by two factors: first the latent fears of reunification shared by all of Germany's neighbours (fears long exploited by the Soviet Union); and second, the West Germans' continual insistence that reunification should remain a major objective of their policy. In effect, the Germans were the one people who did not accept the political as well as the strategic *status quo* in Europe.

This was a troubling exception. Indeed, for the first few years after *détente* began, the major unsettled question in the Western Alliance related to this problem of West Germany's concern to change a basic pattern of political organization on the Continent. After all, what chance was there that *détente* could proceed if there were not some firm understanding in East and West on the future of Germany? And which of the following objectives was more important for the other Allies: a hope of German reunification in the distant future, or practical steps towards *détente* with the East?

Put simply, there was doubt that the interests of all the Western Allies in exploiting the possibilities of *détente* would coincide. Rather, there was concern that there would be major strains in the Alliance as the result of diverging interests. This study has already considered some of these problems, which are intrinsic to any alliance that tries to change the basis on which it has been organized. But the question of differing perspectives during the early stages of *détente* went even beyond the normal strains to be expected in a multinational coalition of disparate powers. Indeed, in the years following the Cuban Missile Crisis, when there began to be widespread perceptions of *détente*, considerable diplomatic activity within NATO was centred on this one problem of relating German interests to those of the other Allies. How could the West Germans best be kept in step with the process of *détente*, without having to be granted the assurance that every step would be subject to their veto?

This was largely an American problem, but not exclusively so, for in the period 1962–68, the general interest of West Europeans in *détente* roughly coincided with that of the Americans. On the one hand, the former hoped that *détente* could help to bring about a change in the pattern of confrontation. *Détente* was already showing signs of furthering East-West contacts, including some liberalization of Communist régimes in the East. The latter, on the other hand, came to see the utmost benefit in turning away from the fears, tensions and sheer economic costs of an uncontrolled arms race, and a continuing series of European crises with the Russians. The Russians, of course, also shared this interest. And, at least until the summer of 1968, they seemed to accept that the maintenance of *détente* also required them to permit some semblance of internal liberalization in the Eastern *bloc* countries. In retrospect, it appears that this assumption rested more on hope than on analysis, especially since the Russians had had little reason before the development of the Prague Spring to assert their own view of internal changes in Socialist countries in such a bold way.

But for West Germany, there was not the same correspondence of view with that of other West European states and the superpowers. Indeed, this different perspective also applied in somewhat different form to the German Democratic Republic, a state still lacking the full panoply of legitimacy conferred on the Bonn Government. There were acute fears in West Germany that either the United States or some grouping of West

European states would be willing to sacrifice, or at least to postpone, the interests of German reunification. This would be done either for the sake of arms control, in the case of the United States, or for the sake of a form of reunification in Europe, generally.

General de Gaulle was quick to identify this problem. He did what he could both to reassure the West Germans and to gain diplomatic leverage *vis-à-vis* London and Washington, by seeming to help Bonn to secure its overriding objective. Indeed, he had long worked to conclude a Paris-Bonn Axis, the central formal element of which was the Franco-German Treaty of 1963. Except on rare occasions since then, however, this treaty has had little effect except to symbolize one of the goals of the original European Coal and Steel Community. This was that war between France and Germany should be made impossible, and that the 90-year old quarrel should be formally brought to an end. Even then, de Gaulle sought a clear recognition that France was the dominant power in the partnership. Of course, by the end of the decade, with the departure of President de Gaulle and the assertion of German economic power, even this symbolic effect of the Franco-German Treaty was no longer seen as particularly important.

This problem of reconciling West German ambitions in *détente* with those of the other Allies was also apparent in the debates about nuclear sharing and the Multilateral Force. These debates were less about actual strategic matters than they were about the position that Germany would occupy in the Alliance. They were, in effect, in large measure efforts to reassure the West Germans that they continued to have an active and influential role to play in a Western association— as had been developing since 1955. And they were efforts to meet some German political needs without making everything in *détente* contingent upon an active prosecution of the Bonn Government's interest in reunification.

Most important, however, the West Germans were still concerned about American intentions towards Europe and *détente.* After all, as noted earlier, only the Americans (in conjunction with the Russians) could really sanction a change in the status of the division of Europe and of Germany. The French might seek *rapprochement* with Bonn, and couple it with diplomatic efforts in Moscow on West Germany's behalf. But Paris still could not change the fundamental and continuing US role as the dominant power in Western Europe. Even the Russians (with rare lapses) have acknowledged this fact. Indeed, they have often insisted upon it.

Yet as the process of *détente* seemed to gain momentum—at least as far as US-Soviet relations were concerned—the emphasis in West German policy began to shift. There was, to begin with, a gradual change in the old Adenauer policy of playing the role of 'good Germans' in the West. This change began under Chancellor Erhard, but it was accelerated under Dr Kiesinger, a new figure who was even better able to see the movement in recent years towards a divergence between American and European interests in the process of *détente*.

The two Chancellors began a basic shift in the emphasis of West German interests towards connections with France. For example, Germany accepted readily the continued stationing of French forces in the Federal Republic, almost regardless of the status of these forces. But this shift toward a more European focus was reinforced by another event: namely, a major redefinition of American policy towards Europe and the process of *détente* that was made by President Johnson in October 1966. The essence of this redefinition of policy represented only a reversal of priorities: no longer, Mr Johnson implied, would German reunification be seen as an event to take place on its own. Nor would it remain a goal to be seen in isolation. Rather, it was to be seen as part of a process of change throughout Europe. Indeed, it might be necessary to find conditions for ending the artificial division of Europe, before making approaches to settling the more parochial German problem.

This redefinition of American policy was undoubtedly the most forward-looking and realistic assessment of the actual conditions required for change in patterns of European confrontation. As such, it did not lead to a radical realignment of political forces in the Alliance, with the Continental Allies grouped on the one hand, and *les Anglo Saxons* on the other. But it did create a potential for disagreement across the Atlantic if there should emerge a divergence of opinion or interest as between the Americans and the others about the worth of continuing *détente* with the Russians. After all, here were the Americans once again prescribing strategies for Western Europe, however much the approach of placing German interests second might have appealed to other West Europeans.

Yet even more important, this redefinition of the US attitude towards *détente* also implied an American desire to proceed with purely bilateral US-Soviet relations. This was particularly true with regard to measures like the Non-Proliferation Treaty, and efforts to reduce the likelihood of superpower confrontation in various parts of the world, including Europe. Of course, this process of improving US-Soviet relations would coincide with West European interests only so long as there were corresponding gains in terms of improved West European relations with the East. In the general climate of international relations surrounding the Johnson speech of 1966, however, only the West Germans seemed to be losing something by the course to be taken in *détente*.

Then, following the Soviet invasion of Czechoslovakia in August 1968, the inevitable happened. US interests began to diverge from those of the West European states in general. Almost immediately, two basic interests in *détente* ceased to be complementary: namely, the US interest in developing as wide an agreement with the Russians as possible, and the West European interest to see that the benefits of increased contacts with the East applied to all the Allies. The prospects for the latter interest were rapidly disappearing while, ironically, the Russians were simultaneously making new approaches to the United States about ending the strategic arms race.

For Europeans, therefore, a fundamenal question arose: how

could they accept *détente* while the Russians demonstrated that they were still willing to go to any lengths to reverse liberalization movements in places like Czechoslovakia? This would be very difficult indeed. At the same time, the Russian invasion also seemed to end the prospect that there could be a gradual erosion of political barriers which would eventually lead to a political reconstitution of the Continent. This was true even though this erosion would be taking place within a context of strategic stability that was clear to all. Thus as far as many West Europeans were concerned, the Russians apparently did not share the hopeful view that *détente* could apply to relations between the East European states and the outside world. At least it could not apply to the extent that the East European states would have increased autonomy in their own internal political development.

Disillusionment in Western Europe was widespread and deep. But it stemmed in part from a faulty concept in the West of the conditions needed to bring about a change in the pattern of confrontation. As had been true in views held of Soviet-American relations before 1962, the West had been focusing too much attention on the nature of the strategic environment in relations among European states across the old East-West barrier. It was true that East-West relations on the political level had improved with almost startling ease. But there were grave errors of judgment in the West—for once, almost universally shared. In short, there was a failure to assess the extent to which political relations could develop without efforts being made to define the significance of their relations within a context of Soviet interests. And the broader context was one that only the Russians, themselves, could construct.

After *détente* had been under way for some time, there developed in the West a concept to explain the process. According to this concept, very considerable political changes would be possible in Europe, provided only that neither the Western Powers nor the Soviet Union threatened the newly-accepted strategic *status quo* on the Continent. For some time, this concept proved to be valid. As a result, Western observers contrasted the process of liberalization under Mr Dubček with the almost totally different set of changes which were taking place in Roumania. Roumania was a state which remained essentially Stalinist while challenging Soviet leadership within the Warsaw Pact. In the West, therefore, this Roumanian challenge was regarded as posing the more fundamental challenge to Russia, because of the Western emphasis on Russia's security rather than on its political interests that went beyond security.

Thus the Soviet invasion of Czechoslovakia upset Western calculations about the extent to which strategic stability in Europe would alone automatically provide the basis for profound political changes. After all, the Dubček government had been generally scrupulous in reassuring the Russians that nothing that was being done in Czechoslovakia would jeopardize Soviet security interests. In this way, the Czechoslovaks hoped to avoid the fate of the Hungarian 'Revolution' of 1956, in which there appeared to be a threat to Hungary's position in the Warsaw Pact.

In retrospect, however, there has emerged a precedent for judging Soviet interests in terms that go beyond these simple strategic questions. The 1948 *coup* in Prague also did nothing to change the strategic *status quo* in Europe. Even then, Czechoslovakia was almost universally considered to be within the Russian sphere of activities for any strategic purpose. In 1948, as well, West Europeans, at least, had been almost as astonished at Soviet behaviour as they were twenty years later. This was astonishment that the Russians thought it necessary to bring about a *coup* in a country which already stood firmly on their side in the slowly coalescing strategic balance in Europe.

In any event, it was apparent after August 1968 that the process of *détente* was going to be much more difficult than had earlier been presumed. At least it would be more difficult for the nations of West and East Europe. It appeared that the Russians would insist on having a free hand on their side of the strategic frontier. That is, the Russians would try extending the tentatively-accepted concept of a *strategic* sphere of influence beyond the bounds that had been reaffirmed (rather than invalidated) by their invasion of Czechoslovakia. They would extend the concept to encompass what had always been for them a *political* sphere of influence, with implications that were more far-reaching than the West had ever before realized.

As a result, the West Europeans could expect to gain little directly from accepting the American definition concerning the need to conduct a Western search for areas of accommodation with the Soviet Union. West Germany was even worse off. The prospects of gaining reunification seemed even more remote. This was so whether it was to be achieved as a by-product of general changes in Europe, or through the eventual success of a direct functional approach to East Germany that had been part of the Federal Republic's *Ostpolitik*.

As discussed in an earlier chapter, it was significant that the NATO countries rejected the notion that the Soviet invasion of Czechoslovakia should be countered by a major build-up of forces. Such a move would have implied that there was a real increase in the Russian threat. Indeed, there was not even a general NATO alert during the invasion, and Moscow took the most scrupulous care to inform Western Governments that they were not being threatened with attack. These facts led some sceptics to inquire whether the invasion of Czechoslovakia was like the building of the Berlin Wall: that is, in reducing a source of instability in East-West relations. As such, was it possible that the United States found the invasion not unwelcome in terms of its broader interests of preventing instability on the Continent?

Be that as it may, the NATO countries did decide to make some military build-ups. But these were designed primarily as a way to let the Russians know that continuing *détente* with the Americans required a major change in their attitude

The Development of *Détente*

towards Czechoslovakia and the two other principal apostate powers, Roumania and Yugoslavia. At the same time, there were strong verbal attacks from long-standing opponents within NATO on the concepts of political warning time and of the distinction between Russian military capabilities and political intentions. These attacks also helped to create the climate necessary to make Russia aware of the price to be paid for continuing *détente* with the United States. Fortunately, however, the concepts of political warning time and intentions *versus* capabilities have remained part of NATO doctrine.

Furthermore, nowhere in the Alliance was there a real scare about an increased threat to NATO. Even in West Germany, it was apparent that the logic of military confrontation had worked itself out. Even for the Germans the mould seemed to have been broken. The logic was unlikely to be revived without some very concrete evidence of new Soviet aggressiveness. Nor did this mean aggressiveness against Russia's nominal Allies, or even against peripheral Western interests elsewhere in the world, including those in the Mediterranean. It meant aggressiveness against the NATO Central Front itself—a situation which has not materialized.

For a time, the American Government also seemed to acccept the reasoning of its Allies on the requirements for continuing with *détente*. The US ceased pressing for the arms control measures to which it had been so firmly committed a few months before. In a way the Russians made this inevitable. By reaffirming their interest in an arms agreement at the same time they were invading Czechoslovakia, they underscored the sudden divergence between US and West European interests in *détente*. This may have been simply an effort to reassure the US, but it might instead have been a Russian attempt to divide the Allies politically. This is a method that Moscow employs from time to time, often when it least suits its own interests in broader topics like *détente*.

For several months, therefore, the Americans felt constrained to resist their desire to begin arms limitation talks with the Russians. Instead, they treated with the Allies' anxieties that the invasion of Czechoslovakia should in no way appear to be rewarded. It was only after the American election campaign, and President Nixon's early visit to Western Europe in February 1969, that the Americans felt they could reconcile these two competing needs and desires.

In the meantime, the NATO Allies took a formal step of their own. They issued a warning to the Soviet Union about the consequences of possible Soviet moves against certain un-named countries. These certainly included Yugoslavia at the very least. This warning by NATO was also widely seen in relation to what seemed to be a real threat to at least one Eastern European country—namely, Roumania. But it was really concerned with something more basic than a Soviet threat to any particular state. Rather, the NATO warning concerned the conditions the Russians would have to meet in order to be regarded as 'playing the game' of searching for a new pattern of European security arrangements. Put simply, few West Europeans would want to try going beyond NATO, if this process left the Russians with the impression that they were free to invade countries in the Eastern *bloc* when Russian security, even broadly defined, was not really in danger.

The NATO declaration in the autumn of 1968 therefore seemed to make up for an earlier mistake. This was the mistake of believing that understandings about the political nature of the strategic *status quo* had been fully accepted by the Russians. And it was a mistake of believing that these understandings covered circumstances, such as those obtaining in Czechoslovakia, that the West Europeans deemed important if *détente* were to have much significance for them at all. By their declaration, the NATO Allies demonstrated a much more sophisticated attitude towards the relationship between a strategic *status quo* and political understanding than they had shown before. Potentially, this was a good sign of more effective progress in the future towards finding means of changing the pattern of confrontation in Europe and its essential political dimensions.

There was, however, the existence of the so-called Brezhnev Doctrine, first proclaimed by Moscow in September 1968. This doctrine, which seeks to justify Russian intervention in other socialist states, contrasted sharply with the conditions of behaviour demanded by the West European Allies as the price of pursuing *détente*. Yet to date, there has been no formal modification of the Brezhnev Doctrine by the Soviet Union—a doctrine the Russians anyway refuse to acknowledge—and little resolution of West European anxieties about Soviet intentions in the East.

The exception occurred in September 1971, during Mr Brezhnev's visit to Yugoslavia. There, he accepted that socialist states should have greater freedom to chart their own internal course. This apparent concession may herald a major change in Soviet behaviour. Or it could be only a more sophisticated way of opposing Yugoslavia's independence. That is, the Russians may recognize that Soviet hostility would be the greatest obstacle to the heightening of internal tensions and possible divisions among Yugoslavia's competing republics after Tito's death. A warm sun from Moscow, therefore, may in this case be no more than a ruse. And, indeed, a closer look at the documents coming out of the Brezhnev-Tito meetings indicates that the Doctrine has certainly not been abandoned.

The scope of Soviet intentions, and the limits of Soviet patience, may soon be tested in another way. The riots in Poland at the end of 1970, for example, appeared to strain Soviet forbearance. What happens now will be seen in the West as an indication of future Soviet behaviour in the Eastern European states, generally. At the time of writing, it is still not clear whether the new régime of Edward Giereck will succeed in steering Poland between the rigidities of the past and a new liberalization that will provoke Soviet wrath and action, though Mr Brezhnev's visit to Warsaw in December 1971 seemed to indicate that the Russians are reconciled to

Security in Europe

Poland's policies. In any event, upon the outcome of this continuing Polish uncertainty will hang much of the chance for a generalized *détente* on the European Continent.

Whatever happens in Poland, or in East Germany following the departure of Herr Ulbricht in May 1971, the rift between the United States and its West European Allies over the conduct of *détente* has not been entirely healed. It will open up again if the United States at some point—such as at SALT—deals directly with the Soviet Union over matters affecting Europe.

In recent months, however, there has been less pressure from the West Europeans to secure better Soviet behaviour in East Europe as the price of Soviet-American *détente*. For a time, this reflected pessimism about the possibility that anything of broad-scale importance could happen in Europe, itself, for the immediate future. Strain between differing interpretations of the meaning of *détente* is more likely to appear when there is hope of a breakthrough that pits European interests against those of the US. As will be discussed below, such a time may shortly be upon us.

Furthermore, until recently, progress in the *Ostpolitik* practised by the Government of Chancellor Willy Brandt in Bonn on a narrow front—an exploratory operation, so to speak—reduced some of the pressures for such broader-scale efforts elsewhere. This was so even though West German efforts were stalled for several months, partly because of Soviet and East German intransigence over Berlin, and partly because of warning noises from Washington. Nevertheless, the very existence of a West German *Ostpolitik* has helped to reconcile many West Europeans to the continuing Soviet-American talks at Helsinki and Vienna. In this sense, West German efforts have been in support of the interests of other West European countries, since *Ostpolitik* may be building the broader climate needed for forward motion elsewhere.

In addition, anxieties that the West Germans may get 'out of step' have been less prevalent. This has been so in part because *Ostpolitik* has not gone too far; in part because it has involved an effort by West Germany to settle anxieties on the part of its Eastern neighbours that have also given its Western neighbours 'sympathy pains' from time to time; and in part because of West Germany's active role in the Western-oriented European Community. Still, the prevailing attitude has remained one of 'wait and see', especially following the haste with which Chancellor Brandt journeyed to the Soviet Union after the signing of the Berlin Agreement in September 1971.

The potential divergence between US and West European views of *détente* has also been less significant during 1971 than might have been expected because there has been a reordering of priorities in West Europe, itself. In general, there has been a new emphasis on putting relations with the Soviet Union ahead of direct bilateral relations with individual East European states. The experience of Czechoslovakia has reduced the tendency in West Europe to think wishfully, and has led to a more pragmatic effort to deal with the source of the problem. This is Moscow, and, as a result, the West German approaches to Moscow during 1970 were seen to lead to a later treaty with Poland. This seemed to vindicate the view, noted in Chapter 3, that 'the road to Prague (for example) lies through Moscow'.

Whether these attitudes will continue to hold remains to be seen. Yet, it is very unlikely that West Europeans will much longer be content with the kind of approach that plays down their interests in East Europe. This is particularly true now that there has been a Four-Power Agreement on the status of Berlin. Following the success of diplomatic contacts between East and West Germany, this agreement in theory clears the way for the Bonn-Moscow and Bonn-Warsaw Treaties to be ratified.

Subsequently, there will likely be a reversion to the earlier concern that the Soviet Union permit broad, general contacts between East and West. There will be emphasis placed on using the Four-Power Agreement as the basis for further steps in *détente*, with the implication these will have for a divergence in US and European attitudes. There will also be increased anxiety in Western Europe over US intentions, as a result of the economic crisis surrounding the suspension in August 1971 of the dollar's convertibility into gold. And there should be a renewed concern that the United States take the problem of Soviet behaviour in East Europe as seriously as the prosecution of the SALT talks beyond an initial agreement slated for early 1972.

These problems of US and West European interests in *détente* were among the products of the invasion of Czechoslovakia and of the events leading up to it. But there were other problems, of which one in particular had been the source of some anxiety in the West for several years. This was the whole question of the manner in which *détente* could progress and include political changes in Eastern Europe. But how could this be done without the changes producing turmoil and a breakdown of political and strategic understandings that had been reached during the two decades of confrontation? Only if this question could be answered would it then be possible for NATO and the Warsaw Pact to begin a process of change within a general sense of stability.

There have been essentially two schools of thought on this matter of reconciling change with order. On the one hand, it can be argued that the continued existence of NATO and of Western military preparations can help to ensure that domestic disturbances in Eastern Europe would not bring about new East-West tensions and instability. For example, riots like those that took place in East Berlin in 1953 would not increase anxieties in the West that Soviet reactions would spill over into Western Europe. In turn, the Russians would be reassured that their forbearance, leading to change in Eastern Europe, would not threaten stability across the East-West division. The Russians might therefore be more willing to let internal change take place.

On the other hand, it can be argued that the continued existence of two armed camps dividing the Continent between them would merely exacerbate the problem of change in Eastern Europe. This could happen if the Russians were led to hold down change because of fears that it would be exploited by the West, backed by a formidable military force. In turn, pressures would build up for change—pressures that could lead to turmoil and internal conflict within individual East European countries. Or the Russians might simply panic in the face of these internal changes and take foolish risks in the direction of the West.

The debate between these schools of thought was interrupted by the Soviet invasion of Czechoslovakia, which seemed to bear out the latter view: namely, that the presence of an armed confrontation did not reduce the Russians' view of their need to employ repression. Rather it may actually have heightened Russian concern lest the liberation movement in Czechoslovakia should get out of hand. As noted earlier, the Russians seem to have defined their concept of security so broadly that it could preclude change of almost any sort, however unrelated this change was to actual military security.

By this standard, therefore, the situation in Czechoslovakia was indeed 'getting out of hand' from the Russian point of view. Of course, Russian behaviour may have been primarily due to the fulfilling of a fear that had sometimes been expressed in the West. This was the fear that a process of liberalization, once begun, would proceed too fast and inflame Soviet anxieties. Nevertheless, the continued existence of an armed confrontation also seemed to have narrowed the scope of those changes that the Russians would be prepared to accept anywhere in the Eastern *bloc*. By this logic, the Soviet invasion of Czechoslovakia could not really have been prevented by threats from the West; only some reduction of the size of the two armed camps in Europe would serve to broaden the scope of change in Eastern Europe that would be acceptable to Moscow—if anything at all would lead Moscow to change its attitude.

Security in Europe

In so far as the armed confrontation actually influenced the
Soviet decision to invade Czechoslovakia, this argument comes
down to a simple proposition about the possibility of change
in Eastern Europe and the emergence of conditions under
which *détente* will have as much meaning for West Europeans
as it does for Americans. That is, these possibilities can only
be realized after real efforts are made to reduce the dependence
of the present confrontation on armaments and troops. In
other words, it is possible that change in Eastern Europe would
be more acceptable to the Russians if it were not for the mass
of NATO and Warsaw Pact forces facing one another. This
view may be over-optimistic, though it is neither implausible
nor inconsistent. However, we can only really say that the
Soviet invasion indicated that the Russians will go to some
lengths to preserve political influence and the communist
system in Eastern Europe as Moscow defines that system.
This appears to be true even though the invasion of Czechoslovakia may have taught the Russians that invasion is a
particularly expensive way of ordering relations with the East
European states.

Unfortunately, there has been no way of testing this proposition about the relationship of Russian tolerance to the role of
military confrontation. Furthermore, the considered reaction
by the NATO powers to the invasion—not the initial acceptance of it—seemed to make it even less likely that a mutual
process of reducing the role of armaments in confrontation
would be begun soon. The NATO Powers may have been
taking the right approach to the Russians by warning against
similar behaviour elsewhere in Eastern Europe. This was
deterrence, and an effort to get the Russians to accept the
conditions necessary for *détente*.

But in a longer view, the warning might have been the
wrong approach. This would be so if the question is really
one of reducing the element of force remaining in East-West
relations—both in attitudes and in actual forces—as fast as
possible in order to bring about conditions for greater East

European liberalization. This proposition, too, cannot be demonstrated without being tested. But if it is true, then the increasing preoccupation of NATO with military force levels and organization in 1970 and 1971 has also been unfortunate. As discussed in Chapter 4, this preoccupation has been a product chiefly of the Allies' inability to find other ways of ordering their relations, and their falling back on the tried-and-true issues and relations of the military Alliance. In addition, of course, if this proposition is true it increases the incentives the Allies have to begin negotiations on Mutual and Balanced Force Reductions, despite the difficulties of beginning such a process this early in *détente* (see Chapter 4).

This discussion illustrates a further point about *détente*—namely, the difficulty of determining what steps will lead from the present arrangements for security in Europe to some new political position. Ideally, in this new position there will be less dependence upon forces and a greater degree of political and economic contact throughout the whole of Europe. But given the political climate prevailing in Eastern Europe after the invasion of Czechoslovakia, how will it be possible to reduce forces on both sides in Europe? Here, again, NATO's response in the autumn of 1968 was significant. NATO used a military instrument, including appeals for limited increases in force levels, in order to give diplomatic signals. This failure to find a non-military way of indicating a political point showed how difficult it will be to change the military-political context of confrontation back into one that is strictly political. In this sense, too, the use of a military means of signalling may have been unfortunate. It may only have helped to delay any serious consideration of the problems entailed in ending the formalism of the military context; it may also have delayed reductions in the forces that are physically in position on both sides, and made these changes even more difficult to achieve.

Before getting to the details of force reductions, it is worth exploring some further political complications, partly because the idea of force reductions has always begged certain central questions. What, for example, should be the role of Soviet forces in East Germany in supporting a régime that has needed support, at least in part because of the failure of the West to recognize its legitimacy? In other words, the West has wanted to accomplish two contradictory purposes at the same time. It has wanted to take steps that would advance a concept of *détente* and reduce the military residue of the Cold War. Yet at the same time it has wanted to deny a major objective in *détente* to a country that definitely exists as an economic and political unit. It is also a country that has exerted considerable influence in the East to stifle change, in part because it is denied the legitimacy that is granted the Government in Bonn even by the Soviet Union. East German promotion of the invasion of Czechoslovakia was a case in point.

There is a matter of choice, here. Yet the burden of argument is shifting as current speculation indicates there is a real possibility of mutual force reductions—reductions that would create one of the major conditions for a real reconstitution of European politics. Thus the strength of argument now lies with those who favour the recognition of East Germany by the West.

Of course, the debate on this problem has always been somewhat artificial, since East Germany is a fact to be reckoned with. Failure in the West to affirm this fact is one of the strongest forces acting against change in the East. It also still tends to promote some anxieties, real or manufactured, in Eastern Europe and the Soviet Union about West Germany and Western intentions in general. Paradoxically, recognition of the Pankow régime by the West may even be the best way for the West Germans to proceed, step by step, towards a form of functional 'reunification' that is impossible so long as an East German Government has to search so desperately for legitimacy.

The role of the East Germans in progress towards *détente* was particularly noticeable in the politics that followed the negotiation by Bonn of treaties with Warsaw and Moscow. For reasons of domestic politics, the Federal Government felt impelled to make ratification of these treaties contingent upon progress towards clarifying the status of West Berlin. Therefore, for a time, both the Soviet and the East German governments appeared to have gained a form of veto over the progress of specific steps in Bonn's *Ostpolitik*, because each supposedly could prevent progress on Berlin. There was also an opportunity, not to be missed, for East Germany to slow West German prosecution of *détente* with other Eastern states, thereby by-passing Pankow.

The Soviet Union, however, had too much at stake to exercise its veto for long or to indulge the East Germans. Most importantly, under the Treaty of Moscow with Bonn, it would gain greater access to West German (and other Western) technology—access it needs in order to have any chance of bringing its economy to the 'second industrial revolution'. Apparently, therefore, the Russians were not content with the effective ratification by West Germany of their control over Eastern aspects of *détente* that the mere signing of the Moscow and Warsaw Treaties represented; they were also sufficiently concerned to have the Moscow Treaty ratified by the Federal German Parliament that they resisted East Germany's intransigence on Berlin.

This conflict between Soviet and East German objectives in *détente* seemed to explain the halting of traffic on the Autobahns linking West Germany to West Berlin in early 1971. This act appeared to be an effort by the East Germans to put pressure on the Russians to give greater attention to East German interests in the Berlin talks. Had this effort worked, Pankow would indeed have secured an effective veto on *Ostpolitik*—a veto that would have remained viable so long as the West German Government needed to seek agreement on Berlin as a condition of taking other steps in *détente*.

This position was acceptable to neither superpower—not to the Russians, for reasons stated above. Nor was it acceptable to the Americans, who wished to use what appeared to be

Soviet interest in the Moscow Treaty both to end the 'Berlin question' for once and for all and to extract a price for the 'concessions' that the West Germans were in process of making to the East. The Soviet interest here may largely explain the departure of Herr Ulbricht, and his replacement by a man more attuned to Soviet interests.

Thus the Berlin talks reached a fairly expeditious conclusion, leading to the signing of an agreement on September 3, 1971, by the Quadripartite Powers of Britain, France, Russia, and America. (See Appendix X.) This signing seemed to resolve a significant dilemma that had appeared earlier. Quite simply, the Allies had permitted the fulfilling of the West German desire for a Berlin Agreement to become the test of all Soviet intentions in *détente*, thus giving the Russians even greater control over its progress. In May 1971, the North Atlantic Council even reaffirmed that an agreement on Berlin had to precede movement towards a European Security Conference.

There was some merit in supporting the need of the West Germans to have such an agreement for its internal purposes. But there was little to be gained by the other Allies—and by the US in particular—in promoting that policy, if the result would only be a slowing of progress on other fronts. Thus there would be another failure to see that US-Soviet *détente* must be matched by progress on the Continent itself. As argued earlier, the chances of friction within the NATO Alliance would increase, and, in any event, the symbolic nature of the whole Berlin question argued for its being resolved at a later stage in *détente*, rather than at this early stage. Otherwise the issue of Berlin could prove a stumbling block to other, more fruitful, approaches to *détente*.

In the event, this dilemma did not emerge with full force, and was apparently removed altogether by the Quadripartite Agreement. Yet this was true only in a short run diplomatic sense. After all, the Agreement did not settle the status of Berlin—and especially that of West Berlin. In fact, it deliberately left that question an open one. Nor did it give the West Germans all they wanted, even though issues like the travel of West Berliners to East Germany and of communications between West Germany and West Berlin seemed to be resolved. At least the Russians accepted responsibility for seeing that these matters are taken care of, to be supplemented by having the East Germans join in giving assurances.

The Russians also implicitly agreed to abandon any return to their periodic threats of an earlier time of turning over to the East Germans complete authority in areas reserved to the Four Powers (a 'separate peace treaty'), which would, indeed, have given greater leverage to Pankow. But since this had always been a hollow threat, there was not much of a concession here. Yet there were some important concessions on the part of the West. That there should be a Soviet Consulate in West Berlin wasn't terribly significant, but there was also a retrenchment on the part of the West on acts of sovereignty that the Federal Government could exercise in West Berlin. While agreeing that Bonn could reach international agreements on behalf of West Berlin, and provide West Berliners with Consular services abroad, the Four Powers also restricted the scope of Bonn's claim that West Berlin should be seen as part of West Germany.

Who benefited more from the Berlin Agreement—the West or the East—is therefore an open question. It is possible to argue that, in the most practical terms, the East got the better bargain: it gave up certain practices that were anyway becoming increasingly unlikely in an age of *détente* (such as the closing of the Autobahns in fits of petulance); it agreed to the freer circulation of West Berliners (a West German, but not an Allied interest); while it gained some assurances on the only real issue of diplomatic substance—the future status of West Berlin. In future, the ties between West Berlin and West Germany may be strengthened—as the Western Powers affirmed. But any West German desire to move progressively towards including West Berlin as a 'constituent part of the

Federal Republic of Germany', to be 'governed by it', were prohibited. Immediately, perhaps nothing was given up here; but the possibility of using ambiguity as a tool for linking West Berlin more closely to West Germany from year to year was reduced by this act of clarification.

Be that as it may, the Berlin Agreement seems most important as an 'agreement to agree', that allows US-Soviet *détente* to proceed, if not also European aspects of *détente* now represented formally by preparations for negotiations on MBFR. In a way, however, the partial settlement of the Berlin question— i.e. getting enough of the irritants out of the way so that the final settlement of West Berlin's status can be put off—has increased the need of the United States to take seriously its Allies' interests in *détente*. The West Germans have been partially satisfied; the Americans and the Russians (with Britain and France looking on) have shown that they can agree on matters of their mutual interest. But can the Americans now demonstrate that what the rest of the Allies want fits within Washington's plans for *détente*, as well?

This problem of East and West Germany is only one complication involved in the search for *détente*—a complication which was raised by the anomalous status of Germany, and made even more complex in 1955 when both Germanies were formally included in the context of military confrontation in Europe. Ever since then, the question of Germany has remained central to any concept of a reconstituted pattern of security on the Continent. This has been true even when other problems have been left aside, such as the diplomatic problems in both East and West, and the difficulties, mostly in the West, of arriving at common Alliance positions on anything. As a result, therefore, American involvement on the Continent remains as important as ever, if only to reassure everyone (including the West Germans) about the Federal Republic's good behaviour. This role was emphasized by the departure of de Gaulle.

The basic question that flows from this discussion is a simple one: where would a reunited Germany stand? Would it stand in the East, or in the West? On the one hand, if a reunited Germany were to gravitate to one direction, there would no longer be any value in *détente* for the other side. Indeed, there would most likely be a crisis of extreme proportions in reaction to such a radical disturbance of the strategic balance.

On the other hand, would it be possible for Germany to be reunified and left as a neutral country in the centre of a Europe that was still divided as between NATO and the Warsaw Pact? This is not an easy question to answer. In particular, the context of conflict has now included the idea of two Germanies for a long time. Weapons policies, troop deployments, strategies, and diplomatic relations both within NATO and the Warsaw Pact have also been based on the existence of two Germanies and on the integration of the Federal Republic and Democratic Republic in their respective Alliances. As a result, this solution also seems unthinkable. It might have been possible if both Germanies had been kept out of the two alliance systems, or if the process of tying up the loose ends in Germany during 1947–48 had not led to the formalizing of Germany's division. But that time is long since past.

A third alternative may be the most promising: namely to find a means for a reunified Germany to take its place within a Europe that is itself no longer divided. Under this scheme, the political goal could be stated in a fairly straightforward way. That is, the Continent should be unified without that process benefiting either the Russians or the Americans strategically. Furthermore, this reunification must not mean that either superpower could extend its political influence into today's strategic sphere of the other at the other's expense.

This formulation may appear to place undue emphasis on the role of the superpowers in shaping the future of Europe. This is not a trivial objection, especially in view of the difficulties that both Alliances would have in agreeing on specific steps to take in pursuing *détente* and, eventually, reunification of the Continent. Yet the central point remains: little will happen in Europe that either the US or the Soviet Union feels is a threat to its political or strategic prerogatives, *vis-à-vis* the other. Of course, some West Europeans worry that the Russians could one day 'Finlandize' West Europe—that is, while retaining their hegemony in East Europe, the Russians would subject West Europe to influence that would effectively neutralize that part of the Continent. But unless the Americans take leave of their political senses and retreat from Europe with no concern at all for US interests—and especially the need for Atlantic economic co-operation—this idea is vaguely ridiculous.

Be that as it may, this third alternative way of reunifying Germany could reduce but not eliminate the significance of there being one or two Germanies. In any event, this approach, too, is unlikely to be pursued very far in the near future. Indeed, there would still remain the problems posed by attempts of a Western social-democratic country more or less to amalgamate with a communist one. More important, there is also the matter of the roles played by the two Germanies in their respective economic *blocs*, even if they left the two military alliances in a reunified Continent. Both are now powerful economic partners with their immediate Continental Allies. In the case of West Germany, the development of the European Community is also opening political possibilities that will make anything more than limited approaches to the DDR very difficult.

Nevertheless, there can at least be some small steps in the direction of this functional reunification even now, without a broader understanding of where this process will lead. Progress was made in this direction when the Federal Government enunciated its concept of two German states in a single nation. So far, however, this formulation has not been enough for the DDR in its search for legitimacy. Indeed, in mid-1971, Herr Honecker, the new East German leader, rejected the approach to functional cooperation, in a clear effort to affirm that East Germany sees its immediate future within the Warsaw Pact. This may also have been another East German attempt to counter Bonn's direct approaches to Moscow and East European capitals.

Whatever transpires, of course, some means must be found to ensure that any new arrangements between the two Germanies, even guaranteed by the two superpowers, do not permit 'Germany' itself to upset the balance of political and economic influence in Europe. In this regard, the two Germanies' membership in economic *blocs* is actually a safeguard for the rest of Europe.

This search for such a means to preserve the strategic *status quo* in Europe and the balance of political influence will also involve an active role to be played by the nations of the Warsaw Pact, as well as those of NATO. This will be so regardless of the direction taken by *détente*. But what will this role be? At the moment, the answer to this question must remain somewhat obscure, if only because of the extremely broad terms in which the Soviet Union has chosen to define its own security. This Soviet attitude has given a false air of cohesion to the Eastern *bloc* Alliance that, as argued earlier, might *not* be evident if there were a general erosion of both NATO and the Warsaw Pact. Of course, this statement implies that neither side will retain an equivalent system. Such a system now exists in the network of Soviet bilateral treaties, which also helps Moscow to retain considerable control over the foreign and domestic political development of its Allies.

The East European Allies clearly have only limited influence within the Warsaw Pact. This has been especially true since the Brezhnev Doctrine has introduced new uncertainties concerning the possible Russian response to change in these states. The Russians have been a bit more cautious since then; but this limited unbending has still not led to appreciably greater influence for the Pact states.

Yet there remain some major identities of interest among most of the Warsaw Pact powers concerning the terms of any possible restructuring of European security. It is not just the greater geographical cohesion of the Pact as compared to

NATO; nor is it just the fears of West Germany, real or artificial, that are evident within the Northern Tier nations in the Pact. It is also a recognition that the Soviet Union is in no position to choose a policy of isolating itself from the European continent. The Soviet Union is rooted there by geography and by the memory of Soviet policies during the inter-war years—from Rapallo and the *cordon sanitaire* imposed by the West to the Nazi-Soviet Pact. None of these policies provided the Soviet Union with any lasting security.

Partly because of this understanding about the necessary involvement of the Soviet Union in problems of European security, there has never been a real crisis of confidence in Eastern Europe about the willingness of the Russians to use nuclear weapons in risking all on their Allies' behalf. Even more important, there is also no practical way for the Eastern *bloc* states to contemplate new patterns of European security that do not take a greater notice of Russian attitudes than would be necessary for West European states in relation to American attitudes. Even Roumania has been somewhat more circumspect in its challenges to security aspects of the Russian Alliance than the French under President de Gaulle were with regard to the American Alliance.

At the same time, however, there is a greater sense within Eastern Europe that forms of independence, sought in order to pursue national policies of internal development, are more likely to be realized within the context of a Europe that is not so closely dependent upon the military trappings of two military *blocs*—bearing out the view presented earlier in this chapter. Even if these developments continue to be closely monitored by the Soviet Union, most East European states would prefer to have this monitoring take place on a bilateral basis rather than as a by-product of a military confrontation with the West.

For some time, therefore, there has been considerable support in the Eastern *bloc* for the diplomatic initiatives taken by the Warsaw Pact—initiatives directed towards dissolving both itself and NATO. Recently, however, this particular objective has largely ceased to interest Moscow since West German *Ostopolitik* became a major effort, and it was omitted from the 1970 Warsaw Pact declaration (Appendix IX). The omission may reflect Soviet concern to contain a West German diplomatic effort within the only sure structures for ordering East-West relations in Europe. There might continue to be support in the East for reducing the role of military alliances; but there would be extreme caution in actually taking that step.

At one time, the Warsaw Pact's interest in dissolving both Alliances also reflected the strategic advantages which the Soviet Union would enjoy over the United States in an undivided Europe. But then it became clear that some basic understandings had been achieved, at least concerning the strategic division of the Continent. As a result, there emerged concern in the East as well as in the West to see European security restructured on a basis that does not require such a high level of costly forces. Such changes would also fit within the general Russian attitude that the settling of political differences can be a means of achieving stability. This attitude is in contrast to the greater emphasis placed by the Americans on stability that derives from strategic balances, although, as noted in Chapters 2 and 4, this contrast is now less sharp. Of course, Moscow might still try to use such a process to gain a more important political position in Europe, both East and West.

It is from this perspective of achieving stability and reducing costs that we should see specific proposals advanced by the Warsaw Pact powers. Perhaps the most important of these proposals was for the convening of a European Security Conference. This proposal was contained in the communiqué issued by the Pact's Political Consultative Committee, following its meeting in Bucharest during the summer of 1966 (Appendix V). It was repeated in roughly similar terms after the Warsaw Pact summit in March 1969, and taken even further in 1970 (Appendix IX). But even in 1966 the idea was not new: it had appeared as early as 1954, when the Soviet Union had tried to forestall both West Germany's entry into a Western Alliance and the final act of formally dividing Europe that this step represented. At that time, the proposal was firmly rejected by the West.

When the Warsaw Pact proposed in 1966 that a general European Security Conference be held, it was not simply making a gesture that recognized that there was a condition of strategic *status quo* prevailing across the Continent. Indeed, the proposal was obviously conceived very much with the problem of West Germany in mind. After all, this was a time when the nuclear-sharing issue within NATO had hardly begun to disappear. In other words, the promise of such a conference might tempt the West to put the potential resolution of East-West conflict ahead of solving an internal political problem of the Atlantic Alliance. The Warsaw Pact initiative also seemed to represent attempts to exploit divisions in NATO following the withdrawal of France from Allied Command Europe.

But despite these ambiguous motives, there was a strong sense in the 1966 communiqué of a view of security problems similar to that advanced here. That is, the continuation of East and West German armies, and of two armed camps generally, could actually increase political uncertainties. At some point it might even pose threats to the continuation of European security itself.

On the face of it, this concept is not very far from that advanced by the NATO nations, beginning in the mid-1960s, when they began giving some consideration to a process of Mutual and Balanced Force Reductions (see Chapter 4). Beginning with the North Atlantic Council meeting in Reykjavik in June 1968, the NATO Allies made the discussion of MBFR a cardinal element in any agenda for a European Security Conference. The Americans, in particular, insisted on this point. It was made part of a formal appeal addressed, indirectly, to the Warsaw Pact Powers after the North Atlantic

Council meeting of May 1970. Surprisingly, the Warsaw Pact Foreign Ministers in June responded favourably to the idea that the 'question of reducing foreign armed forces' should be discussed (see Appendix IX). This should take place, however, not at an all-European Conference, itself, but rather 'by the organ proposed to be established by the all-European conference or in any other forum acceptable to interested states'. At least this was some progress, although its value was depreciated by the North Atlantic Council in December 1970.

This step has since been taken further, building on proposals by the Soviet Union in March and May 1971 that negotiations take place to see about troop reductions in Europe—even before a European Security Conference. At the very least, the very fact that MBFR is a topic for discussion may help reduce the likelihood that any future East-West political crisis in Europe will translate rapidly into one complicated by anxieties about the role of military forces. This will be so even if the latest Soviet proposal, and Western support for it, comes to naught. And if it doesn't, negotiations on MBFR could become part of a continuing process of *détente* in which the growth of political understandings in any one area help in the search for these understandings in other areas. This may not be the ideal time to discuss this subject of force reductions; but if they are to be discussed by East and West, the most should be made of them in the interests of other efforts and the general climate of *détente*. Indeed, it is this 'confidence-building' aspect of negotiations on force reductions that is most important, even if details of an agreement are many years off. The step-by-step approach would help the negotiations become a way of reducing tensions even further, rather than a potential source of disruption, either within the Western Alliance or across the line of confrontation.

There are thus two sets of proposals: for a European Security Conference, and for separate negotiations on Mutual and Balanced Force Reductions. The former is preferred by the East, though MBFR could be included. The latter is preferred by the West. The difference lies mainly in the scope of these approaches. On the one hand, the Warsaw Pact states were advocating a formal conference to discuss a broad range of political and other problems. On the other hand, the West proposed a series of careful steps limited at first to the military realm.

Yet in the spring of 1971 the Soviet Union appeared to accept the Western approach, at least at the outset, while continuing to press for a European Security Conference that could parallel (or subsume) talks on MBFR. Why Mr Brezhnev made this proposal is not clear. He may have wished to exploit Western desires for lower defence budgets in order to weaken resolve to maintain today's level of forces or increase their effectiveness. He may have been genuinely concerned to see *détente* move forward in an area promising some budgetary savings, and permitting the Soviet Union to pay some greater attention to China. He may have seen this proposal as a device for gaining greater access to Western technology. He may have wished to gain specific Western recognition of the Soviet 'sphere of influence' in Eastern Europe, in part as a way of reducing the effects of the West's attractiveness for the East. Or he may have simply been concerned to show that the Soviet Union, in contrast to China, was concerned with arms control and relaxation of tensions. This would help in the internal debates taking place within the communist world, and could reflect Soviet anxieties over a possible Sino-American *détente*. Indeed, if this last-named motive of simply *appearing* to be interested in arms control was the dominant one, the Russians may not have had any clear idea at that time of what would be entailed in negotiations on force reductions. They may not have been prepared for NATO's favourable response.

Be that as it may, there now appears some common ground for going forward with a new element of *détente*. At the same time, however, the West should continue to take a close look at a broader conference, especially since it would only be part of a long process. There could be no one-shot meeting designed to reshape the political map of Europe. Such a conference is clearly impossible at this time. Even the Warsaw Pact Powers foresee a 'series of all-European conferences'. In particular, in the words of the 1966 Warsaw Pact communiqué, there could be progress even if the NATO nations were not yet ready for a 'complete dissolution of both alignments'. The process could begin with an 'understanding on the abolition' of both military organizations; bilateral or multilateral efforts to advance the 'cause of European security'; and the taking of 'partial measures towards military relaxation on the European continent'.

Understandably, NATO has found it difficult to come to terms with proposals like these, partly because of the lack of symmetry in the strategic positions of the two alliances. The 'partial measures' referred to above, for example, included a nuclear-free zone, reduction of German forces on both sides, an end to foreign war bases, and withdrawal of foreign forces to 'within their national frontiers'. As mentioned earlier, for the Russians this would mean a few hundred miles; for the United States, a few thousand. These proposals would have appeal in the East, even for a nation like Roumania, which has sought withdrawal of Russian forces stationed in Eastern Europe. Yet the strategic advantage in all of them still lies with the Soviet Union.

This fact, of course, points to a central weakness contained in almost every proposal for changing patterns of confrontation in Europe. How, indeed, can we get from A to B without the gaining of an advantage by one side or the other? This shift in advantage would stem from an asymmetry in strategic positions and, more particularly, in the political roles played by military forces within the internal politics of the two Alliances.

But at least the 1966 communiqué of the Warsaw Pact Powers introduced ambiguity on one essential point: namely, whether the Americans could take part in the process of restructuring security in Europe. By implication, the US could be included, as one of the 'members of the North Atlantic Treaty'. This was not a complete step away from rejection of US participation, but at least the question was left open. It wasn't until 1970 that the ambiguity disappeared altogether (along with anti-Western propaganda), and the Warsaw Pact Powers formally included the US in their definition of acceptable states. Notably, this declaration was contained in the same sentence as one asserting East Germany's right to take part as well.

This inclusion of the US in the East European proposal for a European Security Conference was an important development. It indicated that a framework is possible within which both the Soviet Union and the United States can be seen as joint guarantors of whatever new system of security is evolved for Europe. Yet despite this hopeful sign that the Warsaw Pact states are concerned to take steps that recognize some basic strategic and political requirements, there is still no clear method of resolving the many dilemmas posed by any effort to change today's patterns of confrontation. This would be true even if a European Security Conference were convened.

In addition, there is a sense in which the Warsaw Pact declarations of Bucharest in 1966 and of Budapest in 1969 can be seen as serving internal needs of the Pact, as instruments of propaganda designed to show that the West was less concerned to end confrontation, and also a sense in which these declarations might indicate a Soviet view of the limits to be placed on liberalization in Eastern Europe. Both documents, for example, contain references to East-West contacts, and appear to sanction them. There is 'the strengthening of economic and trade relations, the multiplication of contacts and forms of co-operation' (1966); and to 'strengthen political, economic, and cultural contacts' (1969). By 1970, the Warsaw Pact was even including the West's most trendy topic, 'questions of the human environment'.

On the face of it, these statements fit neatly within the concept of *détente* as it has become important for the West

The Development of *Détente*

European states. But are these really efforts to legitimize East-West contacts? Or are they merely a formal expression that the Soviet Union could impose limits on the range of activities permitted to the Eastern *bloc* states? The very facts of the Soviet invasion of Czechoslovakia and the enunciation of the Brezhnev Doctrine seem to support the latter view. This is so because both these events took place between the Bucharest and Budapest declarations, yet had little effect on the latter. Most likely, therefore, the Pact has had in mind a combination of propaganda, an effort by the Russians to give a false picture to the West of its intentions, and a realization that the Conference sanctioning these East-West contacts would probably not take place anyway. The Soviet bluff would therefore not be called.

Despite this pessimistic view of Soviet intentions, however, there is considerable merit in the view that the NATO powers should also work towards a European Security Conference, either on its own or in conjunction with talks on Mutual and Balanced Force Reductions. Several of the smaller NATO countries from time to time have urged their larger Allies to accept such a Conference. President Pompidou made this the central theme of his proposals on Europe during the October 1971 visit of Mr Brezhnev to Paris. Again, the US, in particular, has dragged its feet on this idea, on the grounds that it would lead NATO to start 'unravelling' before anything else were there to put in its place. This seems to be an exaggerated fear. It assumes both that there will be no Western input into the way in which the Conference is structured, and that NATO would not 'unravel' anyway, perhaps because of inaction on *détente*.

Most immediately, a European Security Conference should be designed to expand or direct contacts between individual states in Eastern Europe and NATO countries. Admittedly, there are a wide range of bilateral contacts already being pursued. But at some point it would be valuable to assert these as an established part of *détente*, thus helping to make them a part of political behaviour not open to objection by Moscow. Could the Soviet Union deny the legitimacy of contacts that were undertaken in the context of such a Conference? It would have some difficulty in doing so, since it supported the idea of holding it in the first place. Rather, the European Security Conference would establish a method for discussing a broad range of issues, which, taken together, could further the political climate of *détente* and create functional areas of accommodation between East and West.

There would be a drawback in having this conference too soon, thereby emphasizing the existence of informal contacts before the political process was far enough along to merit shoring them up with the legitimacy of a formal sanction. Furthermore, care would have to be taken that contacts were not limited only to those channelled multilaterally. But with skill, the West Europeans should be able to call the Soviet bluff on the whole issue.

For the same reasons, there is much to be said for creating a permanent European Security Commission, either before or after a Conference itself. In fact, its creation before the holding of a Conference would help test Soviet intentions regarding greater freedom of action for the East European states. Thus the pace of this aspect of *détente* could be tied to Soviet willingness to exercise restraint. Perhaps all steps in *détente*, at least at this time, do have to be conducted through Moscow; but, even if so, there is merit in at least challenging this Soviet-imposed need by adopting one of the Warsaw Pact's own proposals.

This Commission would be composed of representatives in many fields from all states concerned with the future of Europe, and could, perhaps, build on the UN Economic Commission for Europe. Such a Commission could also help make legitimate an increase in East-West contacts, even if it did little to sort out problems specifically concerned with European security. It, too, would be a functional approach to *detente*.

Needless to say, the Western Allies would need to exercise due caution here as well. They should insist that individual states be represented on their own, and not simply as part of a larger *bloc*. Indeed, this is one advantage of a Security Conference over negotiations on Mutual and Balanced Force Reductions: the latter more or less require *bloc*-to-*bloc* arrangements, because there is the existence of NATO and the Warsaw Pact, and because the identity of view among Eastern *bloc* states is much greater when military issues are being discussed than when they are discussing political or economic issues. Thus a European Security Conference (and Commission) would help the West better to exploit political differences as between the Soviet Union and its Allies, potentially leading to some greater freedom of action in East Europe and the partial attainment of a primary West European goal in *détente*.

Furthermore, a European Security Conference and Commission would also be an even better framework than negotiating on MBFR for placing *Ostpolitik* in a wider framework. A European Security Conference would not have to focus so directly on the role of the West German *Bundeswehr*—a role that will represent a difficult hurdle in the MBFR talks, and that will only emphasize a source of anxiety with respect to West Germany at the very moment that Bonn is showing by its responsible political actions in *détente* that that anxiety is misplaced.

Be that as it may, at least the discussion about a European Security Conference should be kept alive even after negotiations have begun on MBFR. Just talking about a Conference may, indeed, be one of its chief values. In moving attitudes away from preoccupation with confrontation and helping to lock everyone into a view that change is important, this talk indicates that the West is concerned about what happens in Eastern Europe, that the US takes its Allies' concerns seriously, and that the Soviet Union has to be aware of broader West European interests as it tries to exploit *détente* directly with West Germany and the United States.

In any event, there is a point made earlier: that potential divisions between the Continent and the United States on the future of *détente*, itself, argue for some means to balance the US-Soviet SALT talks with a broad-gauged European effort designed to gain specific West European interests. Either a European Security Conference (and Commission) or negotiation on MBFR serve this function. As argued in Chapter 5, the latter would be better for dealing with difficult issues like the US forward based systems, balancing a discussion of those by a parallel effort to explore ways with the East of promoting a more stable form of security throughout the Continent. But the former method—a Security Conference—would be better for indicating that the concessions required from the Soviet Union by the West Europeans are chiefly economic and political.

Be that as it may, the North Atlantic Council in December 1971 did affirm that multilateral 'conversations' could be begun, leading to a Conference on Security and Cooperation in Europe, 'as soon as the negotiations on Berlin had reached a successful conclusion'. This moment came closer with agreement between the two Germanies on the settlement, and the signing of a protocol by the Big Four Powers. It appeared however that the 'conclusion' also had to wait for ratification of the Moscow and Warsaw Treaties by the West German *Bundestag* in the spring of 1972. At time of writing, this question was still in doubt.

In its December 1971 communiqué, the North Atlantic Council even listed a set of principles to govern the Conference: that it 'should not serve to perpetuate the post-war division of Europe but rather should contribute to reconciliation and co-operation between the participating states . . .'; and that it 'should address in a concrete manner the underlying causes of tensions in Europe and the basic principles which should govern relations among states . . .' These principles were general enough, as were the specific areas to be discussed of security, freer movement of peoples and ideas, economic and

The Development of *Détente*

scientific co-operation, and co-operation to 'improve the human environment'. This was, in effect, a compromise: the Europeans (especially the lesser Allies and France) got a commitment to a Conference, and the United States got the issue of troop reductions placed centrally in NATO's requirement for an agenda. Yet the commitment of NATO to a Conference in any form was at least a step in a direction that could help achieve some of the benefits of a European Security Conference for the West and for *détente*, generally, as outlined above.

Nevertheless, the emphasis in NATO is still on troop reductions. Indeed, circumstances have taken over and created a new set of concerns for holding MBFR negotiations. Indeed, the idea is now so far along that it has entered the accepted canon of NATO projects, and thus would be an issue even if a European Security Conference were to be preferred. So, too, the diplomatic machinery is now in gear—again, with the strong bias that the existence of a North Atlantic Treaty Organization and established patterns of discussions have on deciding issues like this one.

As presented in Chapter 4, MBFR is now important as a possible way of heading off a premature West European strategic separatism that would only place too much emphasis on strategic questions at a time when they could be allowed to diminish in importance. Even more important, however, there is now the prospect of major US troop reductions on the Continent during the next few years, come what may.

The problem is becoming more urgent. In the spring of 1971, for example, Senator Mansfield again set in motion legislative action to reduce US force levels. This time, the issue was binding legislation—not a 'Sense of the Senate Resolution'—to cut US forces to 150,000 men (i.e. by one half). This move should not have come as a surprise. Rather, it was the failure on the part of the Administration to begin a political process leading towards some troop reductions that provoked this Senate effort. Instead of an orderly process, however,

213

filled with direct European participation, the Mansfield action threatened to raise European fears that the US might, once again, take a unilateral step affecting the entire Alliance. Of course, the Amendment might not have passed the House of Representatives, and would have faced a Presidential veto. Still, an expression of sentiment by more than half the US Senate would have had an unsettling impact in Europe.

There was an added irony: the Mansfield Amendment was introduced in the very week that some European states had been forced to make adjustments in their exchange rates to counter the flow of dollars to the Continent. The proposal on troop reductions, therefore, came as a second blow; each seemed to indicate that the US has a declining interest in the future of the Continent. Coming at a time when Europeans can see American disillusionment with Vietnam and with far-flung commitments in general, the Mansfield Amendment could lead to widespread questioning on the Continent about the future role of the US in Europe.

Of course, US forces in NATO can be seen to have value in bargaining with the European Allies. But the diplomatic card of possible troop reductions is only valuable if it is *not* played, at least not in public. Again, the issue is one of European confidence that the US is committed to Europe's future. To threaten a step that could reduce that confidence is not likely, therefore, to lead Europeans to be more forthcoming on matters like reform of the international monetary system. Rather it would lead them to be more anxious about protecting their own interests, and finding ways to decrease their reliance on the US for many elements of security.

In the event, the Mansfield Amendment was defeated in the Senate, but not on its merits. Rather, the fortuitous coincidence of a proposal by Mr Brezhnev for talks on MBFR was used successfully by the Administration as an argument against unilateral US cuts.

What happens now, therefore, is most important. Indeed, in November 1971, Senator Mansfield again introduced legislation, this time calling for a cut of 60,000 US troops by June 15, 1972. The Administration, of course, immediately argued that negotiations leading towards MBFR were sufficiently far advanced to caution against 'rocking the boat', and introduced a Presidential letter into the Senate debate to this effect. The Amendment was subsequently defeated by a vote of 54–39, as compared with the defeat of the earlier Amendment by a vote of 61–36. At some point, however, Senator Mansfield will surely succeed with one of his efforts to reduce US troop strength unilaterally, unless talks on MBFR proceed faster than most observers now believe possible. But at least the Administration has now locked itself into support for these negotiations, by reason of the role its commitment played in the November Senate vote.

Furthermore, the economic crisis that came to a head in August 1971 increased the pressures in Congress for troop reductions, and for greater evidence that Europeans are 'doing their share' for NATO. Needless to say, the latter interest is but a faint hope, at levels that would satisfy the Congress, despite the extra $1,000 million in defence spending pledged collectively by ten European countries for 1972. The mood of Congressional impatience was exacerbated by the tenor of economic nationalism that accompanied Administration elaboration of the so-called New Economic Policy.

For these reasons, steady progress towards negotiations on MBFR has become important in the context of America's demonstrating its continued commitment to Europe. That, at least, is the way the issue has now been structured, because of failure by the Allies to decrease the importance of the military component in assessing the psychological American commitment, and failure to work harder to avoid a clash of economic interests. Therefore, whatever their major drawbacks as discussed above, negotiations on MBFR have gained an added reason for being.

The Allies need to realize, however, that these talks are not enough on their own. There is even more need for a parallel

P

process of requiring better Soviet behaviour in East Europe. It has been argued here that MBFR itself (or any means of reducing forces on the Continent) might reduce the Russians' perceived need to maintain tight control over internal developments in East Europe. There is a contrasting body of opinion in the West, holding that the Soviet Union will not want to proceed to major force cuts—simply in order to be able to maintain today's degree of control in East Europe. Whichever theory is right, however, there is a need to put pressure on the Russians for liberalization while the talks are in progress, especially if MBFR is a long time in coming. Furthermore, American military experts do not want more than 10–20 per cent cuts, largely because of their preoccupation with strategic questions and a failure to emphasize the political value of a process of MBFR, as a way of strengthening mutual understandings about the future of European security. Again, this reluctance to go farther strengthens the case for a European Security Conference as well, as a way of prosecuting West Europe's interest in *détente*.

Finally, the prospect of negotiations on MBFR increases the need for the Western Allies to maintain close consultations on the best way in which NATO force reductions can take place within the compass of an East-West agreement. This is important, not only to help maintain control in the West over MBFR negotiations and to deal with the problem of the *Bundeswehr*, but also to increase Soviet incentives to see the negotiations succeed. It has been argued for example, that the Russians can stall on MBFR, in the belief that Western expectations will lead to an anticipatory reduction in Western forces. Yet, again, the problem is not one of Western force reductions, but of the way in which they are carried out. Indeed, if the Allies can show that this issue can be handled without causing serious divisions—that the Atlantic Alliance remains just as strong politically—then the Soviet incentive to reduce forces, as well, may go up, whether as part of MBFR or in response to unilateral reductions by the West. Or at least a failure by the

Soviet Union to respond to this chance of having a less expensive form of confrontation will not matter as much to the West.

The foregoing discussion indicates that the Mansfield Amendments, for all of their potential short-run disruptiveness, may provide the necessary push to get the Americans, in particular, to recognize the seriousness of providing for an orderly process of force reductions. It has still not recognized that the magic number of 310,000 American troops must be abandoned, though that day may not be far off. At least these issues can no longer be ignored, with their implications for Atlantic understanding and an orderly process of change.

But even if the Mansfield Amendments do have a salutary benefit, they will have it at some cost. Again, there will be testimony to NATO's inability over its entire history to recognize in advance, and come to terms with, problems of the American role in NATO and the need to harmonize conflicts in political policies. This time, however, the interdependent nature of so many processes could exact a higher political toll. SALT, Berlin, *Ostpolitik*, MBFR, forward based systems, a European Security Conference, troop levels, trade bills, multinational corporations, the role of the dollar, Britain's new role in the European Community, and the nature of the international monetary system—all these issues need to be dealt with together as part of a continuing Atlantic Alliance. The test of that Alliance will now rest on the wisdom of statesmen, and on their ability to handle all these complex matters in parallel and together. Of course, strategic stability will likely remain in any event, as will the general East-West understandings about the limits of political activity across the border of confrontation. But the chance for some orderly progress towards change in Europe may have to be postponed yet again.

Be that as it may, it is still true that long-range steps possible in the exploitation of *détente* remain unclear and tentative. Under the best of circumstances, it is still hard to see how a process of *détente* could lead in the near future to basic changes in the nature of confrontation in Europe. This is so partly because of the broad Soviet definition of its own security requirements. Can a context emerge in the near future in which the role of the military *blocs* could be reduced, and then eliminated? Or will there arise significant difficulties concerning the means of sharing political influence in Europe as between the two superpowers? This latter question may be the most critical one of all.

At present, there is no clear picture of an undivided Europe in which the influence of the United States and that of the Soviet Union could be carefully controlled. But there is one possibility worth mentioning. This would entail the development by an undivided Europe of a high degree of unity and potential power in its own right. This could be a form of European Commonwealth, in which there were enough common interest for there to be resistance to political encroachments by either superpower. Or there could be a form of Commonwealth in which economic strength would help reduce superpower influence, even if the two giant outside powers still retained ultimate responsibility for any strategic implications of security.

But even this suggestion is not very possible politically. For one thing it is complicated by the existence of the European Community and COMECON as separate, formal organizations. This suggestion of an independent European Commonwealth would also meet some strategic problems. Put simply, neither the Americans nor the Russians would be particularly comfortable with a strong and united Europe spanning the Continent. Such a Europe would inevitably tend to favour one of today's superpowers at the expense of the other. Even the threat that this might happen would be sufficient to give the US and the Soviet Union a common interest in preserving today's arrangements.

Still, the growth of economic power in each part of Europe does imply that the ability of either superpower to exercise influence anywhere on the Continent will be progressively challenged during the coming years. In the West, this raises problems of dealing with the Americans. There will certainly be strong rivalries and many areas of incompatible interests. Hopefully, there can be a wide area of accommodation. But at least the stresses and strains that will arise in the Atlantic Alliance will not be pulling at a single, integrated, economic framework. These problems will be somewhat easier to handle (though still difficult) because of the existence within the Alliance of two major economic centres. In addition, the strength of the European Community does act in support of American security, even if there are rivalries across the Atlantic.

In the East, however, the assertion of East European economic power will pose grave problems for the established role of the Soviet Union in channelling influence to its Allies primarily through an economic institution. For the time being, it is true that there will be severe limits on the ability of Eastern European countries to exercise economic independence, to say nothing of economic power. Yet for this very reason, a clash of East European and Soviet interests is virtually inevitable at some point. And it will have implications for a Soviet sense of security that is focused in a major way on the role of COMECON as distinct from that of the Warsaw Pact.

As a result, the problems of cohesion that the Soviet Union will face within its economic instrument, COMECON, could lead the Russians to postpone any restructuring of confrontation, even in its military dimensions. This might emerge as a paradox for European security. On the one hand, there is an added incentive to find ways of reducing the level of military forces on the Continent. As argued earlier, this might reduce the likelihood that strains in the Eastern *bloc* would be exacerbated by a continuing military confrontation between East and West. On the other hand, however, the increasing challenge to Soviet economic hegemony within COMECON may lead the Russians to place even more emphasis on the Warsaw Pact and on military forces. They would serve to help maintain that influence and control which COMECON has previously afforded Moscow. The Soviet proposal for talks on force reductions has seemed to indicate that this problem is not a serious one at present. But, as always, it would be well to wait and see whether the talks are held and, if so, what they yield.

The existence of economic *blocs* in Europe may thus complicate the problem of reducing the military element of confrontation. Yet in another way, one of the *blocs*, at least, may help in the pursuit of *détente*. In particular, the growth of the European Community will help it to advance European concepts of the steps required in *détente*, especially with regard to Soviet behaviour in East Europe. As noted earlier, the strength of the Community has already helped to reduce anxieties that West German *Ostpolitik* might not serve a broader West European interest.

The chances may now be uncertain that significant West European efforts in *détente* will succeed as long as problems of Soviet influence in Eastern Europe are producing strains within the Eastern *bloc*. But at least West Europeans will have a greater sense that their interests will not be subjected to an American veto. They will also have less reason to worry that bilateral US-Soviet relations, such as those represented by the SALT talks, will pre-empt pursuit of these European interests. Nor will the West Europeans have to add a major military component to their Community-building. Rather, their economic strength will help them to have major political power within the basic strategic understandings provided by the superpowers. Economics, rather than strategy, could serve as the instrument for pursuing West European interests in security and *détente*.

Despite continuing problems related to the role played by Russian and American influence on the Continent, therefore, at least concepts exist of Europe's strategic unity and stability. This fact leads to speculation about the kinds of changes that could take place in the strategic realm—provided, of course, that some way were found to minimize the impact of the

The Development of *Détente*

political problems mentioned above. As argued earlier, at some point sufficient American and Soviet agreement about the ground-rules of the strategic *status quo* in Europe could develop for them to act as mutual guarantors of a progressively disarmed Continent. Eventually, Europe could cease to be divided, at least in the ways demanded today by the existence of an armed confrontation. And it could be protected against internecine strife and the possibility of a threat to security from one or more Germanies.

This idea may sound too utopian, particularly in view of Soviet attitudes towards the economic and political dimensions of retaining influence in East Europe. Experience with schemes like the League of Nations and the United Nations also suggests caution. But it must be repeated that the United States and the Soviet Union have managed to sort out a wide range of their differences in Europe, at least those expressed in strategic terms. This will almost surely lead them to define their common interests in a far better way than was the case among the League powers, or between American and Russia at the UN in 1945. In these earlier cases, there were almost no commonly accepted understandings about the strategic or political guidelines shaping great power relations on the Continent. In short, therefore, a disarmed Europe would not be one abandoned to its own devices and old insecurities. The nature of warfare and of superpower relations in the nuclear age will almost certainly ensure that America and Russia will be powers to be reckoned with in European affairs into the indefinite future. No new isolationism is now really possible for either country. For Europeans, this is a fact that must be viewed with some ambivalence.

This concept of a disarmed, mutually guaranteed Europe has its attractions. Again, the dominant problem of Germany could cease to have the importance it has today. There would also be a greater focusing on political problems, instead of on the strategic stereotypes that have served to cloud thinking for many years. But still, the problem with this and other models

221

of a Europe of the future lies in getting from A to B—from here to there. As this discussion has made amply clear, the means (if not the ends) of changing the patterns of confrontation in Europe do not seem at all simple or straightforward. Indeed, each step forward seems to bring in a host of complications, many of which had only been dimly perceived before.

For at least the near future, therefore, it seems that NATO and the Warsaw Pact, as political and military alliances, will remain largely as they are now, even though there may be some force reductions on one side or both. They will continue a context of military confrontation that has little real meaning any longer. In lacking the means to get from one situation of strategic stability to another that would be preferable, both the NATO and the Warsaw Pact states have chosen to see the military organs remain largely unimpaired and unready to consider real alternatives. As in the early days of this military confrontation, the formal institutions continue to dominate political patterns of behaviour, and they will probably continue to do so for some time.

As the invasion of Czechoslovakia seemed to indicate, therefore, there will most likely be gradual approaches to political change, interspersed with setbacks. Hopefully, Europeans will get ever closer to some concept of a different means of organizing security and political relations on the Continent. Suddenly one day, perhaps, everyone will realize that the patterns of confrontation have changed in the course of this process, and that the conduct of relations within and between Alliances has shifted to an economic realm. If so, then NATO and the Warsaw Pact could just wither away.

Alternatively, there could be a succession of false starts that founder on the complications of trying to cause change while at the same time accepting the existence of the two alliances. Eventually, political relations across the present division may develop to a point where the two fully-armed camps come to be seen as complete anachronisms, irrelevant to the political and strategic problems of the Continent. At that point, all the nations concerned with the future of Europe may construct an entirely new system of security in one grand effort.

Whichever of these alternatives comes to pass—or other possibilities not yet seen—NATO and the Warsaw Pact are likely to be with us for some time. They will be there with their internal needs and parochial concerns, and with the continuing patterns of Alliance politics that they create. This may not be a very optimistic forecast. But then this system of security has provided an era significant in modern European history: there has been no major war. Of course, this system has its tensions and problems, but to abandon it without first finding something substantially better to put in its place might itself be the surest means of denying Europeans their present hopes. These are hopes for a future of real and lasting security in Europe.

Appendix I

The Brussels Treaty

17 March 1948

The titular heads of the participating States:

Resolved to reaffirm their faith in fundamental human rights, in the dignity and worth of the human person and in the other ideals proclaimed in the Charter of the United Nations; To fortify and preserve the principles of democracy, personal freedom and political liberty, the constitutional traditions and the rule of law, which are their common heritage; To strengthen, with these aims in view, the economic, social and cultural ties by which they are already united; To co-operate loyally and to co-ordinate their efforts to create in Western Europe a firm basis for European economic recovery;

To afford assistance to each other, in accordance with the Charter of the United Nations, in maintaining international peace and security and in resisting any policy of aggression; To take such steps as may be held to be necessary in the event of a renewal by Germany of a policy of aggression; To associate progressively in the pursuance of these aims other States inspired by the same ideals and animated by the like determination;

Desiring for these purposes to conclude a treaty for collaboration in economic, social and cultural matters and for collective self-defence;

Have appointed ... their plenipotentiaries ... who ... have agreed as follows:

ARTICLE I

Convinced of the close community of their interests and of the necessity of uniting in order to promote the economic recovery of Europe, the High Contracting Parties will so organize and co-ordinate their economic activities as to produce the best possible results, by the elimination of conflict in their economic policies, the co-ordination of production and the development of commercial exchanges.

The co-operation provided for in the preceding paragraph, which will be effected through the Consultative Council referred to in

Article VII as well as through other bodies, shall not involve any duplication of, or prejudice to, the work of other economic organizations in which the High Contracting Parties are or may be represented but shall on the contrary assist the work of those organizations.

ARTICLE II

The High Contracting Parties will make every effort in common, both by direct consultation and in specialized agencies, to promote the attainment of a higher standard of living by their peoples and to develop on corresponding lines the social and other related services of their countries.

The High Contracting Parties will consult with the object of achieving the earliest possible application of recommendations of immediate practical interest, relating to social matters adopted with their approval in the specialized agencies.

They will endeavour to conclude as soon as possible conventions with each other in the sphere of social security.

ARTICLE III

The High Contracting Parties will make every effort in common to lead their peoples towards a better understanding of the principles which form the basis of their common civilization and to promote cultural exchanges by conventions between themselves or by other means.

ARTICLE IV

If any of the High Contracting Parties should be the object of an armed attack in Europe, the other High Contracting Parties will, in accordance with the provisions of Article 51 of the Charter of the United Nations, afford the Party so attacked all the military and other aid and assistance in their power.

ARTICLE V

All measures taken as a result of the preceding Article shall be immediately reported to the Security Council. They shall be terminated as soon as the Security Council has taken the measures necessary to maintain or restore international peace and security.

The present Treaty does not prejudice in any way the obligations of the High Contracting Parties under the provisions of the Charter of the United Nations. It shall not be interpreted as affecting in any way the authority and responsibility of the Security Council under the Charter to take at any time such action as it deems necessary in order to maintain or restore international peace and security.

ARTICLE VI

The High Contracting Parties declare, each so far as he is concerned, that none of the international engagements now in force between him and any of the other High Contracting Parties or any third State is in conflict with the provisions of the present Treaty.

None of the High Contracting Parties will conclude any alliance or participate in any coalition directed against any other of the High Contracting Parties.

ARTICLE VII

For the purpose of consulting together on all the questions dealt with in the present Treaty, the High Contracting Parties will create a Consultative Council, which shall be so organized as to be able to exercise its functions continuously. The Council shall meet at such times as it shall deem fit.

At the request of any of the High Contracting Parties, the Council shall be immediately convened in order to permit the High Contracting Parties to consult with regard to any situation which may constitute a threat to peace, in whatever area this threat should arise; with regard to the attitude to be adopted and the steps to be taken in case of a renewal by Germany of an aggressive policy; or with regard to any situation constituting a danger to economic stability.

ARTICLE VIII

In pursuance of their determination to settle disputes only by peaceful means, the High Contracting Parties will apply to disputes between themselves the following provision:

The High Contracting Parties will, while the present Treaty remains in force, settle all disputes falling within the scope of Article 36, paragraph 2, of the Statute of the International Court of Justice by referring them to the Court . . .

ARTICLE IX

The High Contracting Parties may, by agreement, invite any other State to accede to the present Treaty on conditions to be agreed between them and the State so invited . . .

ARTICLE X

The present Treaty . . . shall enter into force on the date of the deposit of the last instrument of ratification and shall thereafter remain in force for fifty years . . .

Done at Brussels, this seventeenth day of March, 1948 . . .

Appendix II

The North Atlantic Treaty

Washington D.C., 4 April 1949[1]

The Parties to this Treaty reaffirm their faith in the purposes and principles of the Charter of the United Nations and their desire to live in peace with all peoples and all Governments.

They are determined to safeguard the freedom, common heritage and civilization of their peoples, founded on the principles of democracy, individual liberty and the rule of law.

They seek to promote stability and well-being in the North Atlantic area.

They are resolved to unite their efforts for collective defence and for the preservation of peace and security.

They therefore agree to this North Atlantic Treaty:

ARTICLE I

The Parties undertake, as set forth in the Charter of the United Nations, to settle any international dispute in which they may be involved by peaceful means in such a manner that international peace and security and justice are not endangered, and to refrain in their international relations from the threat or use of force in any manner inconsistent with the purposes of the United Nations.

ARTICLE II

The Parties will contribute toward the further development of peaceful and friendly international relations by strengthening their free institutions, by bringing about a better understanding of the principles upon which these institutions are founded, and by promoting conditions of stability and wellbeing. They will seek to eliminate conflict in their international economic policies and will encourage economic collaboration between any or all of them.

ARTICLE III

In order more effectively to achieve the objectives of this Treaty, the Parties, separately and jointly, by means of continuous and effective

[1] The Treaty came into force on 24 August, 1949, after the deposition of the ratifications of all signatory states.

self-help and mutual aid, will maintain and develop their individual and collective capacity to resist armed attack.

ARTICLE IV

The Parties will consult together whenever, in the opinion of any of them, the territorial integrity, political independence or security of any of the Parties is threatened.

ARTICLE V

The Parties agree that an armed attack against one or more of them in Europe or North America shall be considered an attack against them all and consequently they agree that, if such an armed attack occurs, each of them, in exercise of the right of individual or collective self-defence recognized by Article 51 of the Charter of the United Nations, will assist the Party or Parties so attacked by taking forthwith, individually and in concert with the other Parties, such action as it deems necessary, including the use of armed force, to restore and maintain the security of the North Atlantic area.

Any such armed attack and all measures taken as a result thereof shall immediately be reported to the Security Council. Such measures shall be terminated when the Security Council has taken the measures necessary to restore and maintain international peace and security.

ARTICLE VI[1]

For the purpose of Article V, an armed attack on one or more of the Parties is deemed to include an armed attack
   —on the territory of any of the Parties in Europe or North America, on the Algerian Departments of France,[2] on the territory of Turkey or on the islands under the jurisdiction of any of the Parties in the North Atlantic area north of the Tropic of Cancer;
   —on the forces, vessels, or aircraft of any of the Parties, when in

[1] As amended by Article 2 of the Protocol to the North Atlantic Treaty on the accession of Greece and Turkey.
[2] On 16 January, 1963, the French Representative made a statement to the North Atlantic Council on the effects of the independence of Algeria on certain aspects of the North Atlantic Treaty. The Council noted that in so far as the former Algerian Departments of France were concerned the relevant clauses of this Treaty had become inapplicable as from 3 July, 1962.

or over these territories or any other area in Europe in which occupation forces of any of the Parties were stationed on the date when the Treaty entered into force or the Mediterranean Sea or in the North Atlantic area north of the Tropic of Cancer.

ARTICLE VII

This Treaty does not affect, and shall not be interpreted as affecting, in any way the rights and obligations under the Charter of the Parties which are members of the United Nations, or the primary responsibility of the Security Council for the maintenance of international peace and security.

ARTICLE VIII

Each Party declares that none of the international engagements now in force between it and any other of the Parties or any third State is in conflict with the provisions of this Treaty, and undertakes not to enter into any international engagement in conflict with this Treaty.

ARTICLE IX

The Parties hereby establish a Council, on which each of them shall be represented, to consider matters concerning the implementation of this Treaty. The Council shall be so organized as to be able to meet promptly at any time. The Council shall set up such subsidiary bodies as may be necessary; in particular it shall establish immediately a defence committee which shall recommend measures for the implementation of Articles 3 and 5.

ARTICLE X

The Parties may, by unanimous agreement, invite any other European State in a position to further the principles of this Treaty and to contribute to the security of the North Atlantic area to accede to this Treaty. Any State so invited may become a party to the Treaty by depositing its instrument of accession with the Government of the United States of America. The Government of the United States of America will inform each of the Parties of the deposit of each such instrument of accession.

ARTICLE XI

This Treaty shall be ratified and its provisions carried out by the Parties in accordance with their respective constitutional processes.

The instruments of ratification shall be deposited as soon as possible with the Government of the United States of America, which will notify all the other signatories of each deposit. The Treaty shall enter into force between the States which have ratified it as soon as the ratifications of the majority of the signatories, including the ratifications of Belgium, Canada, France, Luxembourg, the Netherlands, the United Kingdom and the United States, have been deposited and shall come into effect with respect to other States on the date of the deposit of their ratifications.

ARTICLE XII

After the Treaty has been in force for ten years, or at any time thereafter, the Parties shall, if any of them so requests, consult together for the purpose of reviewing the Treaty, having regard for the factors then affecting peace and security in the North Atlantic area, including the development of universal as well as regional arrangements under the Charter of the United Nations for the maintenance of international peace and security.

ARTICLE XIII

After the Treaty has been in force for twenty years, any Party may cease to be a Party one year after its notice of denunciation has been given to the Government of the United States of America, which will inform the Governments of the other Parties of the deposit of each notice of denunciation.

ARTICLE XIV

This Treaty, of which the English and French texts are equally authentic, shall be deposited in the archives of the Government of the United States of America. Duly certified copies will be transmitted by that Government to the Governments of the other signatories.

Treaty of Friendship, Co-operation and Mutual Assistance[1]

Warsaw, 14 May 1955

The Contracting Parties, reaffirming their desire for the establishment of a system of European collective security based on the participation of all European states irrespective of their social and political systems, which would make it possible to unite their efforts in safeguarding the peace of Europe:

mindful, at the same time, of the situation created in Europe by the ratification of the Paris agreements, which envisage the formation of a new military alignment in the shape of 'Western European Union', with the participation of a remilitarized Western Germany and the integration of the latter in the North Atlantic *bloc*, which increases the danger of another war and constitutes a threat to the national security of peaceable states;

being persuaded that in these circumstances the peaceable European states must take the necessary measures to safeguard their security and in the interests of preserving peace in Europe;

guided by the objects and principles of the Charter of the United Nations Organization;

being desirous of further promoting and developing friendship, co-operation and mutual assistance in accordance with the principles of respect for the independence and sovereignty of states and of non-interference in their internal affairs;

have decided to conclude the present Treaty of Friendship, Co-operation and Mutual Assistance and have for that purpose appointed as their plenipotentiaries; (follow the names of the plenipotentiaries of Albania, Bulgaria, Hungary, East Germany, Poland, Roumania, the Soviet Union and Czechoslovakia), who, having presented their full powers, found in good and due form, have agreed as follows:

ARTICLE I

The Contracting Parties undertake, in accordance with the Charter

[1] Translation published in *New Times*, No. 21, 21 May, 1955 (Moscow).

of the United Nations Organization, to refrain in their international relations from the threat or use of force, and to settle their international disputes peacefully and in such manner as will not jeopardize international peace and security.

ARTICLE II

The Contracting Parties declare their readiness to participate in a spirit of sincere co-operation in all international actions designed to safeguard international peace and security, and will fully devote their energies to the attainment of this end.

The Contracting Parties will furthermore strive for the adoption, in agreement with other states which may desire to co-operate in this, of effective measures for universal reduction of armaments and prohibition of atomic, hydrogen and other weapons of mass destruction.

ARTICLE III

The Contracting Parties shall consult with one another on all important international issues affecting their common interests, guided by the desire to strengthen international peace and security.

They shall immediately consult with one another whenever, in the opinion of any one of them, a threat of armed attack on one or more of the Parties to the Treaty has arisen, in order to ensure joint defence and the maintenance of peace and security.

ARTICLE IV

In the event of armed attack in Europe on one or more of the Parties to the Treaty by any state or group of states, each of the Parties to the Treaty, in the exercise of its right to individual or collective self-defence, in accordance with Article 51 of the Charter of the United Nations Organization, shall immediately, either individually or in agreement with other Parties to the Treaty, come to the assistance of the state or states attacked with all such means as it deems necessary, including armed force. The Parties to the Treaty shall immediately consult concerning the necessary measures to be taken by them jointly in order to restore and maintain international peace and security.

Measures taken on the basis of the Article shall be reported to the Security Council in conformity with the provisions of the Charter of the United Nations Organization. These measures shall be discontinued immediately the Security Council adopts the necessary measures to restore and maintain international peace and security.

ARTICLE V

The Contracting Parties have agreed to establish a Joint Command of the armed forces that by agreement among the Parties shall be assigned to the Command, which shall function on the basis of jointly established principles. They shall likewise adopt other agreed measures necessary to strengthen their defensive power, in order to protect the peaceful labours of their peoples, guarantee the inviolability of their frontiers and territories, and provide defence against possible aggression.

ARTICLE VI

For the purpose of the consultations among the Parties envisaged in the present Treaty, and also for the purpose of examining questions which may arise in the operation of the Treaty, a Political Consultative Committee shall be set up, in which each of the Parties to the Treaty shall be represented by a member of its Government or by another specifically appointed representative.

The Committee may set up such auxiliary bodies as may prove necessary.

ARTICLE VII

The Contracting Parties undertake not to participate in any coalitions or alliances and not to conclude any agreements whose objects conflict with the objects of the present Treaty.

The Contracting Parties declare that their commitments under existing international treaties do not conflict with the provisions of the present Treaty.

ARTICLE VIII

The Contracting Parties declare that they will act in a spirit of friendship and co-operation with a view to further developing and fostering economic and cultural relations with one another, each adhering to the principle of respect for the independence and sovereignty of the others and non-interference in their internal affairs.

ARTICLE IX

The present Treaty is open to the accession of other states irrespective of their social and political systems, which express their readiness by participation in the present Treaty to assist in uniting the efforts of the peaceable states in safeguarding the peace and security of the peoples. Such accession shall enter into force with the agreement of the Parties to the Treaty after the declaration of accession has been deposited with the Government of the Polish People's Republic.

ARTICLE X

The present Treaty is subject to ratification, and the instruments of ratification shall be deposited with the Government of the Polish People's Republic.

The Treaty shall enter into force on the day the last instrument of ratification has been deposited. The Government of the Polish People's Republic shall notify the other Parties to the Treaty as each instrument of ratification is deposited.

ARTICLE XI

The present Treaty shall remain in force for twenty years. For such Contracting Parties as do not one year before the expiration of this period present to the Government of the Polish People's Republic a statement of denunciation of the Treaty, it shall remain in force for the next ten years.

Should a system of collective security be established in Europe, and a General European Treaty of Collective Security concluded for this purpose, for which the Contracting Parties will unswervingly strive, the present Treaty shall cease to be operative from the day the General European Treaty enters into force.

Done in Warsaw on 14 May, 1955, in one copy each in the Russian, Polish, Czech and German languages, all texts being equally authentic. Certified copies of the present Treaty shall be sent by the Government of the Polish People's Republic to all the Parties to the Treaty.

In witness thereof the plenipotentiaries have signed the present Treaty and affixed their seals.

COMMUNIQUÉ ON THE

ESTABLISHMENT OF A JOINT COMMAND

of the Armed Forces of the Signatories to the Treaty of Friendship, Co-operation and Mutual Assistance

Warsaw, 14 May 1955

In pursuance of the Treaty of Friendship, Co-operation and Mutual Assistance between the People's Republic of Albania, the People's Republic of Bulgaria, the Hungarian People's Republic, the German Democratic Republic, the Polish People's Republic, the Roumanian People's Republic, the Union of Soviet Socialist Republics and the Czechoslovak Republic, the signatory states have decided to establish a Joint Command of their armed forces.

The decision provides that general questions relating to the strengthening of the defensive power and the organization of the Joint Armed Forces of the signatory states shall be subject to examination by the Political Consultative Committee, which shall adopt the necessary decisions.

Marshal of the Soviet Union I. S. Konev has been appointed Commander-in-Chief of the Joint Armed Forces to be assigned by the signatory states.

The Ministers of Defence or other military leaders of the signatory states are to serve as Deputy Commanders-in-Chief of the Joint Armed Forces, and shall command the armed forces assigned by their respective states to the Joint Armed Forces.

The question of the participation of the German Democratic Republic in measures concerning the armed forces of the Joint Command will be examined at a later date.

A Staff of the Joint Armed Forces of the signatory states will be set up under the Commander-in-Chief of the Joint Armed Forces, and will include permanent representatives of the General Staffs of the signatory states.

The Staff will have its headquarters in Moscow.

The disposition of the Joint Armed Forces in the territories of the signatory states will be effected, by agreement among the states, in accordance with the requirements of their mutual defence.

Appendix IV

General de Gaulle's Press Conference (Extracts)

21 February 1966

Nothing can cause a law that is no longer in accord with custom to remain in force unamended. Nothing can cause a treaty to remain wholly valid once its purpose has altered. Nothing can cause an alliance to continue as it stands when the conditions in which it was created have changed: The law, the treaty, the alliance must be adapted to the new situation; otherwise such texts, denuded of substance, will, when need arises, be no more than empty words on paper—unless there occurs some brutal rupture between these outdated forms and the living reality.

While France believes that it is today still useful for her security and for that of the West that she should be allied to a certain number of States, and to America in particular, for their defence and for her own in case of aggression against one of them; while the joint declaration in this respect, which took the form of the Atlantic Alliance Treaty signed in Washington on 4 April 1949, remains valid in her eyes she also recognizes that the measures which were subsequently taken to apply it no longer meet the new situation in what, so far as she is concerned, is a satisfactory manner.

I said, 'the new situation'. It is, indeed, clear that as a result of the interior and exterior evolution of the countries of the East, the Western world is today no longer threatened as it was at the time when the American protectorate was organized in Europe under the cover of NATO. But as our fears became less sharp, there was at the same time occurring a reduction in what had been an as good as absolute guarantee of security, bestowed upon the Old Continent by America's exclusive possession of atomic weapons and by the certitude that she would use them without restriction in case of aggression. For, since that time, Soviet Russia has equipped herself with nuclear weapons capable of striking directly at the United States, and this has, at the very least, made the American decision regarding the use of their bombs uncertain, and has, at the same time—I am speaking for France—taken away the justification, not indeed for the Alliance, but for integration.

Security in Europe

On the other hand, while the likelihood of a world war breaking out on Europe's account is decreasing, conflicts in which America is engaged in other parts of the world—the day before yesterday in Korea, yesterday in Cuba, today in Vietnam—by virtue of the famous escalation principle, risk assuming dimensions which could lead to a general conflagration. In that event, Europe, whose strategy within NATO is that of America, would be automatically drawn into the struggle she had not sought. And this would be true for France, if the inclusion in the military system under American command of her territory, her communications, certain of her forces, many of her air bases, and some of her ports, were to be further prolonged. Into the bargain, our country is becoming on its own account and by its own means an atomic power, and is thus led to take upon itself the very wide political and strategic responsibilities implied by this capability, the nature and scope of which render them obviously inalienable. Finally, France's will to be responsible for her own destiny, without which determination she would soon cease to believe in her own role and to be able to be useful to others, is incompatible with a defence organization in which she holds a subordinate position.

Consequently, without reneging on her membership in the Atlantic Alliance, between now and the ultimate date laid down for her obligations, which is 4 April 1969, France will continue progressively to modify the arrangements at present in force so far as they concern her. What she did yesterday in this respect in a number of fields she will do tomorrow in others, while, of course, taking the necessary steps to ensure that these changes are brought about progressively and without causing sudden inconvenience to her allies. Furthermore, she will hold herself ready to work out with them individually, following the method she has already employed in certain cases, the practical co-operative relationships which appear useful to them and to her, both in the immediate future and in the event of conflict. Naturally this goes for allied co-operation in Germany. In the aggregate it is a question of re-establishing a normal situation of sovereignty in which all French forces, whether on land, in the sky, or in the sea, as well as any foreign elements located in France, are in future responsible only to the French Authorities. That is to say, that what is involved, far from being a rupture, is merely a necessary adaptation.

Declaration on Strengthening Peace and Security in Europe[1]

(abridged)

Bucharest Meeting of the Warsaw Pact, 5–8 July 1966

ONE

The safeguarding of a lasting peace and of security in Europe is in accord with the ardent desires of all peoples of the continent of Europe and is in the interests of universal peace. . . .

Now, two decades after the end of World War II, its consequences in Europe have not yet been liquidated, there is no German peace treaty and hotbeds of tension and abnormal situations in relations between states continue to exist.

The socialist states which signed the present Declaration believe that the elimination of this situation and the creation of firm foundations of peace and security in Europe assume that international relations proceeding from the renunciation of the threat of force or the use of force, and the need to settle international disputes only by peaceful means, should be based on the principles of sovereignty and national independence, equality and non-interference in domestic affairs and on respect of territorial inviolability.

The states of Europe should strive for the adoption of effective measures to prevent the danger of the start of an armed conflict in Europe and for the strengthening of European collective security. . . .

TWO

The growth of the forces which are coming out for the preservation and strengthening of peace is one of the determining features of the present international situation. . . .

Tendencies towards getting rid of the features of the cold war and the obstacles standing in the way of a normal development of European co-operation, for the settlement of outstanding issues through mutual understanding, for the normalization of international life and the *rapprochement* of peoples are increasingly appearing and

[1] Reprinted from *Survival*, September 1966, pp. 289–92.

developing in Europe. This course is opposed by imperialist reactionary circles which, pursuing aggressive aims, strive to fan tensions and to poison relations between the European states.

A direct threat to peace in Europe and to the security of the European peoples is presented by the present policy of the United States of America. . . . The United States interferes in the domestic affairs of other states, violates the sacred right of every people to settle its own destiny, resorts to colonial repressions and armed intervention, hatches plots in various countries of Asia, Africa and Latin America, and everywhere supports reactionary forces and venal regimes that are hated by the peoples. There can be no doubt that the aims of the United States policy in Europe have nothing in common with the vital interests of the European peoples and the aim of European security.

The American ruling circles would like to impose their will on their allies in Western Europe and to make Western Europe an instrument of the United States global policy, which is based on the attempt to stop and even turn back the historic process of the national and social liberation of the peoples. Hence the attempts to involve some West European states in military ventures even in other parts of the world, and Asia in particular.

The United States aggressive circles, which have the support of the reactionary forces of Western Europe, are, with the help of the North Atlantic military *bloc* and the military machine created by it, trying further to deepen the division of Europe, to keep up the arms race, to increase international tensions and to impede the establishment and development of normal ties between the West European and East European states. . . .

The US policy in Europe, promoted during the post-war years, is the more dangerous for the European peoples in that it is increasingly based on collusion with the militaristic and revanchist forces of West Germany. These forces are openly pushing the United States to promote an even more dangerous course in Europe. This policy is reflected in the projected creation of a sort of alliance between the American imperialists and the West German revanchists.

The militaristic and revanchist circles of West Germany do not want to take the vital interests of the German people itself into account; they are pursuing aggressive aims which manifest them-

selves in all their actions—in the switching of the country's economic potential to military lines, in the creation of a *Bundeswehr* of
500,000 men, in the glorification of the history of German conquests
and in the nurturing of hatred towards other peoples whose lands
are again being coveted by these circles in the Federal Republic of
Germany.

At present the demand for the possession of nuclear weapons is
the focal point of this policy. The creation in the Federal Republic
of Germany of a scientific, technical and industrial basis that would
serve at a certain moment for the manufacture of their own atomic
and nuclear bombs is being open and secretly accelerated. By
their joint efforts, the peace-loving countries and peoples have so far
succeeded in delaying the creation of a NATO joint nuclear force
which would give the Federal Republic of Germany access to nuclear
weapons; but the plans for this have not been shelved.

The fundamental interests of all the peoples demand the renunciation of the plans for creating a NATO multilateral nuclear force.
If, however, the NATO countries, acting contrary to the interests of
peace, embark on a course of implementing the plans for creating
a multilateral nuclear force or giving West Germany access to
nuclear weapons in any form whatsoever, the member states of the
Warsaw Treaty Organization would be compelled to carry out the
defensive measures necessary to ensure their security.

The territorial claims of the West German revanchists must be
emphatically rejected. They are absolutely without basis or prospects.
The question of European frontiers has been solved finally and
irrevocably. The inviolability of the existing frontiers between
European states, including the frontiers of the sovereign German
Democratic Republic, Poland and Czechoslovakia, is one of the
main prerequisites for ensuring European security.

The states represented at the present meeting confirm their
resolution to crush any aggression against them on the part of the
forces of imperialism and reaction. For their part, the member states
of the Warsaw Treaty Organization declare that they have no
territorial claims whatever against a single state in Europe. The
policy of revanchism and militarism, carried through by German
imperialism, has always ended in fiasco. Given the present balance
of forces in the world arena and in Europe, it is attended by
irreparable consequences for the Federal Republic of Germany.

Security in Europe

The interests of peace and security in Europe and throughout the world, like the interests of the German people, demand that the ruling circles of the Federal Republic of Germany take the real state of affairs in Europe into account, and this means that they take as their point of departure the existence of two German states, abandon their claims for the frontiers of Europe to be carved up again, abandon their claims to the right exclusively to represent the whole of Germany and their attempts to bring pressure to bear on states that recognize the German Democratic Republic, renounce the criminal Munich *diktat*, and acknowledge that it has been null and void from the very beginning. They must prove by deeds that they have really learned the lessons of history and that they will put an end to militarism and revanchism and will carry through a policy of the normalization of relations between states and the development of co-operation and friendship between peoples.

The German Democratic Republic, which is a major factor making for the safeguarding of peace in Europe, has addressed the government and Bundestag of the Federal Republic of Germany with constructive proposals: to renounce nuclear arms on a reciprocal basis, to reduce the armies of both German states, to assume a commitment not to use force against each other and to sit down at a conference table for a solution of the national problems of interest to both the German Democratic Republic and the Federal Republic of Germany which have developed. The government of the Federal Republic of Germany, however, evinces no interest in these proposals. The states which have signed this Declaration support this initiative of the German Democratic Republic.

Having examined all aspects of the present situation in Europe, the states represented at the meeting have drawn the conclusion that in Europe, where almost half the states are socialist, it is possible to prevent undesirable developments. The problem of European security can be solved by the joint efforts of the European states and all the public forces that are coming out for peace, irrespective of their ideological views and religious or other convictions. This task will be all the more successfully accomplished, the sooner the influence of those forces who would like to continue aggravating tension in the relations between European states is paralyzed. . . .

A major factor which increasingly complicates the carrying out of war gambles in Europe is the growth of the influence of these forces in the West European states which are aware of the need to rise above differences in political views and convictions and come out for a relaxation of international tension, for the comprehensive development of mutually advantageous relations between all the states of Europe without discrimination, and for the complete independence of their countries and the maintenance of their national identity.

The states which have signed this Declaration note as a positive feature the presence of circles in the Federal Republic of Germany that come out against revanchism and militarism, which call for the establishment of normal relations with the countries of both the West and the East, including normal relations between both German states, and are pressing for a relaxation of international tension and the safeguarding of European security so that all Germans may enjoy the blessings of peace. . . .

THREE

The states that are signatories to this Declaration hold that measures for the strengthening of security in Europe can and should be taken, in the first instance, in the following main directions:

1. They call upon all European states to develop good-neighbourly relations on the basis of the principles of independence and national sovereignty, equality, non-interference in internal affairs and mutual advantage founded on the principles of peaceful co-existence between states with different social systems. Proceeding from this, they come out for the strengthening of economic and trade relations, the multiplication of contacts and forms of co-operation in science, technology, culture and art, as well as in other areas which provide new opportunities for co-operation among European countries. . . .

The development of general European co-operation makes it necessary for all states to renounce any kind of discrimination and pressure, either political or economic in nature, designed against other countries, and requires their equal co-operation and the establishment of normal relations between them, including the establishment of normal relations with both German states. The establishment and development of good-neighbourly relations between European states with different social systems can make their economic and cultural contacts more active and thus increase the possibilities for European states to make an effective contribution to improving the climate in Europe and the development of mutual confidence and respect.

2. The socialist countries have always and consistently come out against the division of the world into military *blocs* or alliances, and for the elimination of the dangers which flow from this for universal peace and security. The Warsaw Treaty of Friendship, Co-operation and Mutual Assistance—a defensive pact of sovereign and equal states—was concluded in reply to the formation of the military aggressive NATO alignment and the inclusion of West Germany into it. However, the member states of the Warsaw Treaty Organization have considered and consider now that the existence of military *blocs* and war bases on the territories of other states, which are imposed by the imperialist forces, constitute an obstacle along the road of co-operation between states.

A genuine guarantee of the security and progress of every European country must be the establishment of an effective security system in Europe, based on relations of equality and mutual respect between all states of the continent and on the joint efforts of all European nations—and not the existence of military alignments which do not conform with healthy tendencies in international affairs today. The countries that have signed this Declaration consider that the need has matured for steps to be taken towards the relaxation, above all, of military tension in Europe.

The governments of our states have more than once pointed out that in case of the discontinuance of the operation of the North Atlantic Alliance, the Warsaw Treaty would become invalid, and that their place ought to be taken by a European security system. They now solemnly reaffirm their readiness for the simultaneous abolition of these alliances.

If, however, the member states of the North Atlantic Treaty are still not ready to accept the complete dissolution of both alignments, the states that have signed this Declaration consider that it is already now expedient to reach an understanding on the abolition of the military organization, both of the North Atlantic Pact and of the Warsaw Treaty. At the same time, they declare that as long as the North Atlantic *bloc* exists, and aggressive imperialist circles encroach on world peace, the socialist countries represented at this meeting, maintaining high vigilance, are fully resolved to strengthen their might and defence potential. At the same time, we believe it necessary that all member states of the North Atlantic Pact and the Warsaw Treaty, and also the countries who do not participate in any military alliances, should exert efforts on a bilateral or multi-lateral basis with the object of advancing the cause of European security.

3. Great importance is now also assumed by such partial measures towards military relaxation on the European continent as the abolition of foreign war bases; the withdrawal of all forces from foreign territories to within their national frontiers; the reduction, on an agreed scale and at agreed deadlines, of the numerical strength of the armed forces of both German states; measures aimed at eliminating the danger of a nuclear conflict (the setting up of nuclear-free zones and the assumption of the commitment by the nuclear powers not to use these weapons against the states which are parties to such zones, etc.); and the ending of flights by foreign planes carrying atom or hydrogen bombs over the territories of European states and of the entry of foreign submarines and surface ships with nuclear arms on board into the ports of such states.

4. The states must concentrate their efforts on excluding the possibility of access of the Federal Republic of Germany to nuclear weapons in any form—directly, or indirectly through alignments of states—and to exclusive control or any form of participation in the control of such weapons. The way this problem is resolved will largely determine the future of the peoples of Europe, and not only the peoples of Europe. On this question, too, half-hearted decisions are impermissible.

5. The immutability of frontiers is the foundation of a lasting peace in Europe. The interests of the normalization of the situation in Europe demand that all states, both in Europe and outside the European continent, proceed in their foreign political actions from recognition of the frontiers that really exist between European states, including the Polish frontier on the Oder-Neisse line and the frontiers between the two German states.

6. A German peace settlement is in accord with the interests of peace in Europe. The socialist states which are represented at the meeting are ready to continue the search for the solution of this problem. This solution must take into consideration the interests of the security of all the countries concerned and the security of Europe as a whole.

Security in Europe

A constructive approach to this question is only possible if it proceeds from reality, above all, from recognition of the fact of the existence of two German states—the German Democratic Republic and the Federal Republic of Germany. At the same time, such a settlement requires recognition of the existing frontiers and the refusal of both German states to possess nuclear weapons. . . .

As for the reunion of both German states, the way to this lies through the relaxation of tension, through a gradual *rapprochement* between the two sovereign German states and agreements between them, through agreements on disarmament in Germany and Europe, and on the basis of the principle that when Germany is reunited, the united German state would be truly peaceful and democratic and would never again be a danger to its neighbours or to peace in Europe.

7. Convocation of a general European conference to discuss the questions of ensuring security in Europe and organizing general European co-operation would be of great positive importance. The agreement reached at the conference could be expressed, for example, in the form of a general European declaration on co-operation for the maintenance and strengthening of European security. Such a declaration could provide for an undertaking by the signatories to be guided in their relations by the interests of peace, to settle disputes by peaceful means only, to hold consultations and exchange information on questions of mutual interest and to contribute to the all-round development of economic, scientific, technical and cultural relations. The declaration should be open to all interested states to join.

The convocation of a conference on questions of European security and co-operation could contribute to the establishment of a system of collective security in Europe and would be an important landmark in the contemporary history of Europe. Our countries are ready to take part in such a conference at any time convenient to the other interested states, both members of the North Atlantic Treaty and neutrals. Neutral European countries could also play a positive role in the convocation of such a meeting. It goes without saying that the agenda and other questions concerning the preparation of such a meeting or conference should be decided upon by all participating states together, bearing in mind the proposals submitted by every one of them.

The countries represented at this meeting are also prepared to use other methods available for discussing problems of European security: talks through diplomatic channels, meetings of Foreign Ministers or special representatives on a bilateral or multilateral basis, and contacts at the highest level. They consider that the considerations above cover the principal, the most important, aspects of ensuring European security. They are also ready to discuss other proposals which have been submitted, or may be submitted by any state, for the solution of this problem. . . . The parties to this meeting are convinced that countries on the other continents, too, cannot be indifferent to how things develop in Europe.

The Organization of NATO

Extracted from the *NATO Handbook, January 1971*

THE COUNCIL AND THE DEFENCE PLANNING COMMITTEE (DPC)

The North Atlantic Council is the highest authority of the Alliance. It is composed of representatives of the fifteen member countries. These being sovereign states, equal in status, all decisions of the Council are taken unanimously. The Council may meet at the level either of Ministers or Permanent Representatives (holding the rank of Ambassador). At Ministerial Meetings of the Council, the members of the Alliance are represented by one—or several—of their ministers (for Foreign Affairs, Defence, Finance, Economic Affairs) according to the agenda of the meeting. In December 1957, the Council also met at the level of Heads of Government. The Council meets at Ministerial level at least twice a year: in the spring in the capital of one of the member countries, in the winter at NATO Headquarters in Brussels. Between Ministerial Sessions, the Permanent Representatives meet at least once a week—often more frequently—thus ensuring continuous consultation. The Council can be called together any time at short notice.

Whatever the level at which the Council meets, its chairman is the Secretary General of NATO. Each year the Foreign Minister of a member state is honorary President of the Council. This Presidency rotates annually according to alphabetical order in English.

Since the Organization of the North Atlantic Treaty is not supranational, all decisions taken are the expressions of the *collective will of the member governments*. It is in the Council that the views of governments are exchanged on all major issues. Consultation covers political, military, economic and a wide range of other subjects. (To produce the same results through normal diplomatic channels, involving each country consulting the other 14, would require no less than 105 bilateral exchanges.)

Military policy matters are discussed at the same level in the 'Defence Planning Committee'. As in the Council, member countries are represented on this Committee by their Permanent Representatives. They meet round the same table as the Council and also under the same chairmanship of the Secretary General. Since the withdrawal of France from the integrated military organization in 1966, her representative does not attend these meetings.

THE PERMANENT REPRESENTATIVES AND DELEGATIONS

The Permanent Representatives are assisted by national Delegations also located at NATO Headquarters. The Delegations vary in size but the majority of them include officers specifically charged with representing their countries on the various specialized committees. Before a meeting of the Council notice is given of the agenda and any subjects to be discussed, so that representatives have time to seek the instructions of their governments.

THE COUNCIL COMMITTEES

In carrying out its role, the Council is assisted by Committees, some of a permanent nature, some temporary. Like the Council, the membership of each committee is made up of national representatives drawn from the delegations. They study questions submitted to them by the Council for assessment or recommendation. As in the case of decisions of the Council, committee decisions represent a *collective view of the fifteen governments based on the intructions those governments have sent to their representatives on the committees.* The most important committees are those dealing with the following matters: Political Affairs, Armaments, Defence Review, Economic Affairs, Science, Ecology, Infrastructure, Civil Emergency Planning, Information and Cultural Affairs, Military and Civil Budget Committees. Many other committees deal with specialized subjects, such as NATO pipelines, communications, European air space, etc.

Since 1966 the problems of nuclear defence are dealt with by the Nuclear Defence Affairs Committee (which is composed of all member countries, except France, Iceland, and Luxembourg, and which meets at the level of Permanent Representatives) and the Nuclear Planning Group (a Committee of seven/eight members). The NPG, which meets regularly at Permanent Representatives level and twice a year at Ministeral level, changes its membership so that countries not possessing nuclear weapons have an oppor-

Security in Europe

tunity, together with the nuclear powers, to participate in the planning of the nuclear defence measures of the Alliance as a whole.[1]

For environmental problems the Council established in November 1969, a Committee on the Challenges of Modern Society, chaired by the Secretary General of NATO or his representative, normally the Assistant Secretary General for Scientific Affairs, assisted by the Head of the Economic Directorate.

THE SECRETARY GENERAL AND THE INTERNATIONAL SECRETARIAT

The Secretary General is both Chairman of the North Atlantic Council and of the Defence Planning Committee at all levels. He is the head of the International Secretariat, whose staff is drawn from all member countries.

The Secretary General has the right to propose items for NATO consultation and he is generally responsible for promoting and directing the process of consultation. He has the authority to offer his good offices informally at any time in cases of disputes between member countries, and with their consent, to initiate or facilitate procedures of enquiry, mediation, conciliation or arbitration (for example with Greece and Turkey over Cyprus).

The Deputy Secretary General assists the Secretary General in his function and deputises for him in his absence. Under the Secretary General are four Assistant Secretaries General, each in charge of a division, as follows: Political Affairs, Defence Planning & Policy, Defence Support, and Scientific Affairs. Each Assistant Secretary General is normally chairman of the main committee dealing with his subject.

The Executive Secretary is Secretary to the North Atlantic Council and the Defence Planning Committee. His office provides the secretariat for the Council's main committees and working groups.

There is a separate Office of Administration under a Director. The Financial Controller, who is appointed by the Council, is responsible for the control of expenditure.

[1] On January 1st, 1971, the members of the Nuclear Planning Group were: Canada, Federal Republic of Germany, Greece, Italy, Netherlands, Norway, United Kingdom, United States.

THE MILITARY COMMITTEE

The Military Committee is the highest military authority in the Alliance and is responsible for making recommendations to the Council and Defence Planning Committee on military matters and for supplying guidance on military questions to Allied Commanders and subordinate military authorities. It is composed of the Chiefs-of-Staff of all member countries, except France. Iceland, having no military forces, may be represented by a civilian. The Chiefs-of-Staff meet at least twice a year—and whenever else it may be found necessary. However, to enable the Military Committee to function in permanent session with effective powers of decision, each Chief-of-Staff appoints a Permanent Military Representative. Between meetings of the Chiefs-of-Staff, their Permanent Military Representatives deal with and settle questions which come within the province of the Military Committee, except those which, by their nature and scope, require the approval of the Chief-of-Staff. Liaison between the Military Committee and the French High Command is effected through the Chief of the French Military Mission to the Military Committee.

The Presidency of the Military Committee rotates annually in the alphabetical order of countries. The Chairmanship is held by a Permanent chairman, elected by the Committee for a period of two to three years. There is a Deputy Chairman who is also specifically responsible for the coordination of nuclear matters within the International Military Staff.

The Military Committee is represented on the North Atlantic Council and has a number of NATO military agencies under its authority.

THE INTERNATIONAL MILITARY STAFF

The Military Committee is assisted by an integrated International Military Staff which is headed by a Director, selected from any of the member nations. The Director is assisted by six Assistant Directors of flag or general officer rank, and the Secretary of the International Military Staff. The six Assistant Directors head the Divisions for Intelligence; Plans and Policy; Operations, Training and Organization; Logistics; Communications and Electronics; and Command, Control and Information Systems. As the executive agency of the Military Committee, the International Military Staff is charged with ensuring that the policies and decisions of the Military Committee are implemented as directed. In addition, the International Military Staff prepares plans, initiates studies and recommends policy on matters of a military nature.

THE NATO COMMANDS

The strategic area covered by the North Atlantic Treaty is divided, taking account of geographical and political factors, among three Commands: the Atlantic Ocean Command, the European Command and the Channel Command. (Defence plans for the North American area are developed by the Canada-US Regional Planning Group). The authority exercised by these Commands varies in form, being affected by the geographical and political factors and by the situation under peace or war conditions.

The forces of member countries remain under national command in peacetime; some of them may either be assigned or earmarked to NATO Commands.

The NATO Commanders are responsible for the development of defence plans for their respective areas, for the determination of force requirements and for the deployment and exercise of the forces under their Command.

The organization of these Commands is flexible enough and the liaison between them close enough to allow for mutual support in the event of war, and the rapid shifting of the necessary land, sea and air forces to meet any situation likely to confront the North Atlantic Community.

The European Command

Allied Command Europe (ACE) covers the area extending from the North Cape to the Mediterranean and from the Atlantic to the eastern border of Turkey, excluding the United Kingdom and Portugal, the defence of which does not fall under any one major NATO Command. ACE is subdivided into a number of subordinate Commands.[1]

---

[1] ACE subordinate Commands are: *the Northern Europe Command* (Kolsas, Norway); *the Central Europe Command* (Brunssum, the Netherlands); *the Southern Europe Command* (Naples, Italy); *the UK Air Defence Region Command* (Stanmore, UK); and *the ACE Mobile Force* (Seckenheim, Federal Republic of Germany).

The European area is under the Supreme Allied Commander Europe (SACEUR), whose headquarters, near Mons in Belgium, are known as SHAPE (Supreme Headquarters Allied Powers Europe).

The Supreme Commander has also under his orders the ACE Mobile Force. This force is composed of both land and air force units supplied by different member countries. It can be ready for action at very short notice in any threatened area and in particular on the northern and southern flanks of the European Command.

In peacetime SACEUR'S main functions are to prepare and finalize defence plans for the area under his command, and ensure the combat efficiency of forces assigned to him in the event of war. SACEUR also makes recommendations to the Military Committee on matters likely to improve the organization of his command.

He would, in time of war, control all land, sea and air operations in this area. Internal defence (including that of Sardinia and Sicily) and defence of coastal waters remain the responsibility of the national authorities concerned, but the Supreme Commander would have full authority to carry out such operations as he considered necessary for the defence of any part of the area under his Command.

Thirteen of the North Atlantic countries maintain a National Military Representative (NMR) at SHAPE, providing military liaison with the Allied Chief-in-Staff. France has a military liaison mission at SHAPE.

SACEUR and his Deputy Supreme Allied Commander are assisted by political and scientific advisers in addition to the usual military staff advisers.

The Atlantic Ocean Command

This Command extends from the North Pole to the Tropic of Cancer and from the coastal waters of North America to those of Europe and Africa, except for the Channel and the British Isles. The Atlantic Ocean Command is subdivided into a number of subordinate commands.[1]

[1] Commands subordinate to the Supreme Allied Commander Atlantic are: the *Western Atlantic Command* (Norfolk, US); the *Eastern Atlantic Command* (Northwood, UK); the *Striking Fleet Atlantic* (Afloat); the *Submarines Allied Command Atlantic* (Norfolk, US); the *Iberian Atlantic Command* (Lisbon, Portugal); and the *Standing Naval Force Atlantic* (Afloat).

The Supreme Commander Atlantic also has under his order the NATO Standing Naval Force Atlantic (STANAVFORLANT). This force is composed of an international squadron of ships from NATO countries normally operating in the Atlantic.

The Supreme Allied Commander Atlantic (SACLANT), like the Supreme Allied Commander Europe, receives his directions from the Military Committee.

SACLANT'S peacetime responsibilities consist of preparing and finalizing defence plans, conducting joint training exercises, laying down training standards and supplying the NATO authorities with information on his strategic requirements.

The primary task in wartime of the Allied Command Atlantic is to ensure security in the whole Atlantic area by guarding the sea lanes and denying their use to an enemy. SACLANT has responsibility for islands in this area, such as Iceland and the Azores.

SACLANT'S responsibilities are almost entirely operational. STANAVFORLANT is permanently attached to his Command in peacetime. In addition, for training purposes and in the event of war, forces earmarked by the nations involved are assigned to his direction. Although these forces are predominantly naval, they also include ground forces and landbased air forces.

The Channel Command and the Channel Committee

The Channel Command covers the English Channel and the southern areas of the North Sea. Its mission is to control and protect merchant shipping in the area, co-operating with SACEUR in the air defence of the Channel. In emergency the forces earmarked to the Command are predominantly naval but include maritime air forces. The Allied Commander-in-Chief has a Maritime Air Adviser who is also the Commander Allied Maritime Air Force Channel.

The Channel Committee consists of the Naval Chiefs-of-Staff of Belgium, the Netherlands and the United Kingdom, and acts as an advisory body to the Allied Commander-in-Chief.

Canada-United States Regional Planning Group

This Planning Group, which covers the North American area, develops and recommends to the Military Committee plans for the defence of the Canada-United States region. It meets alternately in Washington and Ottawa.

Appendix VII

Future Tasks of the Alliance

Report of the North Atlantic Council, *December 1967* (The Harmel Report)

1. A year ago, on the initiative of the Foreign Minister of Belgium, the governments of the fifteen nations of the Alliance resolved to 'study the future tasks which face the Alliance, and its procedures for fulfilling them in order to strengthen the Alliance as a factor for durable peace'. The present report sets forth the general tenor and main principles emerging from this examination of the future tasks of the Alliance.

2. Studies were undertaken by Messrs Schütz, Watson, Spaak, Kohler and Patijn. The Council wishes to express its appreciation and thanks to these eminent personalities for their efforts and for the analysis they produced.

3. The exercise has shown that the Alliance is a dynamic and vigorous organization which is constantly adapting itself to changing conditions. It also has shown that in its future tasks can be handled within the terms of the Treaty by building on the methods and procedures which have proved their value over many years.

4. Since the North Atlantic Treaty was signed in 1949 the international situation has changed significantly and the political tasks of the Alliance have assumed a new dimension. Amongst other developments, the Alliance has played a major part in stopping Communist expansion in Europe; the USSR has become one of the two world super-powers but the Communist world is no longer monolithic; the Soviet doctrine of 'peaceful co-existence' has changed the nature of the confrontation with the West but not the basic problems. Although the disparity between the power of the United States and that of the European states remains, Europe has recovered and is on its way towards unity. The process of decolonization has transformed European relations with the rest of the world; at the same time, major problems have arisen in the relations between developed and developing countries.

5. The Atlantic Alliance has two main functions. Its first function is to maintain adequate military strength and political solidarity to

deter aggression and other forms of pressure and to defend the territory of member countries if aggression should occur. Since its inception, the Alliance has successfully fulfilled this task. But the possibility of a crisis cannot be excluded as long as the central political issues in Europe, first and foremost the German question, remain unsolved. Moreover, the situation of instability and uncertainty still precludes a balanced reduction of military forces. Under these conditions, the Allies will maintain as necessary, a suitable military capability to assure the balance of forces, thereby creating a climate of stability, security and confidence.

In this climate the Alliance can carry out its second function, to pursue the search for progress towards a more stable relationship in which the underlying political issues can be solved. Military security and a policy of *détente* are not contradictory but complementary. Collective defence is a stabilizing factor in world politics. It is the necessary condition for effective policies directed towards a greater relaxation of tensions. The way to peace and stability in Europe rests in particular on the use of the Alliance constructively in the interest of *détente*. The participation of the USSR and the USA will be necessary to achieve a settlement of the political problems in Europe.

6. From the beginning the Atlantic Alliance has been a co-operative grouping of states sharing the same ideals and with a high degree of common interest. Their cohesion and solidarity provide an element of stability within the Atlantic area.

7. As sovereign states the Allies are not obliged to subordinate their policies to collective decision. The Alliance affords an effective forum and clearing house for the exchange of information and views; thus, each of the Allies can decide his policy in the light of close knowledge of each others' problems and objectives. To this end the practice of frank and timely consultations needs to be deepened and improved. Each Ally should play its full part in promoting an improvement in relations with the Soviet Union and the countries of Eastern Europe, bearing in mind that the pursuit of *détente* must not be allowed to split the Alliance. The chances of success will clearly be greatest if the Allies remain on parallel courses, especially in matters of close concern to them all; their actions will thus be all the more effective.

8. No peaceful order in Europe is possible without a major effort by all concerned. The evolution of Soviet and East European policies

gives ground for hope that those governments may eventually come to recognize the advantages to them of collaborating in working towards a peaceful settlement. But no final and stable settlement in Europe is possible without a solution of the German question which lies at the heart of present tensions in Europe. Any such settlement must end the unnatural barriers between Eastern and Western Europe, which are most clearly and cruelly manifested in the division of Germany.

9. Accordingly the Allies are resolved to direct their energies to this purpose by realistic measures designed to further a *détente* in East-West relations. The relaxation of tensions is not the final goal but is part of a long-term process to promote better relations and to foster a European settlement. The ultimate political purpose of the Alliance is to achieve a just and lasting peaceful order in Europe accompanied by appropriate security guarantees.

10. Currently, the development of contacts between the countries of Western and Eastern Europe is now mainly on a bilateral basis. Certain subjects, of course, require by their very nature a multi-lateral solution.

11. The problem of German reunification and its relationship to a European settlement has normally been dealt with in exchanges between the Soviet Union and the three Western powers having special responsibilities in this field. In the preparation of such exchanges the Federal Republic of Germany has regularly joined the three Western powers in order to reach a common position. The other Allies will continue to have their views considered in timely discussions among the Allies about Western policy on this subject, without in any way impairing the special responsibilities in question.

12. The Allies will examine and review suitable policies designed to achieve a just and stable order in Europe, to overcome the division of Germany and to foster European security. This will be part of a process of active and constant preparation for the time when fruitful discussions of these complex questions may be possible bilaterally or multilaterally between Eastern and Western nations.

13. The Allies are studying disarmament and practical arms control measures, including the possibility of balanced force reductions. These studies will be intensified. Their active pursuits reflects the will of the Allies to work for an effective *détente* with the East.

14. The Allies will examine with particular attention the defence problems of the exposed areas, e.g. the South-eastern flank. In this respect the current situation in the Mediterranean presents special problems, bearing in mind that the current crisis in the Middle East falls within the responsibilities of the United Nations.

15. The North Atlantic Treaty area cannot be treated in isolation from the rest of the world. Crises and conflicts arising outside the area may impair its security either directly or by affecting the global balance. Allied countries contribute individually within the United Nations and other international organizations to the maintenance of international peace and security and to the solution of important international problems. In accordance with established usage the Allies or such of them as wish to do so will also continue to consult on such problems without commitment and as the case may demand.

16. In the light of these findings, the Ministers directed the Council in permanent session to carry out, in the years ahead, the detailed follow-up resulting from this study. This will be done either by intensifying work already in hand or by activating highly specialized studies by more systematic use of experts and officials sent from capitals.

17. Ministers found that the study by the Special Group confirmed the importance of the role which the Alliance is called upon to play during the coming years in the promotion of *détente* and the strengthening of peace. Since significant problems have not yet been examined in all their aspects, and other problems of no less significance which have arisen from the latest political and strategic developments have still to be examined, the Ministers have directed the Permanent Representatives to put in hand the study of these problems without delay, following such procedures as shall be deemed most appropriate by the Council in permanent session, in order to enable further reports to be subsequently submitted to the Council in Ministerial Session.

Appendix VIII

NATO Ministerial Communiqué
North Atlantic Council

May 28, 1970

The North Atlantic Council, meeting in Ministerial Session in Rome on 26th–27th May, 1970, reaffirmed that the Alliance remains indispensable to the security of its members and makes possible their common search for progress towards a more stable relationship between East and West in which outstanding issues dividing Europe can be resolved.

The Ministers again stated their determination to resolve these problems through a process of negotiation. They recognised that, for their part, this search for peace must rest upon a spirit of genuine partnership, the maintenance of the defensive strength of the Alliance, and the practice of full and timely consultation.

The Ministers agreed that it will not be enough to talk of European security in the abstract. The causes of insecurity in Europe are specific, they are deeply rooted in conflicting perceptions of state interests, and their elimination will require patient endeavour. However, the Allies, for their part, remain willing to negotiate, in any suitable forum, those concrete issues whose resolution would enhance the security of Europe. The success of efforts to pursue genuine relaxation of tension will be a test of the willingness of all interested countries to deal meaningfully with real issues of security.

The Ministers affirmed that to endure, peace must rest upon universal respect of the sovereign equality, political independence and territorial integrity of each European state, regardless of its political or social system, and for the right of its peoples to shape their own destinies, free of the threat of external intervention, coercion or constraint. . . .

At their April 1969 meeting in Washington, the Ministers agreed to explore with the Soviet Union and the other Countries of Eastern Europe which concrete issues best lend themselves to fruitful negotiations in order to reduce tension and promote co-operation in Europe and to take constructive actions to this end. The Council thereafter conducted a detailed study of those issues, and at their meeting in December 1969, the Ministers declared that Allied governments would continue and intensify their contacts, discussions or negotiations through all appropriate channels, bilateral or multilateral, and that they remained receptive to signs of willingness on the part of the Soviet Union and other Eastern European Countries to engage in such discussions. Progress, they said, in these discussions and negotiations would help to ensure the success of any eventual conference, in which, of course, the North American Members of the Alliance would participate, to discuss and negotiate substantial problems of co-operation and security in Europe.

The Ministers expressed satisfaction over the launching or continuation of the whole range of talks and negotiations, initiated by members of the Alliance, which they have been actively promoting during the six months since December 1969. At the same time, numerous other East-West contacts have been pursued. The Allies have consulted and will continue to consult closely on all these initiatives and contacts.

With the support and understanding of its Allies, the Federal Republic of Germany has initiated talks with the Soviet Union, Poland and the GDR in order to improve the situation in Central Europe. The Allies consider this to be encouraging. They express the hope that these talks will yield results and will not be compromised by the presentation of unacceptable demands. The efforts being made to solve outstanding problems and to achieve a *modus vivendi* in Germany which would take account of the special features of the German situation, represent an important contribution to security and co-operation in Europe. The Ministers express the hope that all Governments desiring to contribute to a policy of relaxation of tension in Europe will, to the extent possible, facilitate a negotiated settlement of the relationship between the two parts of Germany and the development of communications between the populations.

The Ministers noted with satisfaction that the Four Powers, in the framework of their rights and responsibilities for Berlin and Germany as a whole, began discussions on 26th March about improving the situation with regard to Berlin and free access to the city. They express the hope that the difficulties which exist at this especially sensitive area of the East-West relationship could be overcome by practical measures and that Berlin would be enabled to make its full contribution to economic and cultural exchanges. The conversations detween the United States and the Soviet Union aiming at the limitation of strategic armaments, which began last November at Helsinki, have been continued at Vienna in April. The Ministers welcome these talks, the outcome of which is so important for the security of Europe and the future of humanity....

The members of the North Atlantic Alliance have, over a number of years, proclaimed their interest in arms control and disarmament measures which facilitate a gradual elimination of the military confrontation in Europe. The Ministers recalled the Declarations issued at Reykjavik in 1968, and at Brussels in 1969. They noted that up to now these Declarations had led to no meaningful reply.

The Allies have, nevertheless, carried out intensive studies on mutual force reductions in accordance with the directions given by the Ministers in December 1969. The Ministers examined the detailed report presented to them by the North Atlantic Council in Permanent Session. This has been of great value in clarifying the complex issues involved. The Ministers gave instructions for further relevant studies which would guide policies and explorations in this field.

The Ministers, having examined all these developments, both positive and negative, and having taken note of the Report on the Procedures for Negotiation which they had commissioned from the Permanent Council, stated that they were ready to multiply exploratory conversations with all interested parties on all questions affecting peace.

In so far as progress is recorded as a result of these talks and in the ongoing talks—in particular on Germany and Berlin—the Allied Governments state that they would be ready to enter into multilateral contacts with all interested Governments. One of the main purposes of such contacts would be to explore when it will be possible to convene a conference, or a series of conferences, on European security and co-operation. The establishment of a permanent body could be envisaged as one means, among others, of embarking upon multilateral negotiations in due course.

Among the subjects to be explored, affecting security and co-operation in Europe, are included in particular:

(A) The principles which should govern relations between states, including the renunciation of force;

Security in Europe

(B) The development of international relations with a view to contributing to the freer movement of people, ideas and information and to developing co-operation in the cultural, economic, technical and scientific fields as well as in the field of human environment.

In addition, the Ministers representing countries participating in NATO's Integrated Defence Programme attach particular importance to further exploration with other interested parties of the possibility of mutual and balanced force reductions and have therefore issued a declaration on this subject.

As a first step, the Ministers requested the Foreign Minister of Italy to transmit this Communiqué on their behalf through diplomatic channels to all other interested parties including Neutral and Non-Aligned Governments. They further agreed that Member Governments would seek reactions of other Governments to the initiation of the comprehensive programme of exploration and negotiation which they envisage.

The Ministers reviewed the first Report from NATO's Committee on the Challenges of Modern Society and welcomed the progress made in the six months since the Committee was established as a demonstration of the value of Allied co-operation on the urgent problems of human environment. Intensive studies now in progress will contribute to national and international action on a broad range of environmental issues, including such pressing concerns as air and water pollution.

The Ministers reaffirmed the view that the benefit of the Alliance's work in mankind's environment particularly could become a basis for broader co-operation between East and West in this field of ever-increasing importance. They considered that this could be ensured either through existing international organizations providing a useful framework for enhanced co-operation or by any other appropriate method. . . .

DECLARATION ON MUTUAL AND BALANCED FORCE REDUCTIONS

Meeting at Rome on 26th and 27th May, 1970, the Ministers representing Countries participating in NATO's Integrated Defence Programme recall and reaffirm the commitment of their Nations to pursue effective policies directed towards a greater relaxation of tensions in their continuing search for a just and durable peace.

They recall, in particular, the invitation they have previously addressed to the Soviet Union and other Countries of Eastern Europe to join them in discussing the possibility of mutual and balanced force reductions.

The objective of the work on which their representatives have been engaged has been to prepare a realistic basis for active exploration between the interested parties at an early date and thereby to establish whether it could serve as a starting point for fruitful negotiation. Such exploratory talks would assist those concerned in developing in detail criteria and objectives for substantive negotiations to follow at the appropriate stage in a forum to be determined. They would also provide tangible evidence of the readiness to build confidence between East and West.

The Ministers invite interested states to hold exploratory talks on mutual and balanced force reductions in Europe, with special reference to the Central Region. They agree that in such talks the Allies would put forward the following considerations:

(A) Mutual force reductions should be compatible with the vital security interests of the Alliance and should not operate to the military disadvantage of either side having regard for the differences arising from geographical and other considerations;

(B) Reductions should be on a basis of reciprocity, and phased and balanced as to their scope and timing;

(C) Reductions should include stationed and indigenous forces and their weapons systems in the area concerned;

(D) There must be adequate verification and controls to ensure the observance of agreements on mutual and balanced force reductions.

As a first step, the Ministers requested the Foreign Minister of Italy to transmit this declaration on their behalf through diplomatic channels to all other interested parties, including neutral and non-aligned Governments. They further agree that in the course of their normal bilateral and other contacts Member Governments would seek to obtain the responses and reactions of other Governments. The Members of the Alliance will consult further regarding the outcome of their soundings with a view to enabling the Alliance to determine what further individual or joint exploration might be useful.

Appendix IX

Declaration of the Warsaw Pact Foreign Ministers

June 22, 1970

Memorandum to Interested States

The Governments of the People's Republic of Bulgaria, the Czechoslovak Socialist Republic, the German Democratic Republic, the Hungarian People's Republic, the Polish People's Republic, the Socialist Republic of Roumania and the Union of Soviet Socialist Republics deem it necessary to inform the interested states of their ideas which they believe would correspond to the interests of preparing and convening an all-European conference on questions of security and co-operation in Europe.

They note with satisfaction that in the course of bilateral and multilateral consultations and exchanges of views the positions of the interested states have grown closer on a series of important questions relating to an all-European conference. The balance of consultations and exchanges of views shows that the proposals made in Prague in October 1969 have laid the foundations for the preparation of an all-European conference to be placed on a practical basis in the near future, and, in addition to bilateral negotiations, to be switched over to multilateral forums. It is desirable that the interested states should directly participate in all stages of the preparation and organization of an all-European conference in such forums as will be considered appropriate, including preparatory meetings between representatives of these states.

The question of participation at the conference has been clarified: participation is open to all European states, including the German Democratic Republic and the Federal Republic of Germany on an equal footing with each other and with other European states, as well as the United States of America and Canada. A positive response was received by the initiative of the Government of Finland suggesting Helsinki as the venue of the conference. There is an understanding that the convocation of the conference shall not be made subject to any preliminary condition.

Many countries share the view that the success of the first all-European conference—the preparation, organization and realization of which ought to be a result of efforts by all interested countries—would pave the way for a joint discussion in future of other European problems, particularly those of creating a solid system of European security, and that, in this connection, it would be useful to hold a series of all European conferences and to establish an appropriate organ of all interested states to deal with questions of security and co-operation in Europe.

Discussions continue on the content of work and the agenda of an all-European conference. The two items of the agenda proposed in Prague are in keeping with the interests of bringing about security and developing co-operation in Europe; these are questions on which it is possible to reach wide-ranging agreements. These proposals do not meet with opposition in principle. At the same time, a number of governments come out for broadening the agenda of the conference.

In an endeavour to reach an agreement on an agenda for an all-European conference, acceptable to all interested states, the governments of the People's Republic of Bulgaria, the Czechoslovak Socialist Republic, the German Democratic Republic, the Hungarian People's Republic, the Polish People's Republic, the Socialist Republic of Roumania and the Union of Soviet Socialist Republics recommend to add the following item to the agenda already proposed:

Establishment by the all-European conference of an organ to deal with questions of security and co-operation in Europe.

The Governments adopting this memorandum believe that the interests of reducing tensions and bringing about security in Europe would be promoted by a discussion of the question concerning the reduction of foreign armed forces on the territories of European States. In order to ensure favourable conditions for the discussion of related questions at the all-European conference and to bring to fruition the discussion of the question of reducing foreign armed forces, this item might be taken up by the organ proposed to be established by the all-European conference or in any other forum acceptable to interested states.

They believe further that the question of human environment might be discussed within the framework of the second item of the agenda proposed in Prague, which could also be broadened to include questions concerning the development of cultural relations.

Thus the agenda of an all-European conference might include the following items:

Ensuring of European security and renunciation of the use or threat of force in the mutual relations of European states.

Expansion of commercial, economic, scientific-technical and cultural relations on a footing of equality for the purpose of developing political co-operation between European states.

Establishment by the all-European conference of an organ to deal with questions of security and co-operation in Europe.

The Governments of the People's Republic of Bulgaria, the Czechoslovak Socialist Republic, the German Democratic Republic, the Hungarian People's Republic, the Polish People's Republic, the Socialist Republic of Roumania and the Union of Soviet Socialist Republics express their hopes that the proposals contained in the memorandum and with regard to the views of a number of interested states will be favourably received by the respective governments. These proposals particularly aim at reaching an agreement on an agenda of the all-European conference, acceptable for all interested states, and on the methods of its preparation, which may be started in the near future.

The Governments issuing this memorandum are convinced that the convocation of an all-European conference as a result of joint efforts by all interested states would be a significant contribution towards easing tensions, strengthening security and developing peaceful co-operation in Europe.

ESSENTIAL CONTENTS OF THE DOCUMENT ON THE EXPANSION OF TRADE, ECONOMIC, SCIENTIFIC AND TECHNICAL AND CULTURAL RELATIONS BASED ON THE PRINCIPLES OF EQUALITY, AIMED AT A PROMOTION OF POLITICAL CO-OPERATION AMONG THE STATES OF EUROPE

The states participants of the all-European conference . . . being convinced that the development of relations on equal footing among states without any discrimination in the field of trade, economic, scientific and technical and cultural relations facilitates the attainment of a relaxation of tensions, normalization of relations among all European states and the consolidation of peace and security in Europe;

Proceeding from the fact that the differences in economic and social systems are no obstacle for an expansion of trade, economic, scientific and technical and cultural international relations, relying on full equality of rights and mutual benefits;

Realizing that important changes in the economic relations among European countries, the current scientific and technical revolution, which affects all spheres of social life, and the problems of the human environment necessitate promotion and perfection of the trade, economic, scientific and technical co-operation among European states on which the growth of prosperity of the population of the European continent as well as the preservation of the role of Europe as one of the most important centres of world civilization depend in considerable measure;

Sharing the view that expansion of trade, economic, scientific and technical relations among European states would be beneficial for all participants and would likewise facilitate the advance of economies and raise the living standards of the peoples of those countries;

Taking into account decisions taken by the United Nations General Assembly, the United Nations Conference on Trade and Development and by the Economic Commission for Europe urging the governments of European states to pursue constructive efforts aimed at an improvement of their mutual relations and further development of mutually beneficial co-operation on the basis of the renunciation of discrimination in their trade policies;

Declare that they are resolved to exert further efforts aimed at a promotion of a broader economic, trade, scientific, technical and cultural co-operation among all European states and to take all necessary measures so that the existing obstacles standing in the way of translating such a co-operation into practice be eliminated, which will facilitate the strengthening of mutual confidence and the development of good neighbourly relations among all states of Europe.

Appendix X

Quadripartite Agreement on Berlin

September 3, 1971

The Governments of the United States of America, the French Republic, the Union of Soviet Socialist Republics and the United Kingdom of Great Britain and Northern Ireland,

Represented by their Ambassadors, who held a series of meetings in the building formerly occupied by the Allied Control Council in the American Sector of Berlin,

Acting on the basis of their quadripartite rights and responsibilities, and of the corresponding wartime and postwar agreements and decisions of the Four Powers, which are not affected,

Taking into account the existing situation in the relevant area,

Guided by the desire to contribute to practical improvements of the situation,

Without prejudice to their legal positions,

Have agreed on the following:

PART I

GENERAL PROVISIONS

1. The four Governments will strive to promote the elimination of tension and the prevention of complications in the relevant area.
2. The four Governments, taking into account their obligations under the Charter of the United Nations, agree that there shall be no use or threat of force in the area and that disputes shall be settled solely by peaceful means.
3. The four Governments will mutually respect their individual and joint rights and responsibilities, which remain unchanged.
4. The four Governments agree that, irrespective of the differences in legal views, the situation which has developed in the area, and as it is defined in this Agreement as well as in the other agreements referred to in this Agreement, shall not be changed unilaterally.

PART II

PROVISIONS RELATING TO THE WESTERN SECTORS OF BERLIN

A. The Government of the Union of Soviet Socialist Republics

268

the territory of the German Democratic Republic of civilian persons declares that transit traffic by road, rail and waterways through and goods between the Western Sectors of Berlin and the Federal Republic of Germany will be unimpeded; that such traffic will be facilitated so as to take place in the most simple and expeditious manner; and that it will receive preferential treatment.

Detailed arrangements concerning this civilian traffic, as set forth in Annex I, will be agreed by the competent German authorities.

B. The Governments of the French Republic, the United Kingdom and the United States of America declare that the ties between the Western Sectors of Berlin and the Federal Republic of Germany will be maintained and developed, taking into account that these Sectors continue not to be a constituent part of the Federal Republic of Germany and not to be governed by it.

Detailed arrangements concerning the relationship between the Western Sectors of Berlin and the Federal Republic of Germany are set forth in Annex II.

C. The Government of the Union of Soviet Socialist Republics declares that communications between the Western Sectors of Berlin and areas bordering on these Sectors and those areas of the German Democratic Republic which do not border on these Sectors will be improved. Permanent residents of the Western Sectors of Berlin will be able to travel to and visit such areas for compassionate, family, religious, cultural or commercial reasons, or as tourists, under conditions comparable to those applying to other persons entering these areas.

The problems of the small enclaves, including Steinstuecken, and of other small areas may be solved by exchange of territory.

Detailed arrangements concerning travel, communications and the exchange of territory as set forth in Annex III, will be agreed by the competent German authorities.

D. Representation abroad of the interests of the Western Sectors of Berlin and consular activities of the Union of Soviet Socialist Republics in the Western Sectors of Berlin can be exercised as set forth in Annex IV.

PART III

FINAL PROVISIONS

This Quadripartite Agreement will enter into force on the date specified in a Final Quadripartite Protocol to be concluded when the measures envisaged in Part II of this Quadripartite Agreement and in its Annexes have been agreed.

DONE at the building formerly occupied by the Allied Control Council in the American Sector of Berlin this 3rd day of September 1971, in four originals, each in the English, French and Russian languages, all texts being equally authentic.

For the Government of the United States of America:

KENNETH RUSH.

For the Government of the French Republic:

JEAN SAUVAGNARGUES.

For the Government of the Union of Soviet Socialist Republics:

PYOTR A. ABRASIMOV.

For the Government of the United Kingdom of Great Britain and Northern Ireland:

ROGER JACKLING.

Bibliography

Acheson, Dean, *Present at the Creation*, Hamish Hamilton, 1970

Aron, Raymond, *Peace & War: A Theory of International Relations*, Praeger, 1968: Weidenfeld & Nicolson, 1967

Bader, W. B., 'Nuclear Weapons and the German Problem', *Foreign Affairs*, July 1966

Ball, Margaret, *NATO and the European Movement*, Praeger, 1959

Beaufre, Andre, *NATO and Europe*, Vintage Books, 1966: Faber, 1967

Bell, Coral, *The Debatable Alliance: An Essay in Anglo-American Relations*, Oxford University Press, 1964

Bertram, Christoph, 'West German Perspectives on European Security: Continuity and Change', *The World Today*, February 1971

Birnbaum, Karl E., *Peace in Europe: East-West Relations 1966–1968 and the Prospects for a European Settlement*, Oxford University Press, 1970

Bluhm, Georg, *Détente and Military Relaxation in Europe*, Adelphi Papers, Institute for Strategic Studies (London)

Brodie, Bernard, *Strategy in the Missile Age*, Princeton University Press, 1965

Brzezinski, Zbigniew, *Alternative to Partition*, McGraw-Hill, 1965

Brzezinski, Zbigniew, 'America and Europe', *Foreign Affairs*, October 1970

Buchan, Alastair, *Crisis Management: The New Diplomacy*, The Atlantic Papers, NATO Series II, The Atlantic Institute, 1966

Buchan, Alastair, *Europe's Futures, Europe's Choices*, Columbia University Press, 1970: Chatto & Windus, 1969

Buchan, Alastair, *NATO in the 1960s*, Chatto & Windus, 1963

Buchan, Alastair, *War in Modern Society*, C. A. Watts & Co., 1966

Buchan, Alastair, and Windsor, Philip, *Arms and Stability in Europe*, Chatto & Windus, 1963

Calleo, David, *The Atlantic Fantasy: The U.S., NATO, and Europe*, Johns Hopkins Press, 1970

Camps, Miriam, *Britain and the European Community, 1955–1963*. Princeton University Press, 1964: Oxford University Press, 1964

271

Cleveland, Harold van B., *The Atlantic Idea and its European Rivals*, McGraw-Hill, 1966

Cleveland, Harlan, *NATO: The Transatlantic Bargain*, Harper & Row, 1970

Cottrell, Alvin J., and Dougherty, James, *The Politics of the Atlantic Alliance*. Praeger, 1964

Debré, Michael, 'France's Global Strategy', *Foreign Affairs*, April 1971

Deutsch, Karl W., Edinger, Lewis J., Macridis, Roy C., Merritt, Richard, L., *France, Germany and the Western Alliance*, Charles Scribner's Sons, 1967

Diebold, William, *The Schuman Plan: Study in Economic Cooperation, 1950–1959*, Praeger, for the Council on Foreign Relations, 1959

Djilas, Milovan, *Conversations with Stalin*, Penguin, 1969

Europe and America in the 1970s, Institute for Strategic Studies, Adelphi Papers 70 and 71, November 1970

Fleming, D. F., *The Cold War and its Origins*, Doubleday & Co., 1961: Allen & Unwin, 1961

Gallois, Pierre, *The Balance of Terror*, Houghton Mifflin, 1961

Geyelin, Philip, *Lyndon B. Johnson and the World*, Praeger, 1966: Pall Mall Press, 1966

Green, Philip, *Deadly Logic: The Theory of Nuclear Deterrence*, Schocken Books, 1968

Halle, Louis, J., *The Cold War as History*, Harper & Row, 1967: Chatto & Windus, 1967

Hanrieder, W. F., *West German Foreign Policy 1949–1963*, Stanford University Press, 1967: Oxford University Press, 1967

Hassner, Pierre, *Change and Security in Euope*, Adelphi Papers/ Institute for Strategic Studies, 1968

Hoag, Malcolm W., 'Rationalizing NATO Strategy', *World Politics*, October 1964

Hoffmann, Stanley, *Gulliver's Troubles*, McGraw-Hill, 1968

Hoffmann, Stanley, et al., *In Search of France*, Harvard University Press, 1963

Hunter, Robert E., 'The Strategic Position of Europe,' *European Yearbook/Annuaire Européen*, Volume XV, The Hague, 1967

Hunter, Robert E., 'U.S. Defense Commitments in Europe and Asia during the 1970s: Military and Political Factors in Economic Policy', in *U.S. Foreign Economic Policy for the 1970s: A New*

Approach to New Realities, National Planning Association, Washington, D.C., November 1971

Hunter, Robert E., 'MBFR: The Next Step in *Détente?*', *International Conciliation*, 1972

Hunter, Robert E., 'Troops, Trade and Diplomacy', *Atlantic Community Quarterly*, Fall, 1971.

Ismay, Lord, *NATO: The First Five Years*, NATO, Paris, 1954

Jackson, Senator Henry M., *The Atlantic Alliance: Jackson Subcommittee Hearings and Findings*, Praeger, 1967

Jordan, Robert S., *The NATO International Staff/Secretariat 1952–1957: A Study in International Administration*, Oxford University Press, 1967

deKadt, Emanuel J., *British Defense Policy and Nuclear War*, Humanities Press, 1966

Kahn, Herman, *Thinking About the Unthinkable*, Avon, 1964

Kaser, Michael, *Comecon*, Oxford University Press, 1967

Kennan, George, *Memoirs, 1925–1950*, Hutchinson, 1968

Kissinger, Henry A., 'Strains on the Alliance', *Foreign Affairs*, January 1963

Kissinger, Henry A., *The Troubled Partnership*, McGraw-Hill, 1965

Kitzinger, U. W.. *The Challenge of the Common Market*, Basil Blackwell, 1962

Kleiman, Robert, *Atlantic Crisis*, Norton, 1964: Sidgwick & Jackson, 1965

Knorr, Klaus, *NATO: Past, Present, Prospect*, Headline Series No. 198, Foreign Policy Association (New York), December 1969

Laqueur, Walter, *Europe Since Hitler*, Weidenfeld & Nicolson, 1970

Laqueur, Walter, *The Rebirth of Europe*, Holt, Rinehard and Winston, 1970

Lerner, Daniel and Aron, Raymond, *France Defeats EDC*, Praeger, 1956

Lewin, Leonard C. (intro), *Report from Iron Mountain on the Possibility and Desirability of Peace*, Dell Publishing Co., 1967: Penguin, 1968

Liddell Hart, B. H., *Strategy*, Second Revised Edition, Praeger, 1967

Liska, George, *Nations in Alliance: The Limits of Interdependence*, John Hopkins Press, 1969

Luard, Evan (ed.), *The Cold War, A Reappraisal*, Thames & Hudson, 1964

Mayne, Richard, *The Community of Europe*, Victor Gollancz, 1962

Mayne, Richard, *The Recovery of Europe: From Devastation to Unity*, Harper and Row, 1970

Mendl, Wolf, 'After De Gaulle: Continuity and Change in French Foreign Policy', *The World Today*, January 1971

Mendl, Wolf, *Deterrence and Persuasion: French Nuclear Armament in the Context of National Policy, 1945–1969*, Faber and Faber, 1970

The Military Balance, International Institute for Strategic Studies (Annual)

Moore, B. T., *NATO and the Future of Europe*, Harper & Row, 1958: Oxford University Press, 1958

Mulley, Frederick W., *The Politics of Western Defense*, Praeger, 1962

NATO: Facts about the North Atlantic Treaty Organization, Paris: NATO Information Service, 1962

Newhouse, John, *U.S. Troops in Europe*, The Brookings Institution, 1971

Northedge, Frederick, *British Foreign Policy*, George Allen & Unwin, 1962

Osgood, Robert E., *NATO: The Entangling Alliance*, Chicago University Press, 1962

Pfaltzgraff, Robert L., Jr., *The Atlantic Community: A Complex Imbalance*, Van Nostrand Reinhold, 1969

Pfaltzgraff, Robert L., Jr., *Britain Faces Europe, 1957–1967*, University of Pennsylvania Press, 1970

Pryce, Roy, *The Political Future of the European Community*, John Marshbank Limited in association with the Federal Trust, 1962

Remington, Robin Alison, *The Warsaw Pact: Case Studies in Communist Conflict Resolution*, M.I.T. Press, 1971

Remington, Robin Alison (ed.), *Winter in Prague: Documents on Czechoslovak Communism in Crisis*, M.I.T. Press, 1969

Richardson, James L., *Germany & the Atlantic Alliance*, Oxford University Press, 1966

Riker, William, *The Theory of Political Coalitions*, Yale University Press, 1962

Rosecrance, R. N., *Defense of the Realm: British Strategy in the Nuclear Epoch*, Columbia University Press, 1968

Royal Institute of International Affairs, *Atlantic Alliance: NATO'S Role in the Free World*, 1952

Bibliography

Royal Institute of International Affairs, *Defence in the Cold War*, 1950

Royal Institute of International Affairs, *Survey & Documents*

Schelling, Thomas C., *Arms & Influence*, Yale University Press, 1966

Schelling, Thomas C., and Halperin, Morton H., *Strategy and Arms Control*, Twentieth Century Fund, 1961

Schelling, Thomas C., *The Strategy of Conflict*, Oxford University Press, 1960

Schmidt, Helmut, 'Germany in the Era of Negotiations', *Foreign Affairs*, October 1970

Seabury, Paul. *The Rise & Decline of the Cold War*, Basic Books, 1967

SIPRI Yearbook of World Armaments and Disarmament (Annual)

Stanley, Timothy, *NATO in Transition*, Praeger, 1965: Pall Mall Press, 1965

Stanley, Timothy and Whitt, Darnell M., *Détente Diplomacy: United States and European Security in the 1970s*, The Dunellen Company, 1970

Steel, Ronald, *The End of Alliance*, Viking Press, 1964

Strauss, Franz Josef, *The Grand Design*, Praeger, 1965

Truman, Harry S., *Presidential Memoirs*, New English Library, 1965

Ulam, Adam B., *Expansion & Co-existence: The History of Soviet Foreign Policy 1917–1967*, Praeger, 1968: Secker & Warburg, 1968

Whetten, Lawrence L., 'Recent Changes in East European Approaches to European Security', *The World Today*, July 1970

Windsor, Philip, *City on Leave: Berlin 1945–1962*, Chatto & Windus, 1963

Windsor, Philip, *German Reunification*, Elek Books, 1969

Windsor, Philip, *Germany and the Management of Détente*, Chatto & Windus, for the International Institute of Strategic Studies, 1971

Windsor, Philip, & Roberts, Adam, *Czechoslovakia 1968*, Chatto & Windus, 1968

Wolfe, Thomas W., *Soviet Power and Europe, 1945–1970*, Johns Hopkins Press, 1970

Woodhouse, C. M., *British Foreign Policy Since the Second World War*, Hutchinson, 1961

Index

Index